A Promise of Sweet Tea

THE AZRIELI SERIES OF HOLOCAUST SURVIVOR MEMOIRS: PUBLISHED TITLES

ENGLISH TITLES

Judy Abrams, *Tenuous Threads*/ Eva Felsenburg Marx, *One of the Lucky Ones*
Amek Adler, *Six Lost Years*
Ferenc Andai, *In the Hour of Fate and Danger*
Molly Applebaum, *Buried Words: The Diary of Molly Applebaum*
Claire Baum, *The Hidden Package*
Bronia and Joseph Beker, *Joy Runs Deeper*
Tibor Benyovits, *Unsung Heroes*
Max Bornstein, *If Home Is Not Here*
Felicia Carmelly, *Across the Rivers of Memory*
Judy Cohen, *A Cry in Unison*
Tommy Dick, *Getting Out Alive*
Marian Domanski, *Fleeing from the Hunter*
Anita Ekstein, *Always Remember Who You Are*
Leslie Fazekas, *In Dreams Together: The Diary of Leslie Fazekas*
John Freund, *Spring's End*
Susan Garfield, *Too Many Goodbyes: The Diaries of Susan Garfield*
Myrna Goldenberg (Editor), *Before All Memory Is Lost: Women's Voices from the Holocaust*
René Goldman, *A Childhood Adrift*
Elly Gotz, *Flights of Spirit*
Ibolya Grossman and Andy Réti, *Stronger Together*
Pinchas Gutter, *Memories in Focus*
Anna Molnár Hegedűs, *As the Lilacs Bloomed*
Rabbi Pinchas Hirschprung, *The Vale of Tears*
Bronia Jablon, *A Part of Me*
Helena Jockel, *We Sang in Hushed Voices*
Eddie Klein, *Inside the Walls*
Michael Kutz, *If, By Miracle*
Ferenc Laczó (Editor), *Confronting Devastation: Memoirs of Holocaust Survivors from Hungary*
Eva Lang, David Korn and Fishel Philip Goldig, *At Great Risk: Memoirs of Rescue during the Holocaust*
Nate Leipciger, *The Weight of Freedom*
Alex Levin, *Under the Yellow and Red Stars*
Rachel Lisogurski and Chana Broder, *Daring to Hope*
Fred Mann, *A Drastic Turn of Destiny*
Michael Mason, *A Name Unbroken*
Leslie Meisels with Eva Meisels, *Suddenly the Shadow Fell*
Leslie Mezei, *A Tapestry of Survival*
Muguette Myers, *Where Courage Lives*
David Newman, *Hope's Reprise*
Arthur Ney, *W Hour*
Felix Opatowski, *Gatehouse to Hell*
Marguerite Élias Quddus, *In Hiding*
Maya Rakitova, *Behind the Red Curtain*
Henia Reinhartz, *Bits and Pieces*
Betty Rich, *Little Girl Lost*
Paul-Henri Rips, *E/96: Fate Undecided*
Margrit Rosenberg Stenge, *Silent Refuge*
Steve Rotschild, *Traces of What Was*
Judith Rubinstein, *Dignity Endures*
Martha Salcudean, *In Search of Light*
Kitty Salsberg and Ellen Foster, *Never Far Apart*
Morris Schnitzer, *Escape from the Edge*
Joseph Schwarzberg, *Dangerous Measures*
Zuzana Sermer, *Survival Kit*

Rachel Shtibel, *The Violin*/ Adam Shtibel, *A Child's Testimony*
Maxwell Smart, *Chaos to Canvas*
Gerta Solan, *My Heart Is At Ease*
Zsuzsanna Fischer Spiro, *In Fragile Moments*/ Eva Shainblum, *The Last Time*
George Stern, *Vanished Boyhood*
Willie Sterner, *The Shadows Behind Me*
Ann Szedlecki, *Album of My Life*
William Tannenzapf, *Memories from the Abyss*/ Renate Krakauer, *But I Had a Happy Childhood*
Elsa Thon, *If Only It Were Fiction*
Agnes Tomasov, *From Generation to Generation*
Joseph Tomasov, *From Loss to Liberation*
Leslie Vertes, *Alone in the Storm*
Anka Voticky, *Knocking on Every Door*
Sam Weisberg, *Carry the Torch*/ Johnny Jablon, *A Lasting Legacy*

TITRES FRANÇAIS

Judy Abrams, *Retenue par un fil*/ Eva Felsenburg Marx, *Une question de chance*
Molly Applebaum, *Les Mots enfouis: Le Journal de Molly Applebaum*
Claire Baum, *Le Colis caché*
Bronia et Joseph Beker, *Plus forts que le malheur*
Max Bornstein, *Citoyen de nulle part*
Tommy Dick, *Objectif: survivre*
Marian Domanski, *Traqué*
John Freund, *La Fin du printemps*
Myrna Goldenberg (Éditrice), *Un combat singulier: Femmes dans la tourmente de l'Holocauste*
René Goldman, *Une enfance à la dérive*
Anna Molnár Hegedűs, *Pendant la saison des lilas*
Helena Jockel, *Nous chantions en sourdine*
Michael Kutz, *Si, par miracle*
Nate Leipciger, *Le Poids de la liberté*
Alex Levin, *Étoile jaune, étoile rouge*
Fred Mann, *Un terrible revers de fortune*
Michael Mason, *Au fil d'un nom*
Leslie Meisels, *Soudain, les ténèbres*
Muguette Myers, *Les Lieux du courage*
Arthur Ney, *L'Heure W*
Felix Opatowski, *L'Antichambre de l'enfer*
Marguerite Élias Quddus, *Cachée*
Henia Reinhartz, *Fragments de ma vie*
Betty Rich, *Seule au monde*
Paul-Henri Rips, *Matricule E/96*
Steve Rotschild, *Sur les traces du passé*
Kitty Salsberg et Ellen Foster, *Unies dans l'épreuve*
Zuzana Sermer, *Trousse de survie*
Rachel Shtibel, *Le Violon*/ Adam Shtibel, *Témoignage d'un enfant*
George Stern, *Une jeunesse perdue*
Willie Sterner, *Les Ombres du passé*
Ann Szedlecki, *L'Album de ma vie*
William Tannenzapf, *Souvenirs de l'abîme*/ Renate Krakauer, *Le Bonheur de l'innocence*
Elsa Thon, *Que renaisse demain*
Agnes Tomasov, *De génération en génération*
Leslie Vertes, *Seul dans la tourmente*
Anka Voticky, *Frapper à toutes les portes*

A Promise of Sweet Tea: Memoirs of a Survivor

Pinchas Eliyahu Blitt

FIRST EDITION

THE AZRIELI FOUNDATION · www.azrielifoundation.org

Translations of text from prayer book used with permission from *The Koren Shalem Siddur: A Hebrew / English Prayerbook*. Jerusalem: Koren Publishers Jerusalem, copyright 2017.

Translations of biblical text reproduced from the *Tanakh: The Holy Scriptures* by permission of the University of Nebraska Press. Copyright 1985 by The Jewish Publication Society, Philadelphia.

Cover and book design by Mark Goldstein · Map on page xxiv by Deborah Crowle · Endpaper maps by Martin Gilbert · Art on pages xxv and 171 by Miriam Libicki. Photographs on page 292 reprinted with permission of Ron Diamond.

LIBRARY AND ARCHIVES CANADA CATALOGUING IN PUBLICATION

A Promise of Sweet Tea: Memoirs of a Survivor/ Pinchas Eliyahu Blitt.
Blitt, Pinchus Eliyahu, author. Azrieli Foundation, publisher.
Azrieli series of Holocaust survivor memoirs. Series XIII
Canadiana (print) 20210206225 · Canadiana (ebook) 20210206330
ISBN: 9781989719152 (softcover) · 9781989719213 (ebook) · 9781989719237 (PDF)

LCSH: Blitt, Pinchas Eliyahu — Childhood and youth. LCSH: Holocaust, Jewish (1939–1945) — Ukraine — Kortelisy — Personal narratives. LCSH: Jewish children in the Holocaust — Ukraine — Kortelisy — Biography. LCSH: Holocaust, Jewish (1939–1945) — Ukraine — Kortelisy. LCSH: Holocaust survivors — Ukraine — Kortelisy — Biography. LCSH: Holocaust survivors — Canada — Biography. LCSH: Kortelisy (Ukraine) — Biography. LCGFT: Autobiographies.

LCC DS135.U43 B65 2021 · DDC 940.53/18092 — dc23

MIX
Paper from responsible sources
FSC® C004191

PRINTED IN CANADA

CONTENTS

SERIES PREFACE: IN THEIR OWN WORDS...

In telling these stories, the writers have liberated themselves. For so many years we did not speak about it, even when we became free people living in a free society. Now, when at last we are writing about what happened to us in this dark period of history, knowing that our stories will be read and live on, it is possible for us to feel truly free. These unique historical documents put a face on what was lost, and allow readers to grasp the enormity of what happened to six million Jews — one story at a time.

David J. Azrieli, C.M., C.Q., M.Arch.
Holocaust survivor and founder, The Azrieli Foundation

Since the end of World War II, approximately 40,000 Jewish Holocaust survivors have immigrated to Canada. Who they are, where they came from, what they experienced and how they built new lives for themselves and their families are important parts of our Canadian heritage. The Azrieli Foundation's Holocaust Survivor Memoirs Program was established in 2005 to preserve and share the memoirs written by those who survived the twentieth-century Nazi genocide of the Jews of Europe and later made their way to Canada. The memoirs encourage readers to engage thoughtfully and critically with the complexities of the Holocaust and to create meaningful connections with the lives of survivors.

Millions of individual stories are lost to us forever. By preserving the stories written by survivors and making them widely available to a broad audience, the Azrieli Foundation's Holocaust Survivor Memoirs Program seeks to sustain the memory of all those who perished at the hands of hatred, abetted by indifference and apathy. The personal accounts of those who survived against all odds are as different as the people who wrote them, but all demonstrate the courage, strength, wit and luck that it took to prevail and survive in such terrible adversity. The memoirs are also moving tributes to people — strangers and friends — who risked their lives to help others, and who, through acts of kindness and decency in the darkest of moments, frequently helped the persecuted maintain faith in humanity and courage to endure. These accounts offer inspiration to all, as does the survivors' desire to share their experiences so that new generations can learn from them.

The Holocaust Survivor Memoirs Program collects, archives and publishes select survivor memoirs and makes the print editions available free of charge to educational institutions and Holocaust-education programs across Canada. They are also available for sale online to the general public. All revenues to the Azrieli Foundation from the sales of the Azrieli Series of Holocaust Survivor Memoirs go toward the publishing and educational work of the memoirs program.

~

The Azrieli Foundation would like to express appreciation to the following people for their invaluable efforts in producing this book: Karel Berkhoff, Judith Clark, Ron Diamond, Mark Duffus (Maracle Inc.), Vivian Felsen, Roberta Newman, Susan Roitman, Irina Sadovina, Naomi Seidman, Tobias Wals, and the team at Second Story Press.

EDITORIAL NOTE

This memoir is set during a time when territories in Eastern Europe were frequently changing hands. As borders shifted, names of cities, towns and villages changed, as did official languages. In the period Pinchas writes about, the region of western Ukraine where his village of Kortelisy was situated was ruled by Russia, Poland, the Soviet Union and Germany. After the war, it became part of Soviet Ukraine until Ukraine's independence in 1991. (The map on page xxiv represents the territorial changes in the area from 1939–1945.)

The names of places and various languages used in this memoir reflect the historical conflicts and territorial shifts in the region as well as the author's memories of a particular community, time and place. We have worked to stay true to the author's memory and perceptions, preserving his narrative voice and use of language, while maintaining clarity and historical accuracy. Standardized transliterations of Russian and Ukrainian have been used, and Yiddish words and phrases have been transliterated according to the standard of the YIVO Institute for Jewish Research except where more common or recognizable transliterations give the text more clarity and accessibility. More obscure Hebrew words and biblical phrases have been transliterated with Yiddish pronunciations, as they would have been spoken by Yiddish-speaking Jews in that region.

Foreign-language words and historical terms that may be unclear without additional context have been added to the glossary beginning on page 269.

INTRODUCTION

Pinchas Blitt, the author of these memoirs, was our matinee idol: our Boris Tomashevsky, Jacob Adler and Maurice Schwartz all rolled into one. By "our" I mean those of us lucky enough to grow up in Yiddish Montreal and attend the Folkshule, where once a year the school auditorium on Van Horne was miraculously transformed into a theatre that performed a world-class repertoire of original Yiddish plays and Israeli plays in Yiddish translation. Other than in *Hannah Senesh*, where the heart-stopping Bryna Cytrynbaum, the most beautiful actress I had ever seen, played the leading role, Pinchas always stole the show. He was the faithful father in *Kiddush Hashem*. He was the wily and lascivious Uncle Moses. He was the wise King Solomon. How Dora Wasserman, trained by the legendary Shloyme Mikhoels in Moscow, recruited Pinchas to play the irrepressible matchmaker, Soloveitchik, in Sholem Aleichem's comedy, *Dos groyse gevins* (The Lottery), is something the reader will learn at story's end. Pinchas could sing and dance, and his spoken Yiddish was impeccable — not like ours, which betrayed a Canadian accent.

I played Shloymele, his son, in the 1961 production of *Kiddush Hashem* and can still hum the melody that Pinchas contributed to the script. Like everything else in his memoirs, the fact that this was a Roma beggar song he remembered from his childhood comes as a complete surprise. For among the myriad roles that Pinchas played throughout his life, the role of Holocaust Survivor was not one of them. The Pinchas we knew, both onstage and off, bore no visible scars. He was the life force itself.

A Promise of Sweet Tea is narrated in two voices: one is the voice of an irrepressible little boy who is discovering the world just as that world is changing beyond recognition, and the other is the voice-over of a wise old man, looking back at his former self. At times bemused, at times saddened by it all, he realizes that he is now older than the oldest person in his story. While the child (and later, adolescent) voice is tasked with doing the "showing," with bringing the past to life, the adult voice does all the "telling," as he grapples with its present meaning. This is a delicate balancing act, which many writers have tried before. With the publication of his memoirs, Pinchas Blitt has joined their ranks, and *A Promise of Sweet Tea* invites comparison with other works of literature that are filtered through the consciousness of a Jewish boy or girl who is fated to survive, against all odds.

One major strand in Holocaust literature revisits the harrowing experiences of a Jewish child reaching puberty just as his or her whole world is destroyed. This is what happens to Yurik in Uri Orlev's *The Lead Soldiers* (1956), to Eliezer in Wiesel's *Night* (1958), to Bruno in *The Age of Wonders* (1978) by Aharon Appelfeld and to Appelfeld's *Tzili* (1983). But surprisingly, the character to whom Pineleh bears the closest resemblance is Motl, son of Peysi the cantor.[1] Like Motl, our Pineleh is in his element when out of doors; he loves to catch dragonflies and is as attached to the family horse and cow as Motl was cathected to his calf. One of Pineleh's earliest childhood memories is of working in the green and luscious fields, digging up potatoes. Like Motl, Pineleh has a wonderful ear for languages, idiomatic expressions and parodic speech. (In fact, the dirty songs and off-colour

1 See Sholem Aleichem, *The Letters of Menakhem-Mendl and Sheyne-Sheyndl and Motl, the Cantor's Son*, translated and with an introduction by Hillel Halkin (New Haven; London: Yale University Press, 2002).

jokes that Pineleh retains from childhood are a useful corrective to the oral lore in Sholem Aleichem, which is as clean as the day is long.) Besides his two native languages, Yiddish and Ukrainian, the grownups also speak Polish and Russian, and later, German, English and French, and our Pineleh is a quick study. (There is also a comical episode where they pretend to speak Greek.) Like Motl, Pineleh will learn a great deal and travel the world but will always remain essentially the same. Our latter-day Motl is a spunky, adaptable Jew.

Like Motl, Pineleh is a master of comic discrepancies. Under the Soviets, Pineleh happily attends school wearing the red kerchief of a Young Pioneer, the *galstuk* that becomes "one of the most important pieces of clothing" in his life. He wears it at all times, even in the synagogue on the Sabbath and Jewish holidays. And why not? The only noticeable difference between the Soviet school and the Polish one that he attended before are the portraits on the wall, and Father Stalin looks like someone who cares for little children. But underneath his shirt, our hero does not forget to put on his *laybtsedak* (also pronounced *laybserdak*), "the poncho-like garment" with *tsitses*, or knotted fringes, tied to each corner. For the grownups, the red kerchief and the *tsitses* are irreconcilable; they represent a kind of *shatnez*, or forbidden mixing — so great a religious taboo that much later in the story, God will send a Soviet plane to destroy their makeshift hut in the forest because it was constructed next to two different kinds of trees that were growing together. For Pineleh, mixing and matching are the spice of life. Stalin and Moses may have been two very different people, but the little boy loves them both.

Like Motl, Pinchas Elye (his formal-sounding name) is a prototype of the New Jew, who will bestride the changing world like an explorer. Christian icons are almost as familiar to him as the mezuzah on his doorpost. He is a proud Ukrainian who so wants to pass the "Jew Test" and recite Taras Shevchenko out loud. He is a first-generation Young Pioneer who studies from Communist primers. He is a first-generation survivor of the Holocaust who tries everything, from playing Ping-Pong and roller skating to boxing and soccer, in the Bindermichl displaced persons camp, where he will also master the art of bike riding. He is a first-generation immigrant to Canada who becomes proficient in both official languages. He is the first native of Kortelisy to pass the Quebec bar exam.

Unlike Motl the cantor's son, however, Pineleh is no orphan. His survival owes everything to the resilience of his family: his parents, his maternal and paternal grandparents, his uncles and aunts, and even his kid brother. The shtetl of Kortelisy is so small a place that it doesn't even have its own Jewish burial ground, and to Pineleh it seems like one big happy family. Each member of that family remains indelibly etched in his memory, and therefore in ours, because each has a stake in the boy's well-being. When the going gets rough, when pogrom violence turns to genocide, what they feed him and teach him will make the difference between life and death. And this sense of belonging is what makes Pinchas Blitt a different kind of survivor.

For one thing, Pineleh's family and friends never abandon their faith. The Jews of Kortelisy are salt of the earth and have no great rabbinic authorities to consult when the earth begins to burn under their feet. As observant, halachic Jews, they know that God is always in the details, and adhering to God's laws, even under normal circumstances, is infinitely complex. So what do they do? They put their Jewish religious imagination to work in extraordinary ways. When they must construct a shelter in the forest, Father makes sure to place a makeshift mezuzah at the entrance. In order to salvage their one and only pot, Father is willing to bend the rules of *kashres*. And when newborn triplets have to be hastily buried, not only are all three circumcised at the graveside, but the babies are all given proper Jewish names, and the ceremony is adapted to the cruel realities of wartime. The child observing these ad hoc decisions may not fully grasp what halachic principles are at stake. Thankfully, the adult narrator is there to fill in the gaps. Not for naught did he briefly consider pursuing a rabbinic career — at my academic home of many years, the Jewish Theological Seminary of America.

Besides adhering so resolutely to Jewish law, what do these Jews believe? The core of Pineleh's Jewish education, his catechism, so to speak, is a single phrase, no more than four Yiddish words repeated whenever he comes crying to his parents, whenever he protests the injustice and cruelty they are forced to endure: *Vayl mir zaynen yidn*, this is happening to us "because we're Jews." This is deeply troubling both to Pineleh the child and to Pinchas the adult because it seems to suggest a passive acceptance of fate. Indeed, it reads more like fatalism than faith. As a survivor of the worst that has ever happened to the Jews, however, and in the course of his long life, Pineleh will come to appreciate the life-giving properties of this absolute commitment to *yiddishkayt* (Jewishness). *Vayl mir zaynen yidn* should also be understood as a statement of stubborn, unshakeable faith.

Learning how to live and die as a Jew is not something that can be gleaned from books. So here we come to another major difference: Blitt's "memoirs of a survivor" are grounded in language and lore, whereas muteness and silence are major themes in so much writing on the Holocaust. To survive, the child protagonists are often rendered mute, as in Jerzy Kosiński's *The Painted Bird* (1965) and Appelfeld's *Tzili*. To survive, the protagonists must erase all vestiges of their Jewish speech and mannerisms, as in Orlev's *The Lead Soldiers* and Henryk Grynberg's *The Jewish War/Child of the Shadows* (1965). Pineleh's world, in marked contrast, is alive with the sounds and sensibilities of different languages and cultures.

From the moment he learns to speak, Pineleh is taught to distinguish between high and low cultures, between the spoken vernacular and the language of Scripture, between Low Goyish (Ukrainian), spoken by the locals, and High Goyish (Polish, Russian, German), spoken by the rulers. (Later, in French Canada, Québécois and Queen's English will obey the same hierarchy.) At the same time that Pineleh learns to negotiate the Passover Haggadah in Hebrew, the holy tongue, his father teaches him a parodic way of remembering the precise order of the ten plagues. Instead of using the standard rabbinic mnemonic of *D'tzakh, Adash, B'akhav*, his father "mispronounces" the words as *dreyt zikh a daytsh bay aykh oyfn boydem*, which is Yiddish for "a German is hanging around inside your attic." This movement back and forth between Scripture and reality, the sublime and the ridiculous, is itself a time-tested survival strategy of Yiddish-speaking Jews. Pineleh is also the son of a mixed marriage. "For a village girl," he tells us, "Mother was unusually well-educated. She had graduated from a Hebrew gymnasium, which was the equivalent of a high school. Like her brothers, she spoke Hebrew, Russian, Polish and Ukrainian and, of course, Yiddish." Father, by contrast, graduated the school of hard knocks. But even he, it turns out, will turn his Yiddish to good advantage during the German occupation in World War I by becoming a translator for the German soldiers. His bobeh Freyde, the local barber-surgeon and midwife, had so many customers, Jews and gentiles, that she couldn't keep track of their names, but kept all of them laughing with a good joke. By negotiating languages, in turn, Jews for centuries were able to play a pivotal — indeed, indispensable — role at the centre of a multiethnic society, and Pineleh, despite the total breakdown and eventual destruction of that society, will remain a proud son of the Ukrainian shtetl.

A Promise of Sweet Tea is divided into three unequal parts: Before, During and After the Annihilation. Each part is narrated in sound bites, each chapter a story unto itself. What makes Pinchas Blitt such a great storyteller, besides his ear for languages, his irreverent humour, his total recall and his rich ethnic tapestry, is the way he allows the huge cast of characters to live and love in the present. His story does not backshadow, i.e., diminish the fullness and potentiality of their lives in light of their tragic deaths. To be sure, there are aspects of the past that remain a foreign country: being typecast as a fool just because he was born in the month of Tammuz; the demand to obey one's elders absolutely; the inability of his parents to show overt signs of love; and the refusal to number their years. Contrariwise, there are aspects of his story that still fill him with awe. Why did "Adam and Eve," a Christian couple, join up with fugitive Jews to settle deep in the forest? Why did Sonia, a Soviet citizen who knew nothing about her heritage, choose to die as a *yevreyka*, a Jew? In many ways, *A Promise of Sweet Tea* is a story without an ending — as every true tale of the Holocaust must be.

At the height of the slaughter, Pineleh, his parents and his brother find refuge in a hamlet with a local Jewish family who invite them to partake of a Friday night meal. So great is the disconnect between the serenity and calm of the Sabbath table and the violence of the Jew-hunt they have just escaped that Pineleh simply cannot believe his eyes, and even today, the adult narrator runs through four possible explanations of this scene without arriving at a definitive answer.

It had not even been a year since the brutal massacre in Babi Yar which, if the family or my parents had heard about at all, was probably nothing but a horrible rumour to them. Nothing was said about the murder and destruction of Jewish Kowel and Kortelisy or about the first victims of Ratno, murder that had happened close by and was not just a rumour. Years later, I still think that maybe this sole Jewish family in this little hamlet lived in an illusion and considered themselves immune to German brutality. Or was it fatalism or total helplessness that formed the thoughts and actions of the Jewish family in that hamlet, as well as the thoughts and actions of the Jews in the other villages and even in the big cities? Or maybe it was complete surrender to faith and the will of God, a faith and trust in the Almighty so strong that they left it completely up to Him. Was death no longer a consideration because, notwithstanding all the massacres, God was with them and not with the killers? Or, were they all in a state of denial, knew nothing about what had happened and what was coming and didn't want to know? In any case, it seemed that no one at this Friday night dinner table expected to meet the same fate as the Jews of Babi Yar, Kowel or Kortelisy.

For whatever reason, the adult world has gone crazy, and the child who is the father of the man is trying desperately to figure things out for himself. Yet certain aspects of the event we now call the Holocaust remain unknowable; they defy any received notions of human behaviour or accepted truths about divine providence. As an eyewitness to this event, Pinchas Blitt is committed to keeping the past alive, and in order to do so, the ledger of life and death must remain open.

~

Once memories are committed to paper, they take on a life of their own. They become an open book and as such invite still more questions of the reader. Why did Pinchas Blitt wait so long to tell his story? Why the time lag? True, the native-born Montrealers his age did not want to hear about his wartime experiences, or those of the other survivors with tattooed numbers on their arms. But this was hardly the case in the Yiddish-speaking community where Pinchas played such an important role. Why, Dora Wasserman's troupe put on *Hannah Senesh*, one of the first Israeli plays to deal with the Holocaust, and the same Aba Igelfeld whose unforgettable performance of Peretz's *Bontshe the Silent* Pinchas saw in the DP camp also immigrated to Montreal and would appear regularly at Holocaust commemorations organized by the Jewish Labour Bund. Yiddish culture was a school for healing, but the process of healing can be long and laborious, and Pinchas cannot be blamed for trying to escape the past. Maybe it was granting interviews to the USC Shoah Foundation in 1996 and 2009 that gave him the idea to tell his story at a leisurely pace, one episode at a time, without the cameras rolling, the way it used to be done during long winter nights in Kortelisy. Be that as it may, we are immensely grateful to the Azrieli Foundation for shepherding the memoirs of my fellow Yiddish thespian Pinchas Blitt through to publication and for inviting me to write the introduction.

This book is Pinchas Blitt's command performance. Those who never had the pleasure of seeing him on stage can now hear him play all the roles, male and female, old and young, Jewish and gentile. He manages to speak with native fluency, whether the role calls for Yiddish, Hebrew, Ukrainian, Polish or Russian, and his English isn't bad either, for an immigrant. When on stage, an actor is always "on." He must be in-the-present, on cue at all times, whether he is sipping sweet tea, his favourite drink in the world, or scratching for lice. These memoirs are so full of life, of dialogue, of laughter through tears, that they might easily belong in the Yiddish theatre. In fact, I would say that the reader is getting two books for the price of one. *A Promise of Sweet Tea* is actually a Yiddish memoir that just happens to have been written in English.

David G. Roskies
New York City
2021

A native of Montreal, Canada, and a product of its Yiddish secular schools, David G. Roskies is a cultural historian who has published extensively on modern Yiddish storytelling, Jewish responses to catastrophe, Holocaust literature, and memory. His most recent books are *Yiddishlands: A Memoir, Holocaust Literature: A History and Guide*, co-authored with Naomi Diamant and *Voices from the Warsaw Ghetto.*

Dr. Roskies is the Sol and Evelyn Henkind Professor of Yiddish Literature and Culture at the Jewish Theological Seminary and has also taught at the Hebrew University of Jerusalem, Ben-Gurion University of the Negev and the Russian State University for the Humanities.

In 1981 (with the late Alan Mintz), he co-founded *Prooftexts: A Journal of Jewish Literary History*, and served for eighteen years as editor in chief of the *New Yiddish Library*. He was elected to the American Academy of Arts and Sciences in 2012.

POLAND / WESTERN UKRAINE: 1939–1945

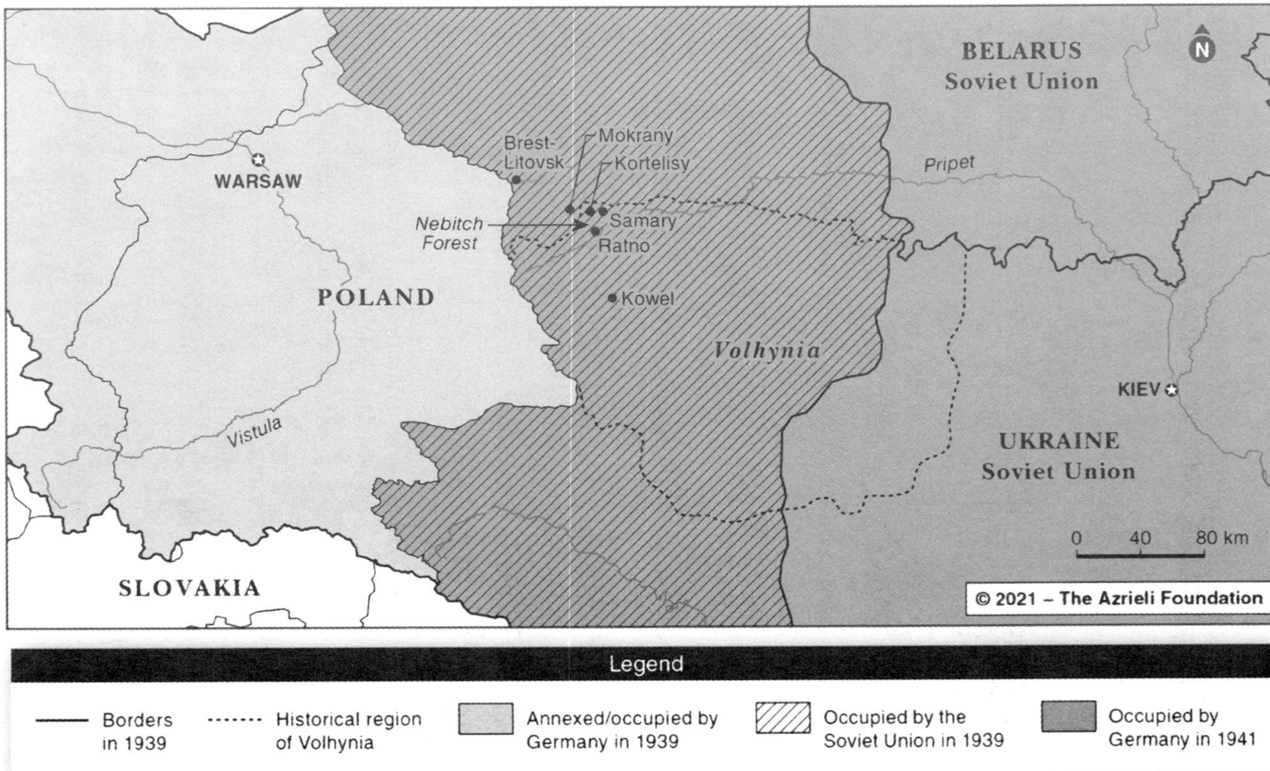

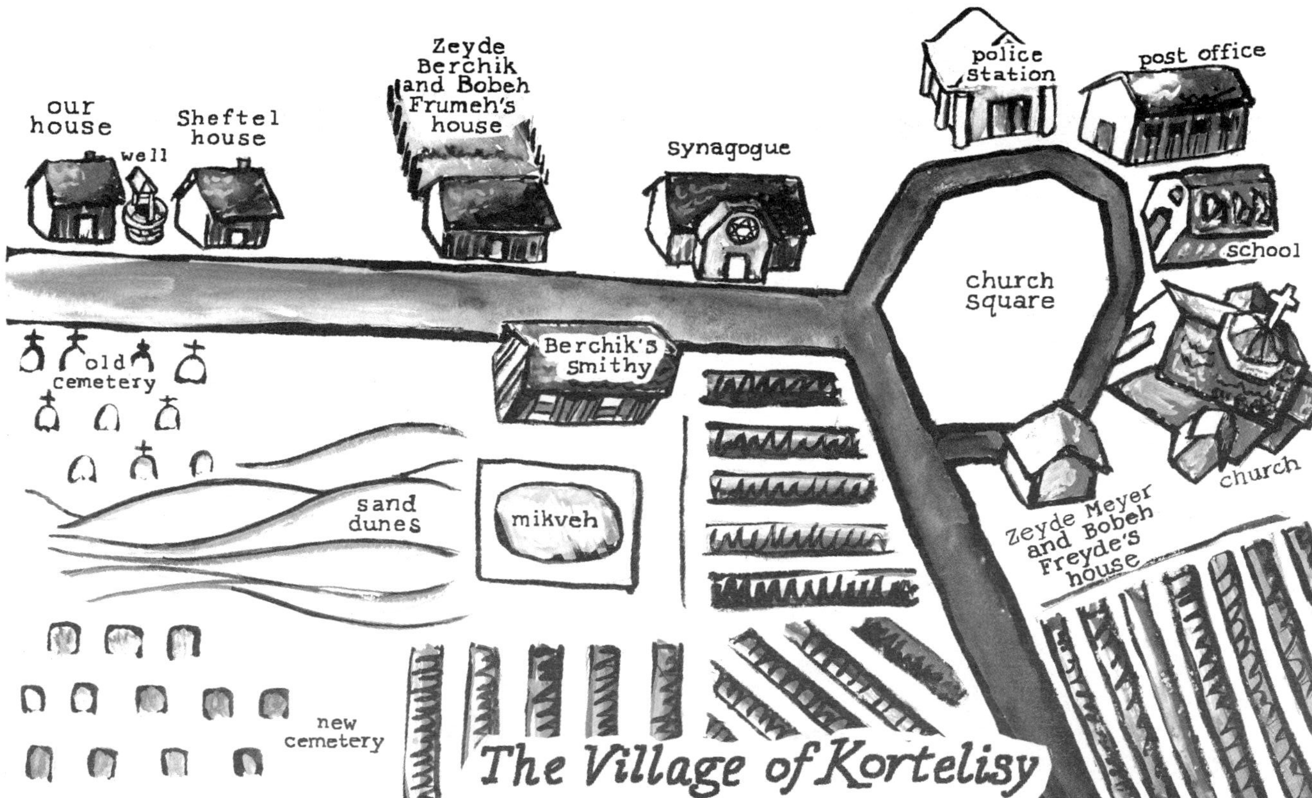

By Miriam Libicki

I wish to dedicate this book to the memory of my murdered grandfather Meyer Blitt and to my grandmother Freyde (née Rothchild), who died of malnutrition and disease during the war; to my murdered grandparents Berchik and Frumeh Ruttenberg; to my murdered uncles Yerakhmiel and Ben-Tsion Ruttenberg and Shmilke Blitt; and to all the Kortelisy victims who perished at the hands of brutal German forces and their Ukrainian collaborators.

To the memory of my dear parents, Mordechai-Leib and Adele, for all the sacrifices and efforts they made, particularly in helping me and my brother survive the war; to my kid brother, Laizer, who went through the struggle of survival with me, and to his family; to the memory of my very best friend, Yekhezkiel Robern Berezniak, who survived Auschwitz but unfortunately died in a skiing accident, and to his wife, Maxine, who predeceased him; and to my late uncle Moyshe-Dovid Blitt, who died before the war.

To my son Jonathan; my son Robert and daughter-in-law Stephanie Kodish and my grandchildren, Noah, Idan and Abraham; to my daughter, Happy, and son-in-law David Lombardy and my grandchildren, Juliette and Rebecca; and to my partner Gisele's son, David Rozin, and his family, whose grandparents survived the war in France and the Soviet Union by virtue of their wits and endurance.

Lastly, I dedicate this book to my beloved partner in life, Gisele Rucker; I never could have written my story without her help and encouragement.

ACKNOWLEDGEMENTS

I wish to acknowledge the Azrieli Foundation for supporting the publication and distribution of this book. Thank you to my wonderful editor, Devora Levin, for carefully crafting a better book from my manuscript. Thank you also to Arielle Berger and Jody Spiegel for their contributions and guidance.

I am thankful for the tremendous help I received from Gisele Rucker, Robert Blitt and Stephanie Kodish for reviewing my numerous drafts and without whose help I could not have finished telling my story. I also wish to thank Edit Kuper for helping me to find the English *mot juste* for Yiddish and Ukrainian words and expressions.

PART I

KORTELISY

Except for the villagers themselves, very few people even knew Kortelisy existed or, if they did and wanted to visit, knew how to find it. There was neither post nor sign, not even an arrow, to direct travellers to it from the main cobblestone highway, the *shosey* that cut through the area's massive Nebitch Forest. The first time I actually saw the name Kortelisy spelled out in Latin letters was in a little corner of the Yad Vashem museum in Israel in 1965.

My beloved village — Kortelisy, called Kortiles by Jews — was located in the historical region of Volhynia (or Volyn), in western Ukraine, which was mostly under Polish control from after World War I until September 1939. Kortelisy was off the highway that connected two major cities: Brest-Litovsk, which Jews called Brisk, to the northwest of Kortelisy, and Kowel, which Jews called Kovle, to the southeast of Kortelisy. Fifty or sixty kilometres north of Kowel, the *shosey* passed through a little town called Ratno, or Ratne to Jews. Ratno was always connected to the Jewish population of Kortelisy in some way. Villagers had either been born in Ratno and moved to Kortelisy, or someone from Ratno had married a Kortelisian and then moved to our village on account of economics; it was always easier to be poor in Kortelisy than in Ratno. Eventually, all Jews from Kortelisy did end up in Ratno, but only after death, in its cemetery.

My grandmother Frumeh used to tell me stories from the time

when she was still a child and Kortelisy sat deep within the forest itself, until the trees were cut and some of the surrounding forest was cleared and turned into farmland. My bobeh recounted that before the forest was cleared, wolves would roam in packs, howling at night. Sometimes they would come close to the windows of the houses and look inside the lit homes. According to Bobeh Frumeh, it was pretty scary to look into the dark, through the window, and suddenly face a wolf's glittering eyes. In those days, no one would venture outside at night, particularly not children. Listening to Bobeh Frumeh's stories, I developed a great fear of and respect for the wolf.

Another menace I lived in fear of was big birds. Bobeh Frumeh would tell me about birds with huge wings and sharp talons so powerful and strong that they could pick up little children with their enormous claws and carry them off. Whenever I was outside, I would look at the sky very carefully for those big birds, even though my bobeh assured me that those birds lived only in a place called Africa. I couldn't wait to gain weight and grow bigger so that no bird could ever pick me off the street.

I think now how lucky I was that Bobeh Frumeh had never heard of pythons and boa constrictors to tell me about and give me something else to worry about. Fortunately, at the time, the only type of snake Bobeh Frumeh and I knew about was the one mentioned in the Bible. That snake had caused a great deal of trouble and was cursed by God for beguiling Mother Eve into eating of the fruit of the tree which was in the midst of the garden. Of course, Eve did not listen to God's instruction not to eat the fruit of that tree, and we still suffer the consequences of being chased out of paradise, including having to get dressed — even though we have improved greatly on the fig-leaf attire that Adam and Eve fashioned after eating the forbidden fruit and experiencing the shame of their nakedness.

Kortelisy, even after some of the forest had been cleared, was well hidden from the rest of the world, separated from the main highway by bulrushes, marshes and large dense forests. It was beloved by no one, except for the local population. Legend has it that besides some saintly rabbis who visited Kortelisy to collect alms, money from the poor for the poor, the most distinguished visitor of Kortelisy was Napoleon. He and his army were on their way to Russia, to their doom, and had to build a special road through our forest to get there. Locals called this earth-packed dirt road by the grand name of "Napoleon's *shlyakh*," Napoleon's road. I recall villagers pointing out remnants of that legendary road, by my time out of use and covered with moss, ferns and weeds.

Kortelisy, with its simple but happy population, was surrounded by pristine and unspoiled nature as far as the eye could see. The sky met the earth in the form of a heavenly cupola, like a yarmulke, but no one in Kortelisy was convinced by this skullcap shape that the earth was round. The one nameless dirt road in Kortelisy had ditches on both sides to help absorb the melted snow and rainwater that flowed off the road. The ditches received a great deal of water, and a plentiful variety of lush green vegetation grew in them. All of it was precious food for the roaming domestic pigs, who enjoyed even the poison ivy that grew in the ditches, along with the tall thistle plants and the wild okra.

But the little prickly bulbs, which we called *shishkes*, growing on top of the thistle plants also served a more sacred purpose on Tisha B'Av, when Jews gathered in the synagogue, took off their shoes, settled down for the night on the floor and recited Jeremiah's Lamentations, weeping over the destruction of Jerusalem and its temple. To augment the pain of this tragic event, Jews in Kortelisy, while praying and lamenting in the synagogue, would throw those prickly, razor-sharp little bulbs of the thistle plant at each other. In Canada many years later, I discovered that okra is a very tasty, nutritious and edible vegetable, good for humans, not only for pigs.

The ditches at the sides of the road did little to keep it dry, as every time it rained or the snow melted, the road would turn mucky; it was pocked with potholes and deep puddles so that even the horses had a hard time pulling their wagons through the thick mud. Of course, there were no sidewalks, and people would walk on the road — which was covered in dung and mud and farmyard manure — together with their cows, sheep, horses and wagons, gaggles of geese and flocks of ducks, passing the occasional cyclist. Cyclists had to be very careful, because our local horses were not used to them. At the sight of a moving bicycle, the horses would get scared, go wild and start galloping like crazy. Sometimes, encounters and collisions between cyclists and horses carrying riders or pulling wagons resulted in serious injuries to both cyclists and horses.

Kortelisy was probably not the most wonderful place on earth. People worked hard, and yet they remained poor and had just enough to live on. They ate what they were able to raise in stock and cattle, and what they could catch, grow or pull out of the ground. Compared to the cities and even the other villages or hamlets in western Ukraine in the 1930s, Kortelisy was pretty backward. Farmers would never buy clothing. They wore what they were able to produce and manufacture for themselves. They made their own shirts, pants, coats and hats, and even footwear. Their shoes, called *postoly*, were made from the soft bark of the birch tree, which would be sliced into long, one-inch-wide ribbons and then plaited. Before putting on these "shoes," the farmers would wrap their feet in strips of cloth or boot rags and then tie up the strips of cloth with a fine homemade binding that was laced up to the knees. On Sundays and holidays, they would wear especially colourful wraps around their feet inside the *postoly*.

The farmers even made their own samogon, a homemade potato vodka, and grew their own makhorka, a kind of tobacco, which

I think were both illegal acts under the Poles and then the Soviets. Under the Germans everything was illegal. It was illegal to live.

I remember working in the green and luscious fields as a child, digging up potatoes. I especially remember the lunch breaks — sitting with the adults, munching on and enjoying sour pickles with freshly boiled or baked potatoes prepared from the very potatoes I'd just dug up with my own tiny bare hands. The freshly dug potatoes were cooked or baked over an open fire in the field. I also remember, quite vividly, the women singing beautifully with wonderful harmonies, as if they had previously rehearsed, as they walked down the road back home after a hard day's work, carrying hoes, scythes, sickles and other farming tools on their shoulders.

Kortelisy, although primitive, had a post office, which housed the only telephone in the village. It also had a fire brigade, which boasted a carriage with a water pump and tank and a huge bell mounted on it, and was drawn by horses with warning bells attached to their necks. There was a primary school and a police station that was run by Polish officers and officials up until 1939. Later, under the Soviets, my uncle Yerakhmiel became the manager of the post office. That was where I first saw and used a telephone. It was pure magic — by holding two pieces of the contraption, one against my ear and another against my mouth, I could hear and talk to my uncle while I was in the corridor and he sat in his enclosed office.

The wooden houses of Kortelisy had thatched roofs consisting of straw, so fires were frequent in the village. Whenever there was a fire, I would sit with my maternal grandfather, Zeyde Berchik, on top of the straw roof of his big wooden house with a bucket of water and rags in hand. When sparks would land on his roof from a nearby fire, we would quickly hit the sparks with the wet rags and save the house from a fiery end. The neighbours, along with homeowners all over the village, would do the same thing.

From the height of my grandfather's roof, reachable by a permanently installed wooden ladder, which I liked to climb before I developed a fear of heights, I could see the lake and surrounding marshes in the distance. I could also see the golden rye fields and cornfields, the tall yellow-rayed sunflower plants bowing toward the sun, the purple and white blooms of the potato and buckwheat plants and the multicoloured fields of lupine stretching before me. The lupine emitted the most wonderful and pleasant fragrance throughout the village.

The population of Kortelisy was about three thousand people, of which approximately 150 people, or thirty families, were Jewish. There were also some wandering Roma and a few Polish administrators and officials during the Polish regime, and the rest were Ukrainian Christians of the Ukrainian Orthodox, or *pravoslavny*, persuasion. They had a beautiful church, a *tzerkve* with a blue-green roof, probably copper, immediately across from my paternal grandparents' little house. As for the small Jewish population in Kortelisy, it had all the facilities and conveniences observant Jews required: a synagogue — though not as imposing as the church — a rabbi-cum-*shoykhet* who took care of all the ritual slaughtering, a cheder, and a mikveh used for ritual bathing built in the wide-open field at the outskirts of Kortelisy.

The only thing the Jewish population of Kortelisy lacked was a cemetery. We had to transport our dead to Ratno for burial. The Christian Ukrainian population, which was substantially larger and outnumbered the Jews by the thousands, had two cemeteries in Kortelisy: the old cemetery with its overturned moss-covered crosses and tombstones that sat across the road from my parents' house on a grassy, pine-tree-covered hill next to the sand dunes; and the new cemetery, surrounded by many birch and pine trees, which sat on the other side of the sand dunes, facing the old cemetery on the hill.

As a child, I used to see the elaborate funeral processions of Ukrainian Christians moving with a great deal of fanfare from the church at one end of the village to the new cemetery at the other end, with men carrying icons and huge flags on long sticks. A Ukrainian Orthodox priest would lead the funeral procession. Wearing a huge hat and heavy colourful attire, he would diffuse incense as he recited prayers loudly and clearly in the haunting and generous voice used for the Ukrainian Orthodox liturgy. His prayers were mixed with the cries and wailings of six or eight professional female wailers, depending on the means of the bereaved, who kneeled on both sides of the casket that sat on top of a wagon pulled by two or three horses. The casket was chiselled out of the bottom part of the trunk of a birch, pine or oak tree, or any other tree with a circumference that could accommodate the deceased.

When I was five or six, I was walking down the village road and I saw a farmer in his front yard chiselling a burial casket out of the bottom part of a tree trunk. It was probably for a relative who had died that very morning or during the night. This sight left me with a permanent sense of awe and sympathy for the dead, especially because I, as a Jew, did not expect to die. Employing my pure and simple childish logic, I had concluded that Jews and Roma don't die. Why? Because I had never seen a Jewish man in Kortelisy or a Roma chisel a burial casket; I had never seen a Jewish or Roma funeral; Kortelisy had neither a Roma nor a Jewish cemetery; and to my knowledge, no one in my family had died. I concluded that there was no Jewish cemetery because Jews don't die. I applied the same logic to the Roma.

Even though my bobeh Frumeh told me, quite often, about the death and murder of her cousins at the hands of marauding Cossacks, and even though I read and studied about the deaths of the Jewish patriarchs and matriarchs and other Jews mentioned in the Bible, I was convinced that Jews don't die. I never asked myself: if they don't die, how do they get to heaven and paradise, which I knew existed for the righteous. I gathered that Jews did have their lives shortened at the hands of murdering Cossacks, as had happened to my grandmother's cousins, but that natural death of Jews was not part of the scheme of things. I had never experienced a pogrom by Cossacks, but I knew all about pogroms. I had heard about the Kishinev pogrom and knew that it involved the killing of Jews, including babies. Thanks to my bobeh Frumeh, I lived in constant fear of wolves, huge flying birds and pogroms, and my fear of Cossacks was not eliminated by the fact that I believed that Jews don't die. When I would ask Bobeh Frumeh, "Why do Cossacks kill Jews?" the answer would always be "Vayl mir zaynen yidn"—*Because we are Jews.* At the time, I thought that this was a non-answer; in retrospect, however, I now believe it was the right and only true answer.

But this naiveté, my belief that Jews and Roma were immune from dying, was soon shattered. Very quickly, at about the age of eight or nine, while still a child, I discovered death — first of Roma, then of Jews — and faced death on a daily basis.

It's not easy to unlearn and discard what you learn when you are a child. It becomes part of your personality, and you have to dispose of part of yourself to shed those beliefs. It took horrific events — death and destruction that took place in front of my eyes — for me to finally realize that Jews and Roma die, even though they didn't have a cemetery in Kortelisy.

VILLAGE BOY

On my many travels with my father, I would see how people lived in the hamlets surrounding Kortelisy. Once, riding through the grass fields, where there were only markings of wheels and hooves to indicate the road, I noticed smoke coming out of the ground. Barefooted children in torn clothing were playing all around this smoked-filled area. I was curious; I had never seen smoke coming out of the ground. Father stopped the horse. It was a house, Father said; people lived there. It was a very strange-looking house, completely underground, a hovel — nothing but a windowless earth pit, flat and without a roof, just covered with straw, moss and grasses, with a barely noticeable pipe protruding out of the centre, emitting the smoke. "Those are very poor people living there," Father remarked. The sight of this underground home in the green fields with little barefooted children running around it seems to have stuck with me forever.

My younger brother, Laizer, and I lived with my parents in a house above ground. Compared to the hovel I had seen, our home was a palace, luxurious and comfortable. Our house, which may have been rented, had the appearance of a log cabin and was situated at one end of Kortelisy's single road. It was the first house one would come upon when entering the village from the west. Right across the road from it was the old Christian cemetery and the sand dunes, where the farmers would bury their potatoes for the winter, covering them with straw to protect them from the winter frost.

Our wooden house with its straw-covered roof had only one very small window looking onto the old cemetery and one fairly large room. In one corner stood a bed, in another the kitchen, and in another the dining area, where we ate on the Sabbath and holidays. The floor was made of clay; it was an unlevelled dirt floor with bumps, crevices and cracks. But on Friday, for the Sabbath, we would spread over the floor a fine orange-brown sand taken from the neighbouring sand dunes. This simple, soft sand would completely refresh the dark and ugly earth floor and provide a sense of renewal. On the Shavuos holiday, we would cover the entire floor with greenery, mainly water lilies and irises that my brother and I would gather from the nearby swamps. The foliage would emit a special and pleasant fragrance and add to the holiday spirit. Naturally, the swamps had leeches, which attached themselves to our bare legs and sucked on our blood. We found a very effective remedy: dropping a tiny pinch of salt on top of the leeches would make them fall off your leg without a fuss. The leeches, without knowing what had happened to them, would fall right back into the water. I always wondered whether they survived or if the salt killed them. I didn't want to be a killer, not even of the bothersome leeches.

For a long time I thought that covering our clay floor with greenery on Shavuos was something done only by my family because I had never seen it done in my grandparents' home or in any other Jewish home in Kortelisy. I later learned that it is an ancient Jewish custom to bring greenery and grasses, even trees, into your house on Shavuos. There were even famous rabbinic disputations on the question of bringing trees into the house on Shavuos.

In the middle of our house stood a tall wood stove, what we called a *hrube*. Built on the floor, it almost reached the ceiling and was covered with white tiles from top to bottom. It provided heating in winter and was also used for cooking. You could also fold your hands behind your back, lean against the *hrube* and warm up just like that. The main wood-burning furnace and stove used for baking and cooking stood in a corner of the house. We also slept on top of the flat wood-burning furnace, where it was very warm, but would sometimes wake up with a horrible headache. We did not realize that the headaches were the result of breathing in carbon monoxide created by the burning wood inside the furnace and that we were putting our lives in danger by sleeping there. There were instances of people dying of asphyxiation by carbon monoxide while sleeping on top of their furnaces. No inquiries were made to discover the cause of death, though, even if the dead were children or babies. People just died in those days and no one knew why.

We had no electricity, but there was a *pripetshik* on the side of the *hrube*, an opening where we lit kindling to provide light for the entire room at night. The light from this hearth was meagre and insufficient. Most of the room remained in the dark. But we were too poor to afford candles, which were used only on Friday nights. And on Friday nights, once the candles burned down, we all went to bed in the dark. We had kerosene lamps, but these were very seldom used because of the expense. Kindling wood was less expensive, or no expense at all, compared to kerosene or candles, even though we made our own candles.

Ours was a village without indoor plumbing, without electricity and without running water. For water, one had to go to a well that was shared with neighbours. It was dangerous, especially in the winter, to fetch water from a well. Some wells didn't have barriers around them, and the opening was level with the ground, so when water spilled around the well and turned to ice, careless water fetchers would slip and fall headfirst into the well.

None of the homes had an indoor toilet, and very few even had an outhouse. Zeyde Berchik had an outhouse, but for me the wooden outhouse had terrifying associations. For a child used to the comfort of the potty, the outhouse was like walking into a cruel death trap.

First of all, I was bothered by the swarms of brown house flies buzzing all around, touching me. The flies acquired their brown colour from contact with the feces in the outhouse pit, which attracted and nourished them. Secondly, and more seriously, I was always in fear that the wooden structure and the toilet seat built over the pit full of feces would collapse and I would fall into the pit and drown in shit. I always dreaded using the outhouse and preferred to do my business behind the stables; I felt safer and more comfortable there, even though it was public. Those without outhouses would usually relieve themselves behind the stables, and the feces would be devoured with great relish and gusto by the same roaming domestic pigs that cleared the lush vegetation on the sides of the road. Watching the pigs consume human feces, I felt that that was sufficient reason for Jews being prohibited by the Bible from eating pork.

Of course, pigs not being kosher, I stayed away from them, but I will always remember the very distinct and childish pleasure, mixed with fear and guilt, of holding a snorting, screaming, chubby, non-kosher, one-week-old piglet in my arms. The little baby porker refused to be held and struggled to extricate itself from my arms, screeching violently. I held on to it firmly, torn between guilt and pleasure. Later in life, when I stopped observing all the biblical and rabbinic commandments, I discovered lobster, which is as un-kosher as pork, and yet, I was able to devour every part of it, including the lobster's stomach contents, which must have contained digested food turned to lobster feces. I guess I had been too quick to condemn the porkers for just enjoying their meal of choice.

THE CURSE OF BEING BORN IN THE MONTH OF TAMMUZ

I was born in the backwoods of western Ukraine in a village on the periphery of history and geography in 1931, or maybe in 1932, according to my mother's calculations, but for sure in the Hebrew month of Tammuz, which usually corresponds to June–July in the Gregorian calendar. I was named Pinchas Elye after two of my late great-grandfathers: Pinkhes Ruttenberg on my maternal grandmother's side and Eliyahu Rothchild on my paternal grandmother's side.

The blessed event of my birth, along with my given names, was duly recorded on the blank leaf inside the front cover of our family's prayer book. Thereafter, no one even glanced at the inscription, even though the *sider* was diligently and religiously used by the entire family, including me, for daily prayers. Unfortunately, the prayer book with all its inscriptions — recording my birth and many other family events, births and deaths — would not survive the events that were to come.

I suspect that later, when we were in Linz, Austria, and I had to apply for an identity card, Mother made me a year or so younger than I was — she chose July 19, 1932 — so that I could get extra milk and other special rations distributed by the American Jewish Joint Distribution Committee.

But, in any event, birthdays were not remembered or celebrated in our home or in any other Jewish home in my village. Celebrating a birthday was *farbotn*, taboo, and even mentioning age was a possible invitation to the evil eye, maybe even — God forbid — Satan or the wicked Ashmeday himself, the king of all demons. Celebrating birthdays involved counting, and counting — particularly of Jews and their birthdays — was truly dangerous, a prohibition going back to biblical days. If one absolutely had to count, the word "not" would always precede the number. The counting would then go as follows: not one, not two, not three, not four and so on. Somehow, by employing the word "nisht"(not) before the number of one's age, all evil spirits would be cast away, as if the age had never been stated.

Laizer and I didn't even know about birthday celebrations. We never received birthday greetings, blew out birthday candles, had birthday cake or received birthday presents. However, we always received Chanukah gelt, cash gifts on the Chanukah holiday. On Chanukah there were special visits to grandparents and other relatives, even strangers in the village, for the sole purpose of collecting Chanukah loot. And though we didn't know much about birthdays, we never felt deprived or missed celebrating them. Despite not celebrating our birthdays, our childhoods were complete and fulfilled by what we had.

My mother affectionately dubbed me with a diminutive and called me Pineleh, as did the rest of the family. However, whenever I was in trouble or fell into mischief, I was always sternly addressed by my formal, full name of Pinchas Elye. My parents would say, "Pinchas Elye, what happened here?" or "Pinchas Elye, can you explain yourself?" or "Pinchas Elye, did you recite the Modeh Ani prayer this morning?" or "Pinchas Elye, you are not listening." I knew I was in trouble when I heard Pinchas Elye.

Notwithstanding the occasional tough talk from my parents and elders, Pineleh, like the king, could do no wrong. My brother and I were pampered and spoiled by uncles and two sets of grandparents who lived practically next door, as did everyone else in the small village with only one street.

My grandmother Frumeh liked to tell, with great relish, a story about how smart a child I was, when at four or five I repeatedly refused her offers of food. Finally, she gave up and stopped asking. Naturally, I wanted to have the food; no child in my village would ever refuse food. But once I had said "no" to several offers, I was too proud to change my mind. I was playing a childish game of hard-to-get; I was, after all, totally spoiled. Eventually, not only did she stop asking, she herself continued munching on the food with great enjoyment, deliberately teasing me. Watching my grandmother smacking her lips, I suddenly developed an even greater appetite. Without necessarily admitting that I had really wanted the food at the outset, I complained to my grandmother, saying, "Had you asked me at least one more time I would have said yes." For years my family repeated this story and were amused, much to my delight, even though I did not understand the humour in it; I was serious about what I had said about her asking me one more time.

It breaks my heart to remember what an obstinate child I was. When I was three or four, I was walking with my mother through a path in the fields toward the stables. She was carrying a huge sack of hay on her left shoulder and supported it with her left hand while holding my hand with her right hand, leading me. When we came upon some puddles of muddy water on the trail, I refused to budge and walk across the puddles. I insisted on being carried.

In my village, kids were used to mud and puddles and even enjoyed walking into them to play and splash. In fact, instead of avoiding them, they would look for them and deliberately jump into them, especially when barefoot. Usually, I too would rejoice at the opportunity of jumping into a puddle, no matter how muddy it was — the muddier the better. This time, for some reason, I refused to walk in the puddles. Pineleh was adamant in the face of all Mother's begging.

My mother, unable to carry both the sack of hay and me at the same time, dropped the sack, picked me up and carried me across the muddy puddles. Once she dropped me off, she left me standing to return to pick up the sack of hay. She repeated these movements again and again until we cleared all the muddy puddles in our way. I still don't understand how Mother tolerated this behaviour, even from a child.

My parents loved their children. Children were considered God-given and a treasure by everyone in the village. When it came to raising children, no sacrifice was too great. The greatest curse was to be a married couple without children. But although my brother and I were pampered and spoiled, we were well disciplined. Strict obedience and respect for your elders was expected from all children, not only by our parents and relatives, but also by strangers, who applied the same standards of behaviour to all children in the village. And, of course, discipline was required by our teachers. Misbehaving was tantamount to hooliganism and resulted in severe punishment and being shamed before your classmates. I was raised with the guiding principle of "mipney seyvo tokum," that one should rise before one's elders as a sign of respect.

~

It was my misfortune to be born in the month of Tammuz, as it led to a hurtful play on words by my dear mother. The word "Tammuz" is apparently of Sumerian and Babylonian origin. It is the name of a Mesopotamian shepherd god, king of biblical Erech, or Uruk. But this is not where my problem began. My problem derived from the first syllable of the name of the month of Tammuz. As anyone who has read about the four sons in the Passover Haggadah will tell you, the third son described in the readings is the *tam*, which means simpleton in Hebrew.

My dear mother, in a talmudic fashion, applied this interpretation to me and forever branded me as the simple son, just like the third son in the Passover Haggadah. I must have been five or six, and this horrible but innocent comment made by my mother in an unguarded moment left a permanent mark on my being: I was a dummy, a fact that was duly established and supported by sacred text, a text in which I myself firmly believed at the time. Throughout my life, each time I faced a challenge, my mother's comment would come to mind and I would ask myself whether I was capable and smart enough to succeed, or was I doomed to failure? My conclusion was always that I was doomed to failure and that in order to succeed I would have to put in a great deal of extra effort — whether it was learning to skate, ski or drive a car, study at university, get married or raise children.

Mother and Father made great sacrifices to raise us, but they never praised us or articulated love or pride about any of our true, though minor, achievements; it was simply expected of us. But I knew, even though they never said so, that they loved us and were proud of us. Praises would come to us indirectly, via reports from others, even strangers, who were subjected by Mother and Father to stories about our achievements.

Upon my mother's death in 1984, I found a newspaper clipping from 1961 in her wallet. It listed the names of the candidates, including me, who had passed the Quebec bar exams. She never told me that she was proud of my graduating from law school and passing the bar exams. But she carried the newspaper clipping in her wallet for over twenty years, till her dying day.

SHAKY WORLD

I still feel and remember even the simple and ordinary events — the touch of my grandmother Frumeh when I was a child with a runny nose and dishevelled attire. She would wipe my nose, wash my face, straighten my clothing and tuck my shirt into my shorts, and she helped calm a hysterical and frightened little boy who started discharging long white parasitic tapeworms while on the potty. As for my other grandmother, Freyde, she must have seen me as gullible and naive, a strong believer. She warned me not to look at the *kohanim* who were covered with their prayer shawls while giving the congregation the priestly blessing because that would bring on blindness. She also told me to avoid encounters with *sheydim un vilde rukhes* and that in order to avoid the demons and evil spirits, I should stay inside the synagogue during Neilah, the final prayer of Yom Kippur. I heeded her warnings then, and they are still part of me. Even though I no longer believe that I will become blind by looking at a man covered in a tallis or that demons and wild spirits roam outside the synagogue during the Neilah prayer, I stay inside the synagogue during Neilah, and I do not look at the *kohanim* while they are blessing the congregation.

My religious education started in the Kortelisy cheder at age three or four, when my father brought me wrapped in a tallis, as was the custom. I learned the *alefbeys*, combining the vowels and letters of the Hebrew alphabet in a singsong: *kometz alef* "*o*," *kometz beys* "*bo*," *kometz giml* "*go*," *kometz daled* "*do*." But after learning the alphabet and then the Chumash (Five Books of Moses) with Rashi's commentary, I had to deal with even more complex issues in Pirkei Avos, the Sayings of Our Fathers. I read and studied what Rabbi Shimon ben Gamliel said: "Al shloysho dvorim ha-oylem kayem — al hadin, v'al haemes, v'al hasholem"—*On three things does the world stand — on justice, truth and peace*. I also memorized the sayings of Shimon Hatzadik, Simon the Righteous, who said that "al shloysho dvorim ha-oylem oymeyd: al hatoyre, v'al ho-avoyde v'al gemilas khsodim"—*on three things the world stands: on the Torah, on divine worship and on acts of loving-kindness*. At the time, the way I saw the world, it was flat like a matzo and, in accordance with the sayings of Rabbi Shimon ben Gamliel and Rabbi Shimon Hatzadik, which I took literally, the matzo-shaped world stood on only three pillars. And so, to my mind, the world on its three pillars was shaky and in danger of collapsing without a fourth pillar to maintain the balance. Unfortunately, I could not think of a proper and meaningful name for the fourth pillar. I may still be searching.

I had an even more difficult time understanding what Rabbi Akavya ben Mahalalel said in the Sayings of Our Fathers: "Reflect on three things and you will avoid transgression: Know where you came from, where you are going, and before whom you will have to give an account and reckoning. 'Where you came from' — from a putrid drop. 'Where you are going' — to a place of dust, worms and maggots. 'And before whom you will have to give an account and reckoning' — before the Supreme King of kings, the Holy One, blessed be He." I had an especially hard time understanding the part about where we came from — the "putrid drop." I also struggled to understand the "place of dust, worms and maggots." But it did not matter whether I understood the meaning of the words; all I had to do was memorize them, which I did diligently, and I was able to recite these verses at the drop of a hat — not only Pirkei Avos, but also large portions of Akdomus, a liturgical poem written in terse Aramaic by Rabbi Meir ben Isaac of France in the eleventh century.

As a child, my heroes were biblical figures: Joshua, Samson, King David and King Saul. I cried like a baby when reading King David's *kine*, his lament over the death of King Saul and his son Jonathan in the book of Samuel II: "Saul and Jonathan, beloved and cherished, never parted in life or in death!" and verse 24, "Daughters of Israel, weep over Saul...."

My favourite book outside the cheder was a children's book in Hebrew with wonderful colourful illustrations. It was called *Reyshis daas* (First knowledge), and my father gave it to me when he returned from one of his trips, sometime before 1939, when we were still part of Poland. It was the only children's book I had and showed a world I had never seen in real life, one in which children wore smart shoes and lived in big cities.

Yiddish and Ukrainian were my mother tongues. Because I learned the Hebrew alphabet in cheder, I could easily read Yiddish books without instruction. I particularly remember reading the Sholem Aleichem story "Chanukah gelt," which was a detailed description of my own family's celebration of Chanukah in every respect — from making and eating potato latkes to receiving cash gifts, lighting candles and singing Chanukah songs in Yiddish and Hebrew. I read other Sholem Aleichem stories that I also felt were about me: "Dos meserl" (The Penknife) and "Di fon" (The Flag). The latter is about a cute and happy little boy, not unlike the little boys I knew in Kortelisy. But this boy, unfortunately, could not pronounce the letter "k" and so was called Topele Tuturitu instead of his real name, Kopele Kukuriku. But Kopele still had a great deal of fun at the synagogue on Simchas Torah, carrying a flag with an apple and candle stuck on top, not unlike me and my friends in real life. I still remember the joy and pleasure I had reading Mani Leib's book-length poem *Yingl Tsingl Khvat*, about a mischievous little boy, full of adventure, with whom I was in complete sympathy and wanted to emulate.

I was introduced to Yiddish stories by my three uncles; all of them had books in many languages, and I recall browsing through their Yiddish books. Based on the illustrations I remember, the books must have been on biology and physics and other sciences; they contained drawings and illustrations that fascinated and startled me, even though I didn't understand the drawings or the words.

I also remember being plagued by the Yiddish song "Der feter Yishmoel vos voynt in Eretz Yisroel" (Uncle Ishmael who lives in the Land of Israel), which I heard so many times at *shaleshudes*, the third meal of the Sabbath, in the late afternoon. What was the *feter* Yishmoel doing in Eretz Yisroel? And why was he such a mean uncle, not allowing Jews to live in the holy land, the land of Abraham, Isaac and Jacob, which, after all, was God-given and belonged to the Jews?

MAGIC CURES AND POTIONS

Kortelisy had no doctors or hospitals, so getting sick in Kortelisy was not a good option. But there were quite a few healers, including my own grandmother Freyde. I remember one such healer very clearly: Dvoyre di alte, The Old Dvoyre, on whose services my parents sometimes relied when my brother or I became sick. Dvoyre di alte was actually quite old and deserved the nomenclature. But she was dubbed Dvoyre di alte not necessarily because she was old, but to distinguish her from another, younger Dvoyre who lived in the village.

Jews in Kortelisy did not rely much on family names. When Jews were given an *aliye* in the synagogue, they were not called up to the Torah by their family name, but by their given name and the given name of their father. Surnames had been imposed on Jews by the gentiles, and therefore they did not count for much. And so, while there were two people in Kortelisy called Yidl, they were distinguished from each other not by their family names but by a special description. One was called Yidl der milkhiker, "Dairy" Yidl, and the other was called Yidl der fleyshiker, "Meat" Yidl. There were also two Zalmens in the village. Again, to distinguish one from the other, one was called by his given name, Zalmen, and the other was called Zalmen der siver, the Grey Zalmen. He was actually grey, so his name appropriately described his appearance.

Dvoyre di alte was short and chubby. She had a round and wrinkled face, but it was soft, pleasant and warm. She always wore black clothes and walked with a cane, carrying a bag containing her own medicines and potions and candy for her child patients — a rare treat for Kortelisy children. By today's standards Dvoyre di alte might not be much of a healer, but children in my village were delighted to get sick, knowing that after a visit from Dvoyre di alte, there would always be candy.

When Laizer was a baby, he was quite sickly. He was sick enough to be taken to Brest-Litovsk to be seen by a real city doctor on numerous occasions. I was jealous because Laizer got to travel by horse and buggy, even by train, and he would see the big city. My jealousy was so great that on one occasion, I pretended to be very sick. Making all the sounds of agony, I told my parents that I was in terrible pain and should be seen by a doctor immediately, which meant we should travel to Brest-Litovsk pronto. I must have listed at least a dozen symptoms. Still, I was apparently not very convincing because I noticed that, instead of being alarmed over my terrible state of health, my parents were not upset at all. On the contrary, they seemed to be snickering and very amused by my complaints. The more I screamed in pain, the more they laughed and delighted in my displays of illness. My father, obviously playing along, topped off the entertainment and harnessed the horse and wagon, ready to drive me to the big city. I guess I must have had some consideration for my parents, or maybe I became fearful of the big-city doctor, but when I saw my father all ready to go, I told my parents, with a great sigh of relief, that the pain had gone and I was feeling much better. They asked me again and again, in a very serious manner, how I felt, showing great concern. The tables had turned, and now I had to convince them that I was well and we didn't have to travel to Brest-Litovsk. The trip was cancelled. I did, however, receive a consolation prize: I was rewarded with a cup of hot milk and cocoa, usually given only to very sick children or offered on other rare occasions.

My little brother, baby Laizer, still in swaddles, cried a lot at night. However, that did not warrant a trip to Brest-Litovsk. Instead, my parents consulted Dvoyre di alte. Without even examining my brother, she prescribed a remedy: she told my mother to place a piece of steel or iron under his pillow. My mother did so and, although it took a while, maybe a year or two, my brother eventually stopped crying and slept through the night. As a healer, no one could equal Dvoyre di alte; she performed magic.

My own experience with Dvoyre di alte happened when I developed a terrible rash on my face. Dvoyre di alte arrived with her usual bag, from which she pulled some pieces of kindling wood. She lit the kindling at both ends, twirled the lit kindling against my face, practically singeing my eyebrows and, after mumbling some incantations I did not understand, spat into my face, spraying warm spit all over my rash. When the fire reached the middle of the kindling, Dvoyre extinguished it and, holding the remnants of the wood in her fingers, continued to spray my face with her drizzly spit several more times while mumbling more incantations. The rash did not immediately disappear, but it worked; after a while the rash vanished completely and never came back. Dvoyre's medicine was effective, and as expected, I received candy from Dvoyre after the treatment.

The Jewish population of Kortelisy did not always rely on healers such as Dvoyre di alte, or even doctors, to help the sick, especially those in truly critical condition and on the verge of death. In addition to prayers as a last resort for the sick, the remedy was to change the name of the sick person so that the Angel of Death would be misled, totally confused and unable to find his victim. Ostensibly, the Angel of Death recognizes the victim only by his or her name and doesn't check passports or identity cards. Unfortunately, the citizens of Kortelisy soon realized that this clever manoeuvre would only delay matters. Eventually, the Angel of Death would do some detective work and discover the plot and, like a good sleuth, find the object of his search, even though he or she was known to the rest of Kortelisy under a brand new name.

Although the Angel of Death could be a good sleuth, devious and clever, Jews in Kortelisy knew that on rare occasions they could outsmart the Angel of Death through their own trickery, not only by changing a name but also through constant prayer and fasting, at least two days a week, either for themselves or via surrogates. There were actual cases of Jews in Kortelisy being very sick and on the verge of death and then recovering fully and living a long life because they had tricked the Angel of Death one way or another.

In Kortelisy we also used the sneeze test to predict the future and test the veracity of an event, any event. If, for example, someone would say that Berl, who had fallen ill, would recover and live a long life, and another person — any person in the vicinity, including Berl — would sneeze, this would confirm the veracity of the statement: Berl would recover and live a long life. A sneeze never failed to be followed by a blessing for health and long life. There was great faith in the sneeze as a sign of good fortune and healing power. I still remember the boisterous reaction of my parents, uncles and grandparents to any of my sneezes: outbursts of hundreds of cries of "To your health and long life!" again and again after every sneeze. And to get the desired attention, I would continue with fake sneezes, with many of my good wishers playing along until I got tired and stopped.

Dvoyre di alte, even though she was a healer and familiar with all the medicines and potions to cure the sick and add years to life, knew that when one reaches a certain age, the various potions or medicines — even changing one's name and all the sneezing and prayers in the world — would not help to avoid the eventuality of death; it is in the hands of God and one must eventually die, sooner or later, as it is written, "Lord, what is man that You care for him, a mortal that You notice him? Man is like a fleeting breath, his days like a passing shadow. In the morning he flourishes and grows; in the evening he withers and dries up." And the end of Man is that he turns to dust and "the dust returns to the earth as it was, but the spirit returns to God who gave it." Those were Dvoyre's articles of faith, and she lived by them, as did every other Jew in Kortelisy.

So, to avoid embarrassment and make sure she arrived in heaven in fine attire and not like a pauper, Dvoyre spared no expense and prepared for herself a set of the finest, most beautiful and expensive shrouds. In contrast to her black street clothes, the shrouds she prepared were white, as white as snow. Now that she had shrouds, she was prepared to die, to leave this temporary, cruel world, meet her Maker and enter the eternal spiritual world of paradise.

A FAILED THIEF

Toy stores and candy shops did not exist in Kortelisy, so children made their own toys and seldom had candy. I remember making my own balloons and kites, which would fly way up into the sky. I also made my own skates, called *konki*, and skis. I discovered many years later that I was more proficient on my homemade skates than I was on factory-made ones. I made my own drinking glasses by popping off the necks of bottles. The process would require at least three people — one holding the bottle tight and the other two wrapping a thin but rough cord around the neck of the bottle and pulling it back and forth to create enough friction to pop it off, resulting in a perfectly shaped drinking glass. But one had to be very careful when using those homemade drinking glasses, as the edges were quite sharp even after they were filed.

I had only one toy, which I made myself. It was a long wire fashioned into an open square at one end, where the iron rim of a barrel would rest. I would roll this iron rim as fast as I could down the only street in Kortelisy. There was only one kid in Kortelisy who had a decent toy, a BB gun that discharged actual projectiles. But he was the son of Tulier, the richest person in Kortelisy, Jew or gentile, who had the liquor monopoly in the village and the only liquor store in the area.

We children also played hide-and-seek. To pick the child who would be the seeker, one of us would point to each of the players while reciting our forefather Jacob's blessing to his grandsons Ephraim and Menashe: "Hamalakh hagoyel oysi m'kol ro yevorekh es haneorim… v'yidgu leroyv b'kerev ha-oretz"—*May the angel who rescued me from all harm bless these boys… and may they increase greatly on the earth.* If the finger was pointing at you while the last word in the verse, *ha-oretz*, was being spoken, you were the seeker. We also played more relaxing and subdued games, like cat's cradle and hopscotch.

The most adventurous game took place on Lag B'omer, a day that falls between Passover and Shavuos. Under the leadership of the village rabbi himself, with Yisroel the yeshiva student playing the part of one of Joshua's *m'raglim*, one of the spies who went "to view the land" of Canaan in biblical times, boys armed with sticks and homemade bows and arrows pretended to be ancient Hebrew warriors, marching in formation like fearless soldiers ready for battle, like true Maccabees. We would explore the fields, woods and marshes — which were plentiful in the neighbourhood — while at the same time trying very hard to avoid vicious dogs and hostile Christian kids, who apparently were always prepared to fight and not just pretend. At the end of the excursion, barring any broken bones and injuries due to an encounter with the gentile kids, we would return to the rabbi's home to celebrate the heroic adventure and enjoy a wonderful feast prepared by the rabbi's wife and the mothers of the adventurous boys.

In the summer of 1937 or 1938, when I was six or seven, I travelled with my grandmother Frumeh to visit relatives in a neighbouring village. We rode in style in a beautiful two-passenger open horse-driven carriage. The horse and *drozhky* were richly decorated with flowers and multicoloured sashes and ribbons and driven by a professional hired coachman. My dear grandmother was dressed in a long black dress with white trim around the neckline, a black coat with a fine fur collar, and a black hat decorated with feathers and flowers. She was beautiful and looked like a queen. I felt terribly important being driven by a coachman with this beautiful lady beside me, particularly when the farmers and peasants on the road stepped aside, treating us like nobility, saluting and waving at us respectfully like we were Polish *pritsim*.

When we arrived at the home of our relatives, I was extremely impressed. Firstly, the house itself was so very big and had many rooms, and its roof was not covered with straw, as houses were in Kortelisy, but had beautiful multicoloured shingles, something I had never seen before. Secondly, to get water, our relatives didn't have to go outside to a well. In their kitchen — which was a separate room — over a tin basin there was a magic handle attached to a pump; all one had to do was pull the handle up and down and water would come gushing from a spout into the basin. To my eyes, it was pure magic. I was so taken by the water pump that I couldn't stop drinking water so that I could use the pump again and again.

There was also a little boy there, probably my age, most likely a cousin. After this visit, I never saw him again. But at the time, I thought he was a lucky little boy. Not only did he live in a beautiful big house with many rooms and water flowing inside the house, he also had many toys to play with, and he was happy to share them and play with me. I was especially taken with his four-wheeled wooden wagon, which could carry three or four kids down the hill and had a long handle in front to steer it. I immediately started formulating plans to relieve that little boy of his wagon, preferably without detection. I finally stumbled on my evil plan. In the back of our *drozhky* there was a substantial amount of hay for the horse. I put the toy wagon in the back of the *drozhky*, covering it completely, thinking that no one would look for it there. I almost got away with it. Our short visit came to an end, and we were on our way, but after we made the turn from the yard onto the street, the father of the boy ran after us. He stopped us, walked to the back of our *drozhky* and pulled the wagon out of the hay. I never found out how he discovered the whereabouts of the wagon at that moment. I did, however, rejoice that I was never accused of theft and, in my mind, I had almost succeeded in my attempt at subterfuge.

I attempted a similar theft of a toy in 1939. After Poland was defeated by Germany, Kortelisy was suddenly discovered by hundreds of Jewish refugee families, called *bezentses* in Yiddish. Unfortunately, in Kortelisy we did not understand the gravity of the situation and the true reasons why those Jews were escaping from the Germans. My parents accommodated at least three or four families in our single-room house for months. They slept on straw and hay on the bare earthen floor. Some of the families decided to return back home to the west, and others took their chances and continued east into the Soviet Union. That turned out to be the better choice.

I recall, with great sadness and regret, an incident involving one little refugee boy who lived with us. He had a big orange ball, and I wanted it. I had never seen a ball before, and I coveted it from this child who was far from his home, who had nothing. I decided to steal it and came up with a clever plan. In a corner of the house near the entrance, my parents kept a large heap of pumpkins. Thinking that the orange ball would be well camouflaged among the pumpkins until the boy and his family left, I threw the ball into the pile when nobody was looking. Luckily for the boy, he detected his ball among the pumpkins and took it with him when they left. In the end, I was relieved that the boy had found his ball and was able to take it with him on that uncertain route he would be travelling with his parents and siblings.

It appeared to me based on this incident and my previous attempt that I was a total failure in the art of theft. And even though I was not accused, and maybe not even suspected, I was certain that God knew what I was up to, and I was plagued by the thought that I may have broken two of the Ten Commandments, the Eighth and the Tenth: Thou shalt not steal and Thou shalt not covet. I lived in fear that God knew what I was doing and that my punishment was on the way.

THIS TOO IS FOR THE GOOD

My father, whom we called Tateh, worked hard and was a good and kind man. I never saw him upset or angry, except on one occasion. When I was about six years old, I suggested to my father that he had nothing to do with my birth and that I didn't have to listen to him and didn't know what he was doing in the house with us. Well, not only did he get angry, he almost strangled me. After this event, he continued to assure me that he truly was my father. Although his assurances were comforting, I really did not understand what my father's function was in my birth, and he had a hard time finding the right words to explain birth, family and relationships to me. I ended up with the confused notion that I came from my mother's stomach and, at the same time, was delivered by the stork. I continued living in the dark about human birth for many years.

My mother was a beautiful woman. In good times, she was elegantly dressed and wore red lipstick and high heels. She was very slim and had a happy round face. Mother wore her hair in the traditional Ukrainian fashion, her thick blond braids wrapped around her head. She loved jokes and sometimes made up her own jokes in conversations with other people. She also enjoyed vodka shots and occasionally sipping cherry liqueur. As a joke, she would puff on a cigarette, which was not in style for a lady of her background and upbringing. She also loved to play pranks and loved laughing.

For a village girl, Mother was unusually well-educated. She had graduated from a Hebrew gymnasium, which was the equivalent of a high school. Like her brothers, she spoke Hebrew, Russian, Polish and Ukrainian and, of course, Yiddish. She would reminisce with great pride about the times when, as a young girl, she had attended lectures by many of the Zionist guest speakers, including the great Ya'akov Zerubavel and many of the Yiddish and Hebrew writers who had lectured in nearby Ratno and Brest-Litovsk. After the war, she learned English and a smattering of French. She even read, in English, many of the world's literary treasures, including Tolstoy's *War and Peace*, which she had read many years earlier in the original Russian.

Unfortunately, Father never received a formal or secular education, unlike Mother or his younger brother, Shmilke. Father never went to school, except for a bit of cheder. From early childhood, he had to help provide for the family. Of course, in cheder, he studied the Pentateuch, as well as the oral tradition as recorded in the Mishnah. As an adult, he even dabbled in the more complex rabbinic discussions in the Gemora. He knew the daily prayer book and Tehillim (Psalms) by heart. Later, in Montreal, when travelling to work by bus, east of Pie-IX Boulevard, he would recite the Psalms in that ancient and haunting tune, loud, proud and clear, in the presence of other passengers who, more often than not, allowed him to enjoy the whole bench to himself.

My father was not a professional *khazn*, cantor, but he was a wonderful *bal tfile*, prayer leader. He loved being a *bal tfile*, from the daily Shacharis, Minchah and Maariv prayers to the most exalted prayer of Kol Nidrei, the opening prayer of Yom Kippur in which all vows are renounced. He sang the prayer in the Volyn *nusekh*, singing the traditional melody in a sweet voice. It was more moving and authentic and heart-warming than any professional cantorial rendition.

Considering his lack of a formal education, Father could only do menial work, so he became a *soykher*, a merchant. He travelled quite often in connection with his work and sometimes dealt in cattle and other livestock. Sometimes he would collect rags or scrap iron. During the Soviet rule he became a government employee, still collecting scrap iron. Although he was only modestly successful, he provided enough for his family. We had shelter, security and never went hungry in Kortelisy.

Even though the neighbouring house of the Sheftel family, with whom we shared the water well, looked like a mansion compared to ours — with its many rooms and a wooden floor — my brother and I never considered ourselves poor or thought that the neighbour's house was better than ours. We were always properly dressed and ate the same staples as the rest of the community. Our candlelit Friday night suppers were always the best meals, and there was a great deal of singing between every course, songs known as *zmires*. On Shabbos morning, for our special Sabbath breakfast, there was always a delicious sponge cake that Mother had baked the day before, accompanied by hot thick brown milk that had simmered overnight, sealed off inside the brick hearth of our furnace-stove. On Shabbos and holidays we always ate delicious and special food. We enjoyed a comfortable life at home and in the synagogue, where most congregants were relatives, neighbours or friends. The Sabbath day always provided particular pleasure and serenity after the hardship and toil of the week.

Father was a *someyakh b'khelkoy*, always happy with what life presented him, and we had a very happy home. My father was the eternal optimist and always looked for a positive spin to any situation. He firmly believed in the saying "gam zu l'toyve"—*this too is for the good* by the first century talmudic sage, the *tane* Nachum Ish Gamzu. Even during the war, daily facing the threat of death, Father always saw a silver lining, no matter how desperate we were.

We had a three-legged cooking pot, called a *drayfus* in Yiddish, which worked on naphtha and was used to boil or warm up food. Once, when I was about ten years old, my parents were not home, and I decided to investigate that fascinating gold-coloured piece of kitchen equipment. Somehow, I managed to unscrew the cover to the container of the very flammable fuel and spilled the naphtha all over the floor until it reached a most precious sack of flour that was on the floor nearby. The entire sack of flour, which would have been enough to bake bread for months and months, was spoiled. When my parents returned and Mother smelled the naphtha and realized what had happened, there was murder in her eyes and heart. It was during the war, and it was not an easy matter to replace all that precious flour. My act had placed my family, without exaggeration, on the verge of starvation. My father tried to console my mother and, in his usual *ish gam zu* fashion, he pointed out the positive to Mother, which made Mother even more angry as, on the face of it, there was nothing positive in what I had done. "A kaporeh oyfn mel," my father said, meaning, *let the flour be the sacrifice* or *to hell with the flour*. Father continued arguing with Mother. "It could have been worse. Imagine what could have happened had he been playing with matches at the same time. And *tsveytns*, secondly," he argued, aggravating Mother even more, "it is really not his fault. He is only a child, and we should not have left the pot there." In every argument, Father always supported his position by making different points: first, second, third — *ershtns*, *tsveytns*, *dritns*, and sometimes even *fertns* and *fiftns*.

In my father's mind, life was too precious to waste time and worry on a sack of flour, even in wartime. Aggravation wouldn't make the flour edible, and punishing and yelling at the child would not replace the flour. Father took me on his lap and talked to me calmly, explaining that I had done something wrong and that it had upset Mother. I knew I had done something wrong and that I was saved by Father, who stopped Mother from tearing me apart. My father may have been right in his argument. Even though I did do something terrible and deserved my mother's wrath, in the end Mother's aggravation, as he said, was *umzist*, for nothing.

Whenever my father argued in this *ish gam zu* way, Mother would accuse him of not being bothered by anything, using this expression in Yiddish to describe his supposed cold and unconcerned character: "Er hot a kaltn lung un leber"—*He's got a cold lung and liver*, meaning he's a cold fish or a thick-skinned person. But Father did have worries. He just dealt with them in his own way — without hysteria or panic; he was always calm, cool and collected.

Many years later, as a lawyer arguing cases before the bar, when I had very little to offer in the defence of my client, I was always able to come up with a most excellent but delightfully flimsy defence using my father's model and logic, just like when he argued in my defence in front of Mother. These arguments were nonsensical, but too charming to be refuted. And I always tried my best, not unlike my father, to keep calm and not to look too perturbed or anxious.

From his birth, my father's life was a struggle. In 1904, his father, my zeyde Meyer, left his wife, my bobeh Freyde, who was pregnant with my father, to seek his fortune in *Amerike*. It was a time when anyone with healthy lungs could immigrate to and work in *Amerike*, and quite a few other Kortelisians had already made the journey. Between the years 1893 and 1923, almost twenty Blitts (or Blits) from Kortelisy, Ratno, Kowel and some other villages in the area, men and women between the ages of fifteen and fifty-five, passed through Ellis Island. Some of them Americanized their names to Bloom. According to the records, the name of my village is always spelled differently; sometimes Kortillis, sometimes Kirtilas and sometimes Kartelisy. It is also listed as being in different countries — sometimes in Russia and sometimes in Poland.

Shortly after Zeyde Meyer's departure, my bobeh Freyde gave birth to my father, on August 17, 1904. She now had to raise two children by herself: Moyshe-Dovid, the eldest son, and my father, Mordechai-Leib or Aryeh. (I believe there was also a son even older than my father and Moyshe-Dovid, named Pinchas, who died as an adult.)

Bobeh Freyde, who had a married older sister already living in

New York City, pleaded with my grandfather: "Bring us to *Amerike*!" He refused. My grandmother then decided to seek the advice and help of her husband's saintly rebbe. My zeyde was the follower of the miracle-working Rabbi of Turzysk, which Jews called Trisk. After listening to my grandmother's pleadings and lamentations, and her recounting of her bitter struggle to survive with her small children without a husband, the rebbe decided to write to my grandfather and ordered him to bring the family to America. My grandfather, who was working in a sweatshop in New York City, completely disregarded the rabbi's order. He wrote back to his wife, with all the disrespect he could possibly muster for his saintly miracle-working rebbe: "I am myself a rebbe. I don't need counsel. We will not settle in *Amerike*. I am coming home."

The problem was that he did not come home immediately. Instead, he returned home sometime in 1913, nearly nine years later, finding the new addition to his family, my father. And this return was short-lived. Zeyde Meyer stayed long enough in Kortelisy to conceive his youngest son, Shmilke, and then quickly departed for the United States again, this time arriving at Ellis Island on September 13, 1913, at age forty. His landing registration declares him to be Hungarian, of Hebrew Nationality, and gave as his last place of residence: Ratno, Russia.

Zeyde Meyer did not like New York or *Amerike*. To him, *Amerike* was a den of wickedness and sin, especially for Jews who had abandoned their faith and were turning into *goyim*. When he spoke to me about *Amerike* many years after his return, I was informed that even though they have *khale indervokhn*, they eat challah on weekdays, *Amerike* is a dangerous place to live. I learned everything I knew about America from Zeyde Meyer. People got shot on the streets of New York, and one of its cities was destroyed like biblical Sodom because of the sins of the people there. My grandfather was probably thinking of the earthquake in 1906 in San Francisco when he told me this. And Jews in *Amerike*, Zeyde Meyer said, have temples and drive cars on the Sabbath. The only reason he stayed there was to earn enough money to build something in Kortelisy. He finally returned permanently in 1918 — after World War I, after my father's bar mitzvah and long after the birth of his youngest son, Shmilke. He preferred the God-forsaken village of Kortelisy, which to him provided the Sabbath peace and tranquility that America could not. He did not care for the hustle and bustle of the city of New York and preferred the solitude of Kortelisy, where he was able to practise his religion without interference and bad influences. The bitter irony of pursuing this Sabbath peace and religious tranquility is that it ensured his murder and the murder of his kin at the hands of the Germans and the Ukrainian police.

While in America, Zeyde Meyer would send some money. But my father, his older brothers, and later on his younger brother, had to survive on their own for many years. Instead of going to school or cheder, the two older brothers and my father had to help support the family. My father was a smart and precocious child. He was pleasant, funny, a good storyteller and an entertainer with a fine singing voice. He had an innate ability to foster warm human relationships, and people liked and trusted him, even into his adulthood and old age. He believed that one could accomplish almost anything by just talking to people, cautiously and quietly, without raising your voice or getting angry, that it is always easier to reach a person with kind words and good deeds.

During World War I, at age ten, Father found himself a job as an interpreter for the enemy, the German soldiers, and got paid handsomely for his service. Through my father's German army connections, the rest of the family became friendly with many of the German soldiers and officers stationed in Kortelisy and the vicinity. In addition to paying my father, they would also bring food to my grandmother's house, turning my father's home into a social club.

Although the Germans of World War I were preferable to the czarist armies, they were still soldiers and dealt harshly with the local population. They acted as occupiers do and rendered arbitrary justice. The farmers and villagers lived in constant fear of the German soldiers, who felt superior and treated the local population like they were subhuman, making life unbearable for them.

As an interpreter, my father got to know many of the farmers he visited with the soldiers. And even though he worked for the Germans, his sympathies were always with the villagers, whom he considered his friends. He would sing loudly to warn farmers that the soldiers were arriving, giving them time to hide some of the items the Germans were looking for. He remained friends with the farmers for many years, even after the war ended. Then, as an adult, he dealt with many of them as a merchant. Those farmers remembered my father well for many years to come, which would also become very useful for us in our years of horror.

One of the stories my father used to tell with great relish and a twinkle in his eye was about some German soldiers who had developed a taste for the ham of one of the farmers. He would tell this story even to a non-ham-eating audience and would generate a great deal of laughter from his listeners.

Ham was a staple for the Ukrainian Christian families of the villages and hamlets in the area. Once a year, mostly on the same day and usually in the fall, farmers would slaughter a hog. In every corner of the village, in the early morning, one could hear the agonized squeals and shrill screams of the poor hogs being slaughtered. The farmers would drive a spike into the hog's heart, then slit its throat and collect the blood for blood sausages. Every part of the pig would be used. After the hog's bristles were gently pulled out, the carcass of the pig was scorched using tightly bound bundles of straw that had been lit. It would take a whole day to render the pig into ham, sausages and other meats, and the farmer would keep the rendered meat, well salted and cool, in a pit in the ground. The rendered meat would provide enough food for the farmer's family for the rest of the year. I recall the frustration of the farmers when, during the war, there was a shortage of salt and they could not preserve their meat. They were worried that without salting, it would be devoured by worms and they would be left with nothing to eat.

These German soldiers of World War I kept taking the ham of this one farmer, and the farmer started to complain to the little Jewish boy who translated for the soldiers; his children would be left without food and would die of starvation. With a straight face, speaking in Ukrainian, my father suggested to the farmer that, in preparation for the soldiers' next visit, he should take a generous piece of ham and treat it well with human feces, wrap it in large leaves and give it to the soldiers with a smile. And so that's what happened. When the soldiers came again, the farmer followed my father's instructions faithfully. The soldiers left the farmer very happily, with my father carrying the parcel.

After leaving the farm, my father told the soldiers that he could not carry the ham. "Why?" inquired one of the soldiers, "Because it's not kosher?" "No," my father said, "worse than that. Because the ham stinks really bad." One of the soldiers checked it out and, sure enough, the parcel, although beautifully wrapped, smelled to high heaven. They dropped the ham in the field and never returned to that farmer again, for ham or anything else.

Even though my father's mother tongue was Yiddish, he spoke Ukrainian like a true native, always punctuating his conversations with Christian references, sprinkling his talk with colourful colloquial expressions and witty bon mots. He also played the fiddle and, in his sweet voice, sang bawdy songs in Ukrainian and Yiddish, much to the delight of his listeners. He also sang the liturgy and hymns of the synagogue and the church and did great imitations of priests chanting liturgical tunes, which entertained Christian audiences. My father even learned to drink like our Christian neighbours and to hold his liquor even better than they did.

I still remember how later, in Ratno, he sang *chastushki* — humorous Russian or Ukrainian verses with a tune — and had vodka-shot sessions in our house with the head of the local NKVD, along with the only judge in town, the principal of the local public school and a female teacher in the same public school. When they were completely inebriated, my father, totally sober, would bring them home, sometimes carrying them one by one.

BOBEHS AND ZEYDES

Kortelisy had a good number of Jewish tradespeople, carpenters, tailors and shoemakers. With the money Zeyde Meyer had managed to save from *Amerike*, he started a business of processing the wool that was sheared annually by the farmers in the area. In one of the rooms in his little house, he installed a huge machine consisting of massive circular brushes that was operated manually. The clipped sheep wool was fed into the machine. After going through the brushes, which would clean the wool of any dirt and impurities, the wool was rolled into equal bundles, ready for the spindle. The business was run by my bobeh Freyde, who was also a healer — a practising and duly registered *feldsher*, and a highly competent midwife. She was always prepared with a good joke and a story to entertain her customers, making them feel at home. Even though she wore a *shaytl* to the synagogue on the Sabbath and Jewish holidays — it was the custom of many religious Jewish women to wear wigs — she was sharp and worldly and quick on the repartee. I still recall her reply to clients who complained when she failed to recognize them: "It's easy for you to remember me. I am only one. But you are so many. How can I remember you all?"

My zeyde Meyer was a warm and cordial man, highly regarded by the community. In the synagogue, he had a permanent seat at the head table, near the ark, which held the holy scrolls against the eastern wall. The *mizrekh* wall was a place of honour and respect.

My paternal grandparents lived in a little house next to the church, off the big church square with the police station across the street. They had a little garden with flowers and a white lilac tree that emitted a beautiful fragrance. On top of their straw roof was a huge storks' nest that was empty during the winter and occupied during the warm seasons, when the storks would suddenly return out of nowhere and settle inside their awaiting nest. This continued from year to year and from generation to generation. According to some in Kortelisy, the storks came all the way from a country called Persia, stayed in Kortelisy for the spring and summer and returned to Persia when it got cold in Kortelisy. The storks laid their eggs, hatched their chicks and discarded the unviable and stillborn chicks by pushing them out of the nest to the ground, leaving my grandfather, with my assistance, to collect the carcasses and bury them.

I can still recall the excitement when my grandfather and I chased a stork that had landed on the ground too early in its life, without first learning how to fly. The stork ran faster than I could, and I was not able to catch it. Eventually, after several attempts, it took off and flew to the nest that sat on my grandfather's roof. I was happy for the young stork but disappointed because I had missed the opportunity to touch a living stork, which did such important things like delivering babies.

My grandfather Meyer was very patient with me; he was always showing and teaching me things and playing with me. He also let me help with the pigeons he raised in the attic of his house. On Fridays he would take me to the ritual bath, and every Shabbos afternoon, without fail, I would be at his house. Naturally, I would disturb his traditional postprandial Shabbos nap, and he would tell me stories and play with me until I fell asleep on top of the warm furnace. Most importantly, we spent a lot of time studying sacred Hebrew texts. He would tell me Bible stories and study Chumash with me and recite from the prayer book, especially Pirkei Avos.

My maternal grandparents, Zeyde Berchik and Bobeh Frumeh, lived on the same street as my parents and paternal grandparents, the one street in the village. In the synagogue, Zeyde Berchik also sat against the *mizrekh* wall, next to Zeyde Meyer. My maternal grandparents demolished their old tiny house, where my crib used to hang from the ceiling, and moved into a big wooden house with a wooden floor in the centre of the village. It was a house with many rooms and a huge vegetable garden that included strawberry plants. My grandmother operated a little store, on her own, out of one little room in the front of the big house. She also sold bread and pastry that she baked every Friday morning. I did not like the new house; I loved the old house and always missed it. But I was compensated for the loss by the strawberries; I could pick and eat as many as I wanted.

My maternal grandfather, who I am sure loved me in his own fashion, from a distance, was a *gingi*, a redhead. A busy, no-nonsense man, he had no patience for children and barely tolerated having me around. Although he was called Berchik der kasn, Berchik the Angry One, I never actually saw him truly angry, and I am convinced he was a good man. He did, however, argue a great deal and liked to give advice to strangers as well as family. For instance, when someone would complain about a health issue or unhappy event, his response would always be that this was nothing, and he would describe worse situations and calamities. His motto was: You think that's bad; it could always be worse.

On one occasion, when I cheerfully announced to my grandfather that the cat had had a bunch of kittens, he shouted angrily, "Drown them!" I burst into tears. But those kittens were never drowned; they continued to live and ran all over the house and garden. In fact, my grandfather loved animals and had a dog called Medyush, which means honey.

On another occasion, my grandfather was making a blessing over a new fruit on the holiday of Shavuos. I was looking at him with wide-open eyes and salivating as he cut into a watermelon that had just arrived from the big city. He gave me a very thin slice of that delicious fruit to eat, though not out of kindness, but to teach me, to make me say the special blessing over a new fruit. I learned to recite the blessing and then tasted watermelon for the first time. Many years later, in Montreal, I learned that one does not have to wait for Shavuos to eat watermelon, that it can be available any day of the year.

Another most delicious food item was introduced to me by my father. One early morning, Father, who had just come home from one of his trips, woke me up, dipped my fingertips in water (*negl vaser* in Yiddish) and made me recite the Modeh Ani prayer, then put something into my mouth that I had never tasted before. It was a most delicious morsel of food with a heavenly taste, like the sweetest and best candy in the world. This must have happened prior to 1939, in Polish Ukraine. I will never forget when I came across a big block of this food under a glass cover on the counter of a store on Park Avenue in Montreal in 1948 and learned that it was called halvah. It had the same sweet, heavenly taste as the stuff I had been treated to by my father those many years earlier.

Like many other Kortelisians, Zeyde Berchik too had lived and worked in America. He had lived in Pittsburgh, where he made railway spikes. When he returned to Kortelisy, he started a smithy and became a blacksmith, making and fitting horseshoes, repairing wagons, ploughs and all sorts of ironwork. At times, curiosity would bring me to his smithy and, eventually, at about age eight, I was charged with the most thrilling job in the smithy: operating the bellows for the furnace that heated the steel. The smithy was an exciting and wonderful place, with lots of people coming with their wagons and horses. Sparks would fly as my grandfather would hit the hot steel over the anvil, fixing or shaping something new, with me busy operating the bellows.

AT HOME IN KORTELISY

The village consisted of different communities, each with their traditions, that lived in relative harmony until the Germans arrived. Kortelisy accommodated a church and a synagogue, as well as the passing Roma who had no permanent address. And even though the communities did not often mix or have nice things to say about each other, they usually dealt peacefully with each other. The Kortelisy Christians, the Kortelisy Jews and the wandering Roma tolerated and accepted one another, as if obeying God's will, without necessarily being in love. On the street and in the church, Jews were called "Crucifiers" or "Christ killers," names that embodied everything evil and repugnant. Nevertheless, the interactions with the Jewish population were usually sufficiently warm that the Ukrainian Christians would forget about their firm conviction that the Jews had cruelly killed Christ, even though they probably never stopped thinking that way. No Jew lived in fear for his life in Kortelisy, whether it was under Polish or Soviet control. It was only upon the arrival of the Germans that being Jewish became life-threatening and a death sentence.

The Roma were colourful and lively. They sang and danced and played various musical instruments, travelling in enormous, beautifully decorated mobile homes and horse-drawn wagons. I remember the coloured paper flowers decorating the windows of their homes. One of the Roma tunes, which I heard only once, has been seared in my memory. A Roma beggar sang it in front of our house when we were living in the hamlet of Hodyn, near Kortelisy. He accompanied himself on an instrument that was like a hurdy-gurdy and was operated by turning a crank. I still nostalgically love to hum the tune and even used it in an amateur Yiddish theatre production I was in that was based on one of Sholem Asch's novels, *Kiddush Hashem* (which means "sanctification of His name," or "martyrdom").

These three communities lived separately and apart, with their own traditions, holidays and religious practices, but they still interacted in many ways. Up until 1939, before Poland was invaded by the Soviets and Germans, there were also some Poles in Kortelisy: the principal of the local elementary school, the post office administrators (a husband and wife team), and the police. They were the upper class — sophisticated, well-educated and Polish-speaking, unlike the surrounding population, which spoke Ukrainian.

I am proud to say that my father and both sets of grandparents had a great relationship with the Ukrainian Christians of Kortelisy. I distinctly remember sitting with my paternal grandparents in the deacon's house at Christmas time, watching the fully decorated Christmas tree with candles and tasting *kysil*, a viscous Jell-O-like fruit dish served on Christmas, which my grandparents did not have but permitted me to eat.

I always felt quite comfortable but was also in awe when visiting the Ukrainian Christian homes. They had the same furnishings and drab appearance as the Jewish homes, with one exception. The walls of my parents' house were white and bare. We had only a tiny round piece of matzo hanging on a nail in the wall as a *zeykher l'mikdash k'Hillel*, a symbol and remembrance of the destruction of the Temple. It was put up on the wall on the second seder night and would be burned with the *khometz*, the leavened foods, on the following Passover eve. The walls of the homes of the Ukrainian Christians were astonishingly decorated with awesome and frightening pictures, icons in beautiful heavy frames under glass. These icons impressed me as a child and aroused my curiosity. They were both beautiful and scary and I looked at them with great perturbation: angels with swords, decapitated bodies, saints with stern-looking faces and round white discs behind their heads, pointing upward with their index and middle fingers. I remember the picture of a huge man dressed in armour holding a massive spear in his hand, killing a giant winged animal with a scaly body, enormous claws and long, sharp teeth. There were also many pictures of a beautiful lady holding a baby in her arms, both figures with discs behind their heads. At the time, I didn't know that this was the Virgin Mary with baby Jesus. It was particularly frightening to look at the picture of a man hanging on a cross, all bloodied and practically naked, with a crown of thorns on his bruised head. I later found out that the man on the cross was actually Jewish and that the Jews were somehow responsible for his death. As a result, the Christian boys teased us and beat us up. In their view, Jews were destined to suffer in the Diaspora and would continue to suffer until we accepted this poor, tortured man as our saviour and God. I did not see any of this in the synagogue. The only pictures hanging in the synagogue were of an eagle, a deer and a lion, and these served as guiding symbols: one has to be as light as an eagle, quick as a deer, and strong as a lion in the worship of the Almighty. For me (and all Jews in the village) there was only one God, as declared in the Shema.

True, as a child, I was occasionally beaten up, mocked and teased by the Ukrainian Christian children and my classmates because I was Jewish. My parents, however, had close friends among many of the Ukrainian Christian families, and we would often visit their homes and work in the fields together, helping each other out.

Jews felt at home and practised their faith freely in Kortelisy. And in general, I was a happy and free child, roaming about with little fear or constraint — at home, at school and in the fields. On one of the frequent trips I took with my father, I saw the strangest and most idyllic scene, like a classical painting of a pastoral setting. I was sitting alongside my father as he drove our wagon when we passed a large hollow oak tree. Inside the hollow of the tree was a group of at least ten adult Jewish male travellers, covered in their prayer shawls and wearing their phylacteries, conducting morning services with Torah scrolls. At the time, seeing Jews pray in the field was not unusual, but seeing them inside the hollow of a tree that they had converted into a synagogue was. The Jews of Kortelisy and the neighbouring villages and hamlets felt free and secure, able to pray openly in public without fear or embarrassment. The land and congregation belonged to each other.

LORDS AND MASTERS

Until 1939, the Polish police in Kortelisy were the lords and masters. Villagers lived in constant awe and fear of them. The police acted as prosecutors, defenders and judges, and ruled by decree, at their sole discretion. I recall how a group of farmers ganged up against a fellow farmer one Sunday after church services. They ran down the road after him with ill intentions, and the pursued farmer ran into my maternal grandparents' house, seeking Zeyde Berchik's protection. The gang of villagers surrounded the house and demanded that my grandfather surrender the farmer.

The scene reminded me of the biblical story of Lot, in which the entire population of Sodom surrounds Lot's house and calls out to him, "Where are the men who came to you tonight? Bring them out to us, that we may be intimate with them." And of course, they weren't just seeking their acquaintance. But the intentions of the villagers of Kortelisy were not as sinister as those of the townspeople of Sodom. In Kortelisy they just wanted to administer the fellow a good thrashing. My zeyde Berchik did not have the heart to surrender the fellow to the mob, not even for a moderate beating, even though the mob was ready to break down the door. But, neither did my zeyde have, as Lot had offered, "two daughters who have not known a man" to pacify the mob. My zeyde Berchik never had two daughters. He had only one daughter, who was my mother, and she already knew my father, so she was unqualified, biblically speaking, to serve the purpose of pleasing and pacifying the mob.

Under the circumstances, there was only one thing left to do — call the police. So, my uncle Yerakhmiel ran to the police station, which was at the other end of the village, near the home of Zeyde Meyer and Bobeh Freyde. One policeman arrived; Ligutka was his name. He pulled out a pole from a nearby fence and walked, pole in hand, toward the crowd. As soon as the crowd saw him, they scattered in all directions, and the problem was solved without a single casualty or shot. I don't think Ligutka even had a gun or pistol on him.

I also remember an incident when quick, arbitrary justice was served by the police to a young boy who had stabbed another youngster in the back. Right there in the yard of the police station, without the benefit of written charges, defence, trial or hearing, the boy was given the most brutal beating by two policemen while the public watched. Strangely, I ended up in the same class as the victim of the stabbing. He still wore the rough cotton shirt he'd been stabbed in. It had a hole in the back and was stained with his blood.

Once, while travelling with my father, I witnessed a policeman horsewhipping a young man, apparently with the help of the young man's father. It was obvious that the young man's only crime was that he had been born with an intellectual disability. The scene made me cry and plead with my father, who knew the family, to stop the beating. But I guess there was nothing my father could do about it, and we just drove on. The scene continued to haunt me and gnaw at my mind.

Ligutka, the policeman who had chased away the menacing crowd from my grandparents' house, was a big, barrel-chested, fleshy man with a beefy face; he looked like a wrestler. I remember him well because he was a frequent visitor at the home of my maternal grandparents, and I dreaded each one of his visits. He had the horrible habit of grabbing me, throwing me on the couch and tickling me violently. I was too frightened to protest or complain to my grandparents. In fact, I could hardly speak. Although I would be in a state of uncontrollable laughter and convulsions, Ligutka would continue tickling me violently while smiling at my grandparents, as if he had their approval and blessing. I could see in the faces of my grandparents an expression of angst; they too were probably afraid to say anything. Finally, I would scream, but it didn't help. He would only stop when he was invited to eat and drink. I would then run and hide.

When the Soviets came to Kortelisy, the Polish police force in Kortelisy, including Ligutka, disappeared. I did not understand the political ramifications, but with Ligutka's departure, I felt total freedom and relief. I thought of the Soviets as my friends and liberators as I no longer had Ligutka to worry about.

THE JEW TEST

I can't stress enough the fact that from my very early childhood, as a Jewish boy in a small village in Polish Ukraine, I lived in constant fear of Cossacks — a fear planted by my maternal grandmother, Bobeh Frumeh. It was as if they lived around the corner. This fear had a profound influence on me and on my attitude to the non-Jewish world. Bobeh Frumeh would tell me the story over and over again, how her cousins, a married couple and the parents of three young children, two boys and a girl, were murdered by Cossacks in a pogrom, and how the orphaned children ended up in separate orphanages — the boys in Montreal and the girl in Chicago. My grandmother and her family had survived the pogrom by hiding behind the stables. This story stuck in my mind, particularly the method of survival. Hiding behind stables would not require too much effort. Survival and Cossacks were always on my mind, even though there were no more marauding Cossacks in Polish Ukraine during my childhood.

Even though I saw many pictures of galloping Cossacks, I never personally encountered a real live Cossack. But, as a Jewish child, I had to deal with all sorts of bullies, relatively benign miniature Cossacks — not lethal ones — but still quite painful and abusive. These were not ordinary bullies; these were bullies with a purpose, raised with a mission of revenge for the supposed killing of their God and saviour, Jesus Christ. When they mocked and attacked us, they were doing the holy work of their church, with a passion, religiously, as if it were God's commandment. Besides being threatened or beaten up occasionally, I was also subjected to some very clever rhyming ditties that delivered a painful message about the great divide between the *goyishe* and Jewish populations of Kortelisy.

Respect for bread was part of the Ukrainian ethos. Friends were welcomed with an offering of bread and salt, and a meal without bread was not a meal. As the Ukrainian saying goes, "bez khliba nema obida"—*there could be no meal without bread*. Jews in Kortelisy may have had a similar attitude toward bread. The expression in Yiddish was "es mit broyt, khazer"—*eat it with bread, you pig*. Whether one was having soup, meat or fish, you always had to eat it with bread, otherwise you were nothing but a glutton. But to the gentiles of Kortelisy, bread was sacred — maybe because of the Great Famine suffered by their brothers in Soviet Ukraine in the early thirties. So, when Passover came around and Jews, following the biblical prohibition not to eat leavened bread, removed bread from their homes, the *goyim* considered it a sacrilege and amused themselves with a little ditty: "Khlibets, khlibets, khody na stilets. Ne protyvsya, shcho zhyd skrutyvsya"—*Little bread, little bread, come to the table and don't be upset because the Jew turned crazy*.

There was another ditty about galloping Tatars and homeless Jews that angered me even more: "Zhydu, zhydu, de tviy dim? Na dorozi pid hivnom. Yikhaly tatary, zhyda roztoptaly"—*Jew, Jew, where's your home? On the road, under the shit. A band of Tatars came along. They trampled all over the Jew*. Kortelisy always had lots and lots of horse and cow manure on the road. It didn't take much imagination to be able to visualize wandering, homeless Jews, without a country of their own, dumped in shit and trampled all over by the vicious, galloping Tatars. I was not offended by the shit so much as by the message that I had no home and no country. I thought that my village and my country were also my home.

The most difficult attack to tolerate was the "Jew test," which supposedly confirmed the truth, according to a well-established Ukrainian myth, that Jews, all Jews, don't know how to speak Ukrainian properly. The taunting accuser would start with a jeering grin, "A nu, zhydu, skazhy kukurudza"—*Come on, Jew, say the word* kukurudza.

I always faced the challenger proudly. I would put my entire heart and soul into pronouncing the word again and again, carefully and with such gusto that even the Ukrainian national poet, Taras Hryhorovych Shevchenko, would be proud of me. But not my tormentors: they would always find fault with my pronunciation. In a desperate effort to convince them of my proficiency in the Ukrainian language, I would recite Shevchenko's immortal poem, "The Testament," *Zapovit*, by heart:

> Yak umru, to pokhovayte
> Mene na mohyli,
> Sered stepu shyrokoho,
> Na Vkrayini myliy....
> *When I am dead, bury me,*
> *In my beloved Ukraine,*
> *With my tomb upon a grave mound high,*
> *Amid the wide spreading plain....*

I expected my tormentors to be moved to tears by my recitation. It did not happen. Even though with the help of my very educated uncles I had learned more about Ukraine and Ukrainians than my tormentors, they were not convinced. I became desperate and angry, and I started taking even bigger risks with my faith to demonstrate my belonging. Short of actually crossing myself, I was forced to compromise my Jewish faith by reciting a prayer in perfect Ukrainian and in the proper church intonation — "V im'ya Ottsya, i Syna, i Svyatoho Dukha," *In the name of the Father, the Son and the Holy Spirit* — while silently praying that God would not hear me and, if He did, that He would forgive this transgression. I tried very hard to convince them that I was just like them. That I was not a wanderer without a country, that their country was also my country. But it was to no avail; they thought of me as a stranger, a pariah and an outcast. No snotty little Jew-boy could speak Ukrainian like a true Ukrainian, without an accent. The experience of being told I didn't belong was always painful and would bring me to tears.

When I asked my parents, "Why do they talk like this, deny our rights, our identity, ridicule us and make fun of us?" there was always the same meaningless answer: "Vayl mir zaynen yidn"—*Because we are Jews*. But the thought of preventing this abuse by giving up my Jewishness, by becoming something or somebody else never entered my mind. I loved being Jewish, but I wanted to belong to the Ukrainian community as well.

The Ukrainian language does not have a hard *g* as in "goose," and Ukrainian songs do not usually have many refrains with *ay, ay, ay* or *oy, oy, oy*. The popular Ukrainian expression "Hospody pomyluy"—*God help me* — an expression I heard often and would say myself, mimicking the adults — is not preceded by an *oy*, as it would be in Yiddish. The Yiddish spoken by most, if not all, Jews at the time in Eastern Europe had plenty of hard *g*'s and plenty of *ay, ay, ays* and *oy, oy, oys*. Besides family names and the numerous Yiddish words starting with "ge" — *gendz* (geese), *gefes* (dishes), *geleger* (bedding), *gesheft* (business) — almost every verb in Yiddish takes on a prefix of "ge" in the past tense: *gegangen* (walk), *geforn* (ride), *geloshn* (put out, as in a fire), *geboyrn* (born), *geblibn* (remain), *geshribn* (write), *getrofn* (meet), *gelofn* (run), *gevidmet* (dedicate), *nisht geshtoygn nisht gefloygn* (never ascended, never flew/useless/a made-up story), *genosn* (benefit), *geshosn* (shoot), *gefangen* (capture), etc.

Naturally, because of the sound of the Yiddish language, with its many hard *g*'s and *ay, ay, ays*, and *oy, oy oys*, Jews were mockingly called *gugugu, gigigi,* or *gegege* and *ay, ay, ay,* and *oy, oy, oy,* even though there are a few Ukrainian folk songs with an *oy* here and there, though not as pronounced or with the significant kvetch as in Yiddish songs. I will never forget the pleasure, joy and satisfaction when, as an adult, I heard for the first time a popular Mexican Spanish song with many *ay, ay, ays* — not unlike the Yiddish *ay, ay, ays*. The discovery of other languages having sounds similar to Yiddish, with similar outbursts in songs, warmed my heart. I developed an affinity to those nations and felt as though I had newly discovered brothers, sisters and friends. And, of course, the first time I heard and learned a language with a hard *g* in it was when the Soviets came to us in September 1939. Hearing Russian spoken, with lots of hard *g*'s, I felt great relief and satisfaction. I felt that I was not alone.

Jew baiting did not change after the Soviets came to our village, except maybe symbolically. The use of the word *zhyd* was permanently abolished and removed from the dictionary by the Soviets, and one could be criminally charged for using it. Even though the use of the word in the Ukrainian language simply means "Jew," calling someone *zhyd* under the Soviets verged on hooliganism or, worse, on criminality. But, at times, even in Ukrainian, the use of the word *zhyd* could be threatening, and the milder word of *yevrey* was used in Russian.

One time, when we were under the Soviets, my father, joker that he was, used the word *zhyd* in jest, when he told another Jew who was sitting at a table in a restaurant to move — "Posunsya, zhyd" — so that he could sit next to him. A police officer overheard my father and dared him to say it one more time: "A nu skazhi yeshchyo raz!" This was no joking matter. My Jewish father was lucky not to have landed in jail and to only have to apologize to his friend. I don't think the Soviet officer, who may also have been Jewish, recognized the irony in the incident. A new reality had been created based on appearances; as soon as the word *zhyd* was banned, the entire issue of Jew hatred was declared to be resolved. Now, we were loved by everyone. The same approach was reflected in a saying used to illustrate how progressive the Soviet Union was: "U nas vsyo yest', dazhe spichki!"—*We've got everything, even matches*! If we had matches, a most insignificant item, we must have everything. Stalin is a great provider.

~

The German and Soviet aggressors defeated Poland just a few weeks after the invasion started on September 1, 1939. Even though the Poles fought bravely and assured their citizens they would never bow to German demands of returning Danzig, with the words "Ani guzika nie oddamy!"—*We won't give up, not even a single button*! — in fact, all of Poland was given up to the aggressors in no time. I remember watching the very sad scene of the defeated Polish soldiers, still in uniform, trying to wash with water from our well. At the time, I did not fully comprehend what I was seeing. With the Germans to the west and the Soviets to the east, Poland was trapped, humbled and defeated. Western Ukraine, which included Kortelisy, was no longer part of Poland; it ended up under Soviet jurisdiction and became part of Soviet Ukraine.

My mother's older brother, Uncle Yerakhmiel, was a soldier in the Polish army. He returned home unhurt, still in uniform, wearing the four-pointed military hat. His return was celebrated at home and in the synagogue by the entire Jewish village; he was given an *aliye* and welcomed as a hero, even though the army he was fighting for was defeated. The Jews of Kortelisy were unaware of what was happening in the part of Poland now occupied by the Germans, that this great joy was but a precursor to tragedy and death.

Immediately after the Soviets arrived, they started building a *mayak*, a tower, outside the village on top of a grassy hill. We did not know the purpose of the tower. It may have been for communication because it had all sorts of protruding wires, antennas and round dishes. It was a true marvel — the tallest structure in Kortelisy. I was with a pack of Jewish Kortelisy boys, and we decided to risk visiting the tower and seeing what the Soviets were up to, as everything the Soviets were doing was strange and suspicious. We didn't walk; we ran — all of us very excited about what we were about to see. But as we neared the tower, we were accosted by a bunch of Ukrainian Christian boys holding sticks and stones and singing the usual ditties. "Zhydu, zhydu, de tviy dim"—*Jew, Jew, where's your home....* We were forced to retreat. There were many more of them, and we Jewish boys didn't even know how to fight back. We had been taught that Jewish boys don't fight: *S'iz nisht sheyn* (It's not nice). *Nor shkotsim shlogn zikh* (Only gentile boys fight). The best way a Jewish boy could spend his time was in cheder, studying. We were lucky to return home without scrapes, bruises or broken bones. I only wished the Soviet officer had been there, the one who almost threw my father in jail for using the word *zhyd,* to protect us and reprimand the boys for attacking us and calling us *zhyd.*

NEW PICTURES ON THE WALLS

The region of Volhynia, along with the rest of western Ukraine, ended up under Soviet occupation. Jewish religious schools were officially cancelled and went underground. Polish school was replaced by Soviet school, which continued in the same building as if nothing had happened, with a new principal and some new teachers. But now we spoke Russian and Ukrainian instead of Polish, and the pictures hung in the classrooms and corridors of the school changed from Piłsudski, Paderewski and Marshal Edward Rydz-Śmigły to Marx, Lenin and Iosif Vissarionovich Stalin. I had never heard of these Russian names before but, except for Stalin, they all looked pretty stern. The men in the pictures looked at us, whether in the classroom or corridors, with a warning: be good, respect your elders and, above all, be obedient, or else! As time passed, the Soviet teachers drilled into us the conviction that Stalin was our best friend. We were convinced that he loved us dearly and that he was kind, warm and fatherly; Stalin had freed us from oppression, and it was Stalin who gave us life, liberty and protection.

I loved school and can still remember walking to school alone on my first day. It was before sunrise, and the huge golden, fiery moon was sitting at the end of the road in front of me, so close I could almost touch it. But I was worried about wolves, always keeping one eye on the side of the road. I walked briskly down the street toward the huge moon, which was getting bigger and bigger as I got closer to the end of the road where the school was located. I was almost running, wanting to make sure I would be on time so as not to miss a thing. I was the first to arrive and sat alone at my desk, full of excitement, waiting for the other students and my teacher to arrive so that I could start learning new things. I was one happy child.

I proudly wore the red *galstuk*, and donning the neckerchief officially made me a Young Pioneer, the first step into membership of the Komsomol movement at fourteen and, eventually, if merited, to membership in the Communist Party. The *galstuk* became one of the most important pieces of clothing in my life, almost as important as the *laybtsedak*, or *tales kotn* — the poncho-like garment I wore as a male Jew, with *tsitses*, or knotted fringes, on its corners. I continued to wear my *tales kotn*, seeing no real contradiction between it and the *galstuk*. I was enamoured with Judaism and with Soviet thinking, and I wore both with great pride at all times; they became part of my identity. My ignorance and confusion were limitless.

But even though the wearing of the *galstuk* was serious business, making the wearer an important person and member of an important group of young people, I also remember reciting a rhyme of uncertain origin describing the "exemplary" behaviour of the Young Pioneer: "Ya pioner, dayu primer: lovit sobak, kurit tabak, dushit kotov vsegda gotov"—*I'm a Pioneer, I show by example: always ready to chase dogs, smoke tobacco, choke cats*. I must have enjoyed and learned this little rhyme well, considering that I still know it now, at the age of eighty-nine, and it still brings a mischievous chuckle and smile to my face when I think about it.

I was taught to recite poems about Stalin that proclaimed his virtues and acknowledged his fatherly love, which was greater than that of my own parents or grandparents. One of the poems about Stalin, in Ukrainian, began with "Stalin, nashe sontse yasne"—*Stalin, our bright sun*, and ended with the lines "Vin uvzyav na ruku Helyu, i zhadav pro vsikh ditey"—*He lifted Helia up, and he remembered all the children.* (I am still not sure who Helia was, and I don't even know how to spell her name but, at the time, I presumed she was his daughter.) Even though I didn't speak to Stalin personally and never met him, he was always there, in the background, alive. I constantly felt his presence and knew that he was thinking about me and providing for me, as he did for all the children. I was certain that when he took his daughter Helia into his arms, as the poem proclaimed, he remembered me as if I were one of his children. To see his sacred picture on the wall was to see love, truth, fulfillment, joy and great inspiration. In song and word we worshipped Stalin as if he were an immortal god who provided us with the air we breathed.

Christmas — next to Passover, Simchas Torah, Purim and Chanukah — became the happiest day of the year. Schoolchildren would be brought to Kortelisy from all the neighbouring hamlets and villages, wherever there was a school. The children, who were from different cultures and ethnic groups and wore different national costumes, put on plays and performances, and sang and danced in different styles and languages. And they never failed to praise Stalin, always emphasizing his special love for obedient children. I recall my participation in these performances, singing and doing the *kazatske*, a lively dance. And, at the end of the shows, all the children would receive gifts, not from Santa Claus but from Ded Moroz, Grandfather Frost. It didn't take much to bring happiness to the children of Kortelisy.

When Jews of Kortelisy died, they were put to rest in the Jewish cemetery in Ratno, but when the Soviets arrived, the cemetery was desecrated, an event that marked the beginning of my understanding that Jews do die like other people, that my great-grandparents had died and were buried in the Ratno cemetery. The desecration started with some of the cemetery land being used as a depot for hay and animal feed. The workers walked all over the cemetery grounds, disturbing the graves and turning over some of the older tombstones. The Jews of Ratno and Kortelisy were upset by this and worried that the cemetery would be destroyed. As a seven- or eight-year-old child, I heard their troubled conversations and saw the agony on their faces as they thought about the place where their loved ones were having their eternal rest. Watching the distressed Jews, I thought to myself, *Why don't they write a letter to Stalin? He will understand their pain. He will understand the whole thing and stop this nonsense, the ruination of a cemetery that is sacred to the Jews.* I had a brainwashed child's faith in the beloved and fatherly Stalin, who loved his people and would not allow the Jews to suffer. Stalin, who was wise and believed only in the good, would resolve the problem. I firmly believed that no evil could come with him as leader.

Many years later I read about the Night of the Murdered Poets, the so-called trial of fifteen Jewish defendants, including the Yiddish writers Leib Kvitko, Peretz Markish, Itzik Fefer, Dovid Bergelson, Dovid Hofshteyn and other prominent Jewish personalities, who were found guilty of "nationalist activity" and espionage. Thirteen of them were executed, along with old-guard Bolshevik Solomon Lozovsky, who was a comrade-in-arms of Lenin and Stalin, going back to 1904. Lozovsky, who was no longer a child and knew Stalin well, had the same childish mindset I did about Stalin. During the "trial" he pleaded with the prosecutor, "Let me write a letter to Stalin. Stalin knows who I am. He knows that I am no traitor or spy." It seems that at age seventy-two, Lozovsky was unaware that Stalin was the one responsible for all his troubles and his eventual execution.

Stalin's party and his constitution had no tolerance for the "other," nor did it provide equal rights under the law. No one could stand in the way of creating the Soviet vision of the New Soviet Man. Anyone showing a smidgen of dissent or discontent would suffer judicial murder, as did the giants in Yiddish literature and theatre and other Jewish intellectuals and professionals in position of Jewish leadership who were executed on August 12, 1952. Neither did the Stalin Constitution protect doctors, who were accused of attempting to poison the leadership of the USSR and who were only saved from another judicial murder by Stalin's demise.

It is now clear, as it should have been at the time, that the destruction of Jewish culture and language — the Jewish thinkers, philosophers, poets, novelists, even Jewish managers and holders of positions of influence — was the beginning of the destruction of the Jewish people. Stalin knew that first you cut off the head and eliminate their culture, and the rest will die too, the natural death of a nation and a distinct people, without the need to commit mass murder the way Hitler did it.

CAUGHT BETWEEN *GALSTUK* AND *TSITSES*

To some degree, I inadvertently betrayed my loyalty to the red *galstuk* and Stalin by still loving and listening to my parents and grandparents, and when I recited the morning prayer of Modeh Ani, pronounced the blessing over the *tsitses* and thanked the Almighty for having returned my soul back to me after a night's sleep. I also recited the evening bedtime prayers, thanking God "who casts the bonds of sleep upon my eyes and slumber upon my eyelids" and saying, "May it be Your will, Lord my God and God of my fathers, that You make me lie down in peace and arise in peace." I do not remember reciting nasty limericks about God, the *tales kotn* or the cheder as I did about the *galstuk*. One did not take lightly and make jokes about those things, as we did about being a Pioneer, even though deep down I was not very upset that cheder was cancelled and no longer officially in existence. However, I was delighted that I had to attend cheder underground and in secret and was ordered never to talk about it to anyone. I particularly liked the clandestine cheder with my grandfather Meyer. First of all, I was his grandson and the other children were not and, secondly, kopecks would fly from heaven whenever I would give the right answer, and I always knew the right answers with a little prompting from Zeyde Meyer.

I never failed to attend my grandfather's cheder after Soviet school to study pages from the *sider*, the Chumash and Pirkei Avos, as well as Akdomus before Shavuos. I failed to see any contradiction in what I was doing, even though I could see and feel that Stalin and Moses were two different people, not necessarily friendly to each other, each telling different stories. But I loved them both — Moses, who was never mentioned by name in the Soviet school, and Stalin, whose name outside of school was prefaced by a curse word by most villagers, Jews and Christians alike.

To this day, I cannot forget the expression on Zeyde Meyer's face, the sadness and fear in his eyes, when I walked into his house, proudly wearing the red *galstuk* for the first time. I know it must have been painful for him to see me with that red piece of clothing wrapped around my neck because I saw tears in his eyes. It must have broken his heart. Children were taught to report on their relatives who were doing or saying things that Stalin did not like. It took a great deal of courage on the part of my grandfather to continue teaching that *galstuk*-wearing little boy — a grandson who might, even innocently, be an informer — the texts written in that sacred, ancient Hebrew language, which was strictly forbidden under the Soviets. Gentle and cautious, he never failed in his mission to make a Jew out of me, notwithstanding the danger and risks involved under the Soviets led by Comrade Stalin. My grandfather knew that I would do nothing to hurt him, but he also knew that I was only a child and feared that I would inadvertently blurt out that I studied sacred Hebrew texts with him, or that I might make biblical references in my conversations with classmates or teachers and mention Moses or King David or the splitting of the sea. Some of the fears may have been without basis, but nobody in Kortelisy really knew what was permitted and what was prohibited, what to fear and what not to fear. I guess Jews in Kortelisy, facing a new regime, were afraid even to ask questions (asking the wrong questions could get one into trouble) and based their conclusions on rumours and speculations. To be safe, people concluded that nothing was allowed. Directives were vague, and we lived in the dark and trod gingerly. We could always proclaim our ignorance when facing government complaints.

In school we were taught to fear one thing: kulak — a new word for us. We were taught to fear and hate kulaks. Kulaks, we were told, are enemies of the nation and are to be liquidated, without mercy. I had a serious problem with the kulaks. I was never introduced to or met a kulak, and the teacher failed to produce a kulak or give a proper description of one. But the way she spoke about them and described them, I didn't think they were people. I thought they were vermin or wild and vicious animals, and to save the nation I was ready to go on a hunt and exterminate every kulak on earth. But, as I discovered later, the teacher was not talking about wild animals, like vicious boars; she was talking about people, entire families. Those enemies included intellectuals, poets, writers, scientists — and also any farmer with a horse, a couple of cows and a plough. The farmers and peasantry who refused to join the kolkhoz, the collective farm, were considered the worst kulaks. They were accused of stifling Soviet power and holding back progress. When I talked to my parents or grandparents about the horrible kulaks, thinking of beasts and vermin or a deadly plague, my harangue would always be met with deathly silence.

The people of Kortelisy tried to understand which way the wind was blowing; they read between the lines and interpreted every occurrence as a sign or message from the government. One day, my uncle Ben-Tsion appeared with a magical box that produced music. Of all things, it emitted Yiddish songs and Jewish liturgical music. I had never seen or heard of anything like this before. The box was a gramophone, and it had a handle that had to be cranked, a turning disc that held records and an arm with a needle on it that was placed on the record. One of the Yiddish songs was "Itsik hot shoyn khasene gehat" (Itzik is now married). One of the lines in that song told us that Itzik was not an ordinary *khosn*, bridegroom; he was a true member of the proletariat: "Itsik iz a khosn, in tash nishto kayn groshn"—*Itzik is a bridegroom, without a kopeck in his pocket* — a happy-go-lucky kind of a guy or, in Russian, *nash brat*, our brother. And there were other songs: "Lomir trinken a lekhayim far dem libn khaver Stalin" (Let us toast to our beloved Comrade Stalin) and "Vu nemt men mel tsu makhn di varnishkes?" (Where do we get flour to make the *varnishkes*?) — a song about making noodles, alluding to the lack of foodstuffs. It went:

> Gevalt! Vu nemt men mel tsu makhn di varnishkes?
> On heyvn un on zalts,
> on fefer un on shmalts,
> vu nemt men mel tzu makhn di varnishkes?
> *Help! Where do we get flour to make the varnishkes?*
> *Without yeast and without salt,*
> *without pepper and without fat,*
> *where do we get flour to make the varnishkes?*

There was even a wonderful religious song about a visiting *khazn oyf shabes*, a cantor for the Sabbath. The song was sung with many different accents, in different pronunciations, styles and voices, and in different Yiddish dialects, reflecting different trades or professions. I recall my uncle going from one Jewish home to another with a group of followers, including me, showing off the wonder and entertaining the Jews of Kortelisy with those delightful songs. Some of the villagers were announcing that there would be a new life under Comrade Stalin. I particularly remember the happy face of the Kortelisy rabbi-cum-*shoykhet*, who was standing in front of the open door of his house with his wife and young daughter, Itke, listening to the songs with great delight.

There was a sigh of relief and jubilation among the Jews of Kortelisy: Comrade Stalin was not only allowing songs in Yiddish, he was making records and gramophones that played Yiddish songs, and even liturgical and cantorial prayers. It was unbelievable. We thought the Soviets might even permit us to reopen the cheder.

Besides the instructions I received on how to worship Stalin and hate kulaks, I also learned how the Ukrainian peasant supposedly suffered under the Polish landlords and nobility, the *pan* and *porets*, from our Russian reader, *Ruskaya Chytanka*. In the book was a drawing that looked so real that it still stands out in my mind. A Ukrainian peasant woman with a baby tied to her back was bent over, perspiring and working hard in the fields — not her own — with her bare hands, digging, and a Polish *pan* was standing over her with a whip. This image left a permanent imprint on my mind and soul. It brought on tears and sadness, and anger at the Poles, the supposed oppressors. The school and the reader did their job well. I was taught and actually believed that Ukraine was liberated from the Polish yoke by the Soviets. The peasant woman with the child on her back was now free. Of course, this was false, but in my youth and ignorance, I learned to despise the Poles. But the sight of the peasant woman also taught me an unintended lesson: to pursue justice, love people and hate oppressors.

Many years later, at the Soviet pavilion at Expo 67 in Montreal, I recognized my old textbook, the *Ruskaya Chytanka*, among a number of books on display. It was like finding an old friend, even though, happily, my rage against the Poles had long vanished. Also, the drawing was no longer there. By then, the Soviets were able to speak of other so-called liberations.

Aside from what I learned from that textbook, I also heard beautiful stories and memorized poems from Russian and Ukrainian literature. The stories "Peter and the Wolf" and "Sonia the Duck" were read to us in class by a female teacher whose face I still so clearly remember. (This was many years before I heard of the composer Prokofiev and his wonderful symphony *Peter and the Wolf*.) She was a very special teacher who loved to tell us stories and read poems. Apparently, she was severely reprimanded by the authorities for singing an old Ukrainian song because it suggested to the class that only

God could make rain. She was also called a kulak, even though she did not have a farm. It was at this point that I discovered that kulaks are not animals to be hunted but regular people who are enemies of the state and are to be liquidated. I thought the teacher was much too nice to be liquidated. This teacher also taught us a very dangerous song, though I didn't realize how dangerous it was at the time: *Shche ne vmerla Ukrayina* (Ukraine Is Not Dead Yet), which turned out to be the Ukrainian national anthem. Later in life I became aware of the great similarities in the lyrics of the Ukrainian national anthem, the Jewish anthem of "Od lo avda tikvateynu"—*We have not lost our hope*, and the Polish anthem of "Jeszcze Polska nie zginęła, kiedy my żyjemy"—*Poland is not lost as yet, as long as we are alive*. There appears to be a certain common existential anxiety about a struggle to live and survive in these anthems.

I also remember a story about a silly monkey who found a pair of eyeglasses and didn't know what to do with them. The monkey tried wearing the glasses on every part of its body, except where it counted, on the eyes. As a seven-year-old, I thought it was very funny and that the monkey was stupid because everybody knew that eyeglasses belong on the eyes, not on the tail or chin or forehead. Anyhow, monkeys don't even wear eyeglasses.

I learned about a silly young man who was the first to discover the potato plant. He boiled and ate the bitter green balls (potato fruits) that grow on top of the potato plant and not the tasty potatoes growing in the ground. To my mind the story was not a joke, it was real. I thought that it must have taken a very clever person to discover that the real food was the potato in the ground, the stuff we now eat, and not the green balls on top of the potato plant.

I also memorized a very funny poem about a young man who brought a package of tea to a friend and asked him to prepare it. The tea maker obviously did not know how to make tea because, in preparing it, the bewildered "chef" and friend added to the boiled water and tea leaves in the pot (*gorshok*) everything that does not belong in a cup of tea: pepper, onion, parsley and some butter. He mixed all this inside the pot with a stick of kindling wood. Naturally, the tea tasted like mud, or maybe like tea soup, and the friend did not like the tea. He mercilessly attacked the incompetent "chef," hitting him on his back and pulling him by his hair. After the beating, the tea maker spent a long time pondering where he might have gone wrong; how had he displeased his friend and patron? In the end, after a lengthy deliberation — and here comes this wonderful and very amusing joke, loved by children and even adults — he realized that he had forgotten to salt the tea. *What a silly cook*, I reflected with seriousness, because I knew that one does not put salt in tea and certainly not pepper, butter, onion or parsley. I knew that you add sugar to tea, and the more sugar the better the tea gets. Everybody knows that.

This poem, as well as the many stories and fables, gave me a great deal of childish pleasure and generated much laughter. I can still recite the poem about the tea maker in almost perfect Russian. My Russian is quite rusty now, as I haven't spoken it on a daily basis since the middle of 1944. Travelling on business to the Soviet Union with a client in the late eighties, when Gorbachev was leader of the Communist Party, I was very gently and politely told by one of the Russian executives that even though we understood each other, I was speaking Russian like his grandmother. "Vy govorite kak nasha babushka." It may have been said as a criticism, but I took it as a compliment.

~

What I had learned before I started in the Soviet school system was ingrained into my persona. What I learned from my parents and grandparents, from the cheder and the synagogue before 1939, and after that, with my zeyde Meyer in his clandestine cheder, had a more lasting influence on me — greater than the Soviet brainwashing. It was too late for Soviet schooling to change the feelings of awe and exaltation I experienced in the synagogue and when reading the biblical stories of King Saul, King David and Elijah the Prophet. They were my friends and the people I admired. The good and also the not so good experiences of my early upbringing were with me permanently, and the Soviet indoctrination at school did not correct or change my Jewish and religious feelings.

The memories of spending time with my grandfather Meyer on Friday afternoons at the mikveh and on Shabbos at his home — when I deprived him of his usual postprandial Sabbath snooze with playing and studying — are my most cherished childhood memories and in complete contrast to what I was taught in the Soviet school. There was no talk of kulaks or liquidation. Thinking back to those days, there was obviously a struggle between Communism and Judaism over my person and soul. I think my grandfather won; I am a Jew. He was subtler in his approach than the Soviets. He did things with love and not because of an order or out of fear — even though the God of Israel was pretty fearsome and vengeful and punished sinners and transgressors without mercy, not unlike the Soviets.

My parents, uncles and grandparents, including Zeyde Meyer, eventually, without necessarily accepting it, got used to the red *galstuk* and realized that I was not an informer, at least not a deliberate informer, as I did not understand the situation and the meaning of the *galstuk* and the difference between Comrade Stalin's Constitution and the Sayings of Our Fathers. In fact, there was a great deal one could have informed the authorities about me and my thinking and my behaviour. I was oblivious to the conflict brewing and the fears that dominated the Jews and Christians in my village. I was not exposed. I wore my *laybtsedak* under my shirt because that was the custom; I wasn't hiding it. I also wore my *galstuk* cheerfully and with great pride. But maybe, just maybe, by accepting Zeyde Meyer's teachings, I myself was a true kulak, even though I never owned or used a plough.

~

I am ashamed to admit that in 1953 — when I was living in Montreal and in my early twenties, and knew about the atrocities committed by Stalin and hated him with a passion — when the news arrived that Stalin had expired, much to my embarrassment, involuntary tears came rolling down my cheeks. I don't think the tears came because I was sad about Stalin's death. I was not. Most certainly, I did not feel fatherless, as some of the people I knew at the time did; Stalin had stopped being my father a long time ago. I could not explain those tears. I could only speculate. They were definitely not sympathy tears, and there was no feeling of loss. I believe the tears came because Stalin's name was so much associated with my wonderful, very short and only childhood, with uncles and grandparents, friends, neighbours and playmates — even those not terribly friendly ones — all part of a happy and beautiful village. It was all under Stalin. All of it happened under Stalin.

STAYING AWAKE

How vividly I remember celebrating the Jewish holidays freely under Polish rule with my parents, grandparents and uncles up until 1939. Our celebrations continued under Soviet rule, even with me proudly wearing the red kerchief on my neck. I wore the red kerchief while dancing with the Torah and carrying a home-fashioned Simchas Torah flag, like Topele Tuturitu in Sholem Aleichem's story, together with the rest of the Jewish community of Kortelisy.

How exciting and lively were the days just before Passover, when the entire Jewish community of Kortelisy would get together to bake the Passover matzo. Each family would come with their sack of wheat flour, and each family would have their matzo baked, with the participation and effort of the entire community. But there was only one young man in charge: Yisroel.

Yisroel was the only one from Kortelisy who had studied abroad in a yeshiva, an institution of religious, rabbinic and talmudic studies that issued *smikhe*, certifying rabbis. Yisroel returned home after his studies, not quite a rabbi but a wise man and talmudic scholar. He took over the leadership of the community and organized it, very carefully under the Soviets, with lectures for the adults. He would deliver sermons (fire-and-brimstone *droshes*) and helped the rabbi with the religious instruction of the Jewish children of the village, with considerable risk to his well-being under the Soviets. Yisroel, probably without remuneration, was also in charge of the communal activity of baking matzo for Passover. As long as my memory endures, Yisroel will stand out because of his unflinching devotion and loyalty to his faith and community. He spoke of God as if He were his next-door neighbour to whom he talked directly on a regular basis. When he spoke about God in his sermons, you were always left with the impression that moments earlier he had left the Almighty at the synagogue entrance, or chatted with Him at the mikveh or left Him after a leisurely walk in the field. Yisroel was also the only Jew in Kortelisy I saw swimming in the nearby lake, in the deep end, far away from the shore. The others never learned how to swim; they would splash with the children near the shore or wade into the shallow part of the lake.

The baking of matzo begins with a slice of dough the size of an adult fist, called a *meyre*, which is flattened and rolled into a thin circular pancake and then pierced through with a perforating roller to get all the air out. The flat pancake is then placed into the hot oven, like a pizza, to bake within a specific time period. But sometimes, in spite of the very strict baking rules and guidelines, a matzo, after being placed into the oven, would get spoiled, by either folding over or puffing up. This would be catastrophic for the owner of the batch, but a blessing for the children, who always gathered around, salivating, waiting for such an occasion. Yisroel, instead of discarding the spoiled matzo, would continue baking it, and when it was at least half-baked, give it to the children. It was the greatest treat. It tasted heavenly. Nothing in the world tastes as good as a soft, fresh, hot, half-baked matzo *kefule*. Yisroel was an expert matzo baker. He could place a matzo in the oven and flip it like a circus performer, and I suspect sometimes he would not wait for a matzo to get accidentally spoiled; he would deliberately do it just to please the children, to give them some earthly pleasure. With time, Yisroel drafted the older kids to participate in the process of baking matzo, either by pouring water or flour, mixing the dough or arranging the baked matzos for pickup.

When the Soviets arrived, we continued to celebrate Passover, with my father conducting the Passover seder, leaving out nothing from the Haggadah, reciting all the prayers and singing all the songs — all very seriously and with great devotion. However, after reciting the plagues and dipping our pinky fingers into the cup of wine and removing a tiny drop for each plague, Father would provide some comic relief by mispronouncing Rabbi Yehuda's acronyms for the plagues. Instead of pronouncing *D'tzakh, Adash, B'akhav*, he would say in Yiddish, "dreyt zikh a daytsh bay aykh oyfn boydem"—*a German is hanging around inside your attic.*

As for me, *galstuk* or no *galstuk*, in total contradiction to the teachings of the *galstuk* and what it represented, I still was trying hard to stay awake for the drinking of the third cup, after which the door was opened, and Father, with great fanfare, welcomed the prophet Elijah to our home to drink from the special cup of wine, which had been prepared for him at the very beginning of the seder. My brother and I were seldom awake long enough to see the arrival of the prophet Elijah. But, when we were successful in our struggle to stay awake, watching the open door and Elijah's cup, we were disappointed when the prophet did not show up. Father always had a good explanation. The reason we did not see Elijah the Prophet, he said, was because, after all, Elijah was invisible. But, how about the cup of wine, we said. It was still full; he did not drink. "Oh yes," Father would say. "He surely drank. But, he drank very little, just a touch, a tiny little sip that could hardly be measured. Remember, he drinks at every visit, in every Jewish home, and if he would drink too much, he would get drunk and that's not the way good people, and particularly prophets, behave." Of course, we believed every word Father said, and we still struggled to stay awake, even though we knew that we would not see Elijah the Prophet. But maybe, just maybe, we would see the wine in Elijah's cup being stirred up or the cup being lifted by Elijah, even if we wouldn't see him. For me, the struggle to stay awake was a great exercise and a precursor of a later life-and-death struggle.

PART II

THE HORROR BEGINS

As soon as the Germans invaded the Soviet-occupied areas in June 1941, with the assistance of the collaborating Ukrainian police, the free-as-a-bird and happy-as-a-lark Roma completely disappeared, never to be seen again; they vanished from the face of the earth. We no longer saw the winding convoys of beautifully decorated horse-drawn homes on wheels. We no longer saw the women and girls dancing in their wide colourful skirts to the sound of drums and fiddles. There were no longer any barefoot children in their torn clothes, boys and girls, with delightful expressions on their beautiful dark faces.

After the local Roma were all gathered in the yard of the police station across from Zeyde Meyer's house, we saw from the relative safety of that house the Roma being beaten and humiliated by Ukrainian police. Many were shot and killed on the spot, and the rest were led away to their final destination, never to be seen again. The crying, wailing and screaming stopped. Also, the begging and praying stopped. Then there was nothing but silence: nothing was said, no questions were asked, and no shouts of horror and protest were heard, not by the victims or by the witnesses to the horrible massacre of the Roma in my village. After all, they were only Roma, who were always abused and, not unlike the Jews, accepted abuse as normal. The Roma fathers probably gave the same answers that the Jewish fathers gave to their questioning children, in the Roma language, or maybe in Ukrainian: "Because we are *tsigani*."[1]

The perpetrators of the horrible crime congratulated each other and celebrated a job well done with pails of vodka, gorging themselves on mountains of food. However, unbeknownst to the Jews of Kortelisy, and to the Christians of Kortelisy, the same destiny was being prepared for them. They too would go the way of the Roma, in total silence, or maybe with just a soft whimper, with nobody left to protest, scream, or even to hear their whimpers when they were led to the slaughter in broad daylight.

We had no radio and we received no news from the time the war broke out. When the German forces were passing close to Kortelisy through a little town called Mokrany (Mokran to Jews), many of the Christian Ukrainians from Kortelisy ran to Mokrany to look at and welcome the Germans. They all returned to Kortelisy excited about the Germans and talking about them with admiration: "Akh, taki krasyvi, akh khoroshi"—*Oh, they are so handsome and so good-looking*. We received the news of the Germans' arrival from those citizens who had run to Mokrany to welcome the Germans with loaves of bread and salt.

Another sign of war in Kortelisy was the pathetic Soviet retreat. We saw many of the defeated Soviet soldiers, now out of uniform and wearing civilian farmers' clothing and carrying farm utensils instead of rifles. They disguised themselves as local farmers, hoping to avoid detection and capture while moving east, trying to reach home. I will never forget the day I looked through the only window of my house, which faced the hilly old cemetery across the street. I saw a group

1 The term "*tsigani*" is considered discriminatory by most Roma people; however, it is likely the word that would have been used by Roma people in Ukraine at the time.

of Soviet soldiers dressed in civilian clothing just resting at the bottom of the hill. I was enthralled and spellbound when suddenly one of them stood up, ran to the top of the hill, stood on his hands and quickly ran down to the very bottom of the hill on his hands. Never in my life had I seen such an acrobatic feat. I was amazed and terribly impressed. Seeing the soldier run down the hill on his hands added a touch of joy and frivolity to a time of great sadness and fear.

It was too late for the Soviet soldiers to get home, as it was too late for us. The German army was way ahead of us, even past the town of Ratno, which was southeast of Kortelisy. My father harnessed our horse and wagon and placed in it some of our most precious belongings, including the butter churn, milking stool, a rolling pin, the coal iron and some pots and pans, as if there was another kitchen already waiting for us. In this way, we started our escape toward the main highway, hoping to outmanoeuvre the German army. But reaching the junction, we were soon informed that the German army was still further ahead of us and had already reached Kowel, some eighty kilometres southeast. We returned home. As sad as it was, it was also comical: our attempt to escape and outrun an advancing army on motorized cars, trucks and tanks with our horse and wagon was an exercise in futility. We had failed to escape the impending horror and were doomed to suffer the consequences.

~

As a child, I was always curious, or maybe just nosy. I would listen in on the conversations of the adults and repeat what they were saying, including rumours and gossip, which would sometimes get me into trouble. After the Germans occupied the area, I picked up for the first time the word "ghetto" when I overheard some talk among the adults about moving Jews from Kortelisy to a ghetto in Ratno or Brest-Litovsk. Jews in Kortelisy were worried and talked a great deal about what the future would bring. The word "ghetto" dominated their conversations. I did not understand what it meant, but I got the message that it involved moving to the big city, which to me was quite exciting. There was no talk of extermination and no one with the knowledge to enlighten us.

As the idea of moving to a big city like Brest-Litovsk or Kowel or even to the town of Ratno appealed to me, I was surprised to hear that the Kortelisy Jews preferred to stay put. The rumours were that the village council had decided, despite the objections of the *starosta*, the village elder (who was obviously a brave and decent man), to send the Jews packing. To the Jews, it was a repetition of Tisha B'Av, the day commemorating the destruction of the ancient temples and the expulsion of the Jews from the holy land. Jews in Kortelisy were worried and in mourning. Considering that the *starosta* was on our side, Jews still had some hope that we would be allowed to stay in Kortelisy. But to my mind, moving to the big city was a great plan, and I didn't understand why everyone was so terribly worried.

There was no more school, nor was there a cheder. One morning I decided to go for a walk on my own. I didn't walk far, just to the outskirts of the village, not too far from my house. I walked leisurely along the edges of the golden rye fields that were bathing in the sun and all ready for the harvest. I chased some butterflies and caught one, examined some muscular grasshoppers and disturbed an anthill with a stick. I noticed a farmer tearing the seed head off the top of a rye stem, rubbing it between the palms of his hands and examining the released grains. He looked satisfied with the grains and even put some in his mouth and started chewing. I walked over to him and began a conversation. I told him how the Jews of Kortelisy were terribly concerned and upset about the situation. I also reported to him the conversations the Jews were having in the village about the good *starosta* and also about the last meeting of the village council and how bravely the *starosta* fought against what the Jews called the expulsion, heaping praises on the *starosta* and cursing the rest of the council. But I made sure to stress to him the fact that I personally had no problem leaving Kortelisy and moving to the big city and that I didn't understand why the Jews were so upset about it, making a big fuss and objecting to something that would, I thought, be beneficial for them. In my critique of the council, I made sure to add that even though I wanted to move, I still loved Kortelisy and the council. The farmer continued smiling as I talked. As it turned out, he knew who I was and he also knew my father, but I didn't know who the farmer was. He was none other than the village elder, the *starosta* of Kortelisy, who later reported the conversation to my father. They both had a good laugh.

I am sure that my praises of the *starosta* had nothing to do with the cancellation of the expulsion order of Kortelisy's Jews. It could be that he was able to change the minds of his councillors, or maybe more sinister plans were already in the works for the Jews of Kortelisy. In the end, there was no need for expulsion or a ghetto.

THE BEGINNINGS OF LAWLESSNESS

Several days after the Germans arrived in the area, the Jews started feeling the lawlessness, even though there were no Germans in Kortelisy yet. In Kortelisy, it began with Ukrainian police killing dogs owned by Jews. No one complained or even questioned this cruelty. First, they shot and killed Medyush, my grandfather Berchik's dog. Later on, they shot and killed our nameless little reddish dog in front of my eyes while my brother and I were playing with him in the sand dunes. The dog was struck by a single bullet fired from a distance by an unseen Ukrainian policeman. He ran for a while, yelping, with blood gushing over the brown sand dunes, and then he just keeled over. My little "Jewish" dog was dead, and I was introduced to death and deliberate cruelty.

My grandparents' house where I had picked strawberries was promised to a Ukrainian Christian family, a transaction I barely understood. The sale was fake, and my grandparents were permitted to continue living in the house. The house could no longer be confiscated because it was now registered in the name of a Christian family and did not belong to a Jew. There must have been a great deal of trust between my grandparents and that family. However, in the presence of my grandparents, the new owner of the house told me to stop picking the strawberries. I was shocked, and I felt that I was being robbed of something that was precious to me, my sacred right to pick the strawberries.

My uncle Shmilke, who was the manager of a co-op and a Soviet government supply store that provided supplies and farm implements to the local farmers, was forced to surrender his keys to a mob, who cleaned the store out of everything, including the shelving, depriving farmers of access to necessary supplies. Without the protection of the law, and with laws that allowed Jews to be molested, robbed and even killed, we were at the mercy of evil people.

One day, a group of people, maybe even neighbours, supposedly decent God-fearing people who believed they were doing God's work but who, in their love of God, hated Jews, entered the home of the healer Dvoyre di alte and her family and just took everything, including her precious shrouds. Death had never been Dvoyre's fear. She knew that there was a much better world after death. Her fear was being buried without her precious shrouds. Her fear was the embarrassment of having to stand before the Almighty like a pauper, in her torn and shabby street clothing. Poor Dvoyre. Her anxiety of being deprived of her shrouds would be short-lived.

Life for the Jews became more dangerous and difficult. Groups of farmers from neighbouring villages started coming to Kortelisy to rob and threaten Jewish homes, until my uncle Yerakhmiel, who had served in the Polish army, organized a group of young Jewish men who confronted the gangs and fought them off, at least for a while.

This was the same uncle who later volunteered to fill out the quota demanded by the Germans for slave labour. The Germans dragged him and three other young men from Kortelisy to Kowel, where he was murdered at the beginning of June 1942 and buried in the Bakhiv Forest in a communal grave, along with thousands of other Jews from Kowel. The three other young men taken to Kowel somehow managed to survive the liquidation and returned home. Uncle Yerakhmiel was the first Jew from Kortelisy to be murdered at the hands of the Germans. My family, especially my poor bobeh Frumeh, Yerakhmiel's mother, was devastated. My grandmother's crying reminded me of the time when my uncle Yerakhmiel was leaving

Kortelisy, when he was drafted into the Polish army a number of years back, when we were still part of Poland. Now, the entire community joined in mourning as my grandparents sat shiva.

Though we lived in fear and were subjected to harassment and humiliating regulations, we still did not know what was in store for us. The mantra was: We won't bother them and they won't bother us. Somehow, all the evil acts we witnessed were rationalized and even pathetically explained away. We thought that all we had to do was avoid provocation and not provide them with a reason to kill, even though they were killing Jews without provocation and without reason. The Jews in Kortelisy lived in a state of denial, refusing to give up hope as long as they were alive, even while death was staring them in the face.

Of course, in Kortelisy we did not know what was going on in the rest of the world. We measured our well-being and chances of survival against local events and myths, and we relied on our strong faith in humanity and the Almighty. We relied also on the goodwill, even love, of our Christian neighbours, even those who were now policemen. After all, those policemen, we knew them well. Some of them were friends, including the chief of police, who was a friend of the family and a classmate of my uncles. But we were betrayed by our own illogical thinking and standards of morality. By the time reality set in and stared us in the face, most of us were dead and it was too late to do anything. We had been outsmarted. It was not unlike the story in Exodus, where Pharaoh, King of Egypt, decided to enslave the Jews: "Hovo niskhakmo lo"—*Let us outsmart them*, he said. And he succeeded, through chicanery and an appeal to patriotism, in enslaving the Jews. Even the Ukrainian Christians should have realized immediately what was happening. But we all failed to wake up to reality and continued to live in a state of denial.

Adult Jews had to wear white armbands with a blue *mogen dovid*, a Star of David, in the centre. We were not allowed to leave the village and were forced to supply orders of clothing, all sorts of material and slave labour — which turned out to be nothing but a death sentence, as in the case of my uncle Yerakhmiel.

Bicycles and certain kinds of furniture were confiscated. We were, however, allowed to keep our animals. We kept our milking cow but, because we could no longer travel outside the village, Father gave away our horse to a farmer. He sadly handed over the harness, wishing the farmer all of the godly blessings, asking him to take good care of the horse as if he was a member of the family. Our horse was a riding horse whom we had treated almost like a pet and family member. We used to clean and brush him and feed him, besides the usual horse staples, apples and raw potatoes, which he enjoyed. The hardest work he ever did for us was to carry a rider or pull a wagon or carriage. It was on this horse that I had learned how to ride. He was too tall for me to get on, so I would try to line him up with a fence; then I would climb the fence and, when I reached the top, I would transfer myself onto the horse. But the horse did not want me on top of him and, even though I would hold him tight, he would always move away from the fence before I was able to climb on. The horse eventually learned to stand still, right up against the fence, and I was able to climb onto him with no struggle. He was not used to farm labour, like pulling a plough or hauling tree stumps out of the ground, or trees that had fallen or been cut down. With his new owner, the horse quickly succumbed to the heavy farm work and expired. Or maybe he was badly treated by the farmer and beaten to death because he was a Jewish horse and the farmer had gotten him for free. In the end, the farmer complained that my father had given him a sick horse. I still did not understand why Father had to give away the horse. I cried bitterly, even though I realized it made no sense to keep and feed an animal we could no longer use.

As for our family cow, which provided milk and milk products for the entire family, we kept her as long as we stayed in Kortelisy. On our last day in Kortelisy, we gave her a last meal of hay, oats and sliced raw potatoes and left her in the stables, knowing full well that she would be picked up by a gentile neighbour or a farmer.

A DOUBLE BEATING

At the very beginning of the German occupation of the area, we continued to live in the village, still in our homes though confined to the village area. We lived in constant fear of the newly established local Ukrainian police, who were the new lords and masters and were always prepared to harass and beat up Jews and rob their homes. We were like cattle to them, and they dealt with us any which way they pleased.

One day, I was visiting a family who ran a tailor shop when the newly appointed chief of the Ukrainian police walked into the shop with a photograph of Hitler in his hand. He showed the photograph to the Jewish tailor and ordered the tailor to sew a jacket for him similar to the one Hitler was wearing in the photo. The tailor was not very happy about the task or about having an image of Hitler in his shop. He told the chief that it would not be easy to create the jacket from just a photograph without the actual pattern, hoping that the chief would be reasonable, abandon his plan and go away. But he didn't; he kept insisting that the tailor sew the jacket.

The tailor, not having much choice, started taking the chief's measurements, knowing full well that he would not get paid for his work. The chief of police was much younger than the tailor and, at one point, in addressing the chief in Ukrainian, the tailor used the familiar term of "*ty*" rather than the formal or polite form of "*vy*" to say "you." The chief angrily responded to the tailor with an old Ukrainian expression: "Did we muck out pig sties together that you have the nerve to address me with the familiar?" The chief was correct. He and the tailor had never taken care of pigs or pig sties together. The Jewish tailor had nothing to do with pigs; he did not own pigs, he did not take care of pigs and he did not eat pigs. However, the chief did; he took care of pigs and was, before he became chief of police for the Germans, a swineherd.

Over the next years, the chief continued doing whatever German collaborators did to their victims and survived the war. He managed to avoid justice and retribution for his evildoing and escaped to the United States, arriving as a refugee, where he apparently is still alive at the time of this writing, most likely enjoying his family in freedom, in the lap of American luxury, while his victims are dead, buried in the marshes and fields around Kortelisy.

On one occasion, I was subjected to a beating by the Ukrainian policemen. After my grandmother's stories about Cossacks and all the humiliations and abuse I had suffered at the hands of Ukrainian Christian boys, I had become a weak, frightened and helpless little person. I was by now well trained to accept being beaten up by a Ukrainian policeman as a normal event. The same mantra explained it all: "Vayl mir zaynen yidn"—*Because we are Jews*. It was as if I had been born with a gene that allowed me to tolerate and accept harsh and cruel treatment, even death, just because I was Jewish. I, along with every Jew, appeared to have been burdened with the Jewish history of accepting suffering, discrimination and death as God's retribution for some personal and ancestral sin. I learned it in cheder: we were in *goles*, in exile, and suffered for our sins and the sins of our fathers. We also firmly believed that the greater the suffering the closer we were to the arrival of the Messiah. This view just reinforced the attitude of the Ukrainian Christians that we were not part of Ukraine and did not belong there.

This particular assault occurred during my walk home along the Kortelisy road after a visit with my paternal grandparents. From a distance, I noticed a couple of Ukrainian police officers coming from the opposite direction. I was a little boy, nine or ten years old, and being Jewish, I smelled trouble. To avoid them, I ran into the yard of one of the houses, but they caught up with me. They didn't accuse me of anything and, without exchanging a single word, they took turns beating me. I was hit several times with a rifle butt by one of the officers and then with a leather truncheon by the other. While they each took a turn, the other one would look on and smile. The whole event was strange. I had no fear. It was as if I were no longer a child seeking protection; I was an adult, completely grown up and accepting of this event as normal, part and parcel of being Jewish. I turned into a piece of stone, without feelings and without pain. I didn't cry "Mother!" or "Help!" I didn't even think of screaming or protesting. I didn't ask myself or my tormentors "Why?" I knew why. *Vayl mir zaynen yidn.* And that was enough of a reason. Maybe it was even God's will. I had been trained and prepared all my life for this treatment, and there was nothing I could do about it but try to quietly survive the ordeal, to live another day. And maybe pray some more that my torment would hasten the arrival of the Messiah.

I couldn't even complain because there was no one to whom I could complain. I had learned very early that my parents couldn't help me. I couldn't complain to my father when I was beaten up by the little Ukrainian kids, and I couldn't complain now, when I was beaten up by big Ukrainian policemen. I already knew what the answer would be if I were to complain: "Because we are Jews." I was taught to associate every calamity and evil act with my being Jewish. Because being Jewish and suffering humiliations and beatings, even being killed, go hand-in-hand.

I became a full-fledged Jew even before I had my bar mitzvah, my induction into the Jewish fold. I didn't have to have a bar mitzvah to become Jewish. I didn't need synagogue instruction. I was taught on the street what it meant to be a Jew. I was young and weak; I lived on hope and fear. I couldn't fight back because I had never been taught how to fight back. I was taught that Jewish kids don't fight; it's not nice to fight. The only thing left for me to do in the event of danger was what my grandmother had done and had advised me to do in order to survive: hide behind the stables. Unfortunately, as I later discovered, stables were not always available when looking down your executioners' gun barrels. And stables are sometimes burned to the ground with people and animals inside.

When I arrived home after the beating, my father was helpless and uncomfortable about handling the situation. He just looked at me and dealt with my wounds. There was nothing he could do and I knew it.

A worse experience, more painful to me than my own beating, was when I saw my parents humiliated, threatened and beaten up by the horrible, ignorant Ukrainian police — the scum of the earth, the dregs of humanity. It happened when we were returning from visiting my parents' friends, the Boyko family, who lived on a big farm not far from Kortelisy. We visited them regularly; it was now dangerous because it was illegal for Jews to be outside the village, but we risked it. I loved to visit the Boyko family and pick the fruit in their huge orchard: cherries, apples, pears and plums — as much as I wanted. I particularly loved to drink the cool and delicious *kvas* made from birch tree sap. This time, we left the farm carrying a large quantity of fruit and vegetables and were starting down the dirt road in the direction of Kortelisy when a horse and buggy appeared with several Ukrainian policemen in it. They jumped off the buggy, screaming obscenities, and started beating my parents with their rifle butts and truncheons.

My parents, without the slightest resistance or protest, just screamed in pain and waved their arms to protect themselves, trying to cover their faces and avoid the blows. My brother and I ran back and forth, crying and pleading with them to stop. They didn't stop. They pointed their rifles at my parents, threatening to shoot them, while blood gushed from my parents' heads as they fell to the ground. As the policemen chambered a round on their rifles, with a horrible sound that signalled the end, our screams escalated. Eventually the policemen stopped and rode off in their buggy.

Much time has passed since that incident, but I can't forget the painful scene or the evil faces of the attackers. It still tortures me to have seen my parents dehumanized like that — the people whom I respected and thought were invincible being treated like helpless animals, clubbed and beaten like non-beings, like pieces of wood.

When we returned home after the ordeal, we all went silently to our separate corners. I could not look into my parents' eyes, and I ran to my bed, hid my face in the pillows and stayed like that for hours, sobbing quietly and bitterly. Maybe it was cowardice, or maybe I thought my parents were ashamed about being beaten up in front of their children but I avoided facing them in order not to hurt them even more. After this, I was angry and forlorn for months.

The last time I saw my mother alive, more than forty years later, I leaned over her hospital bed and she put her hand on my head, giving me a wonderful feeling of safety, love and devotion. The last thing I remember seeing as I looked into her face was the scar on her forehead, the result of that day when I was, in a most horrific way, given another lesson about what it means to be a Jew.

NOTHING CHANGED IN THE SYNAGOGUE

From 1941 and into the first half of 1942, the Ukrainian police did all the dirty work: the humiliations, beatings, robbing, confiscations of property and threats. As yet, no Jew had been killed in Kortelisy. We still lived in our homes and even attended synagogue and celebrated our holidays. During the High Holidays of 1941, every Jew attended synagogue and everyone did a great deal of praying and crying. The old cantor from Ratno, Khazn Velvl (Cantor Velvl), especially hired for the High Holidays, was conducting the services as he had every previous year. Nothing changed in the synagogue except that there was more than the usual crying and hugging, especially of children who, this year, were not allowed to go outside and play and who were permitted, on Yom Kippur, to eat their cold chicken, cake and cookies inside the synagogue, in the presence of the fasting adults. The entire Rosh Hashanah and Yom Kippur services sounded like a Viduy, a deathbed confession, as if everyone was expecting to die. We prayed for atonement, for forgiveness for our supposed sins and offered a plea for life — to survive the bitter humiliations and the war.

During the Rosh Hashanah and Yom Kippur services and at the very end of Yom Kippur, at the end of the final Neilah service, the same prayer is recited, called Ovinu Malkeynu, Our Father Our King, consisting of over forty variations of a plea for God's mercy. Each verse begins with the words *ovinu malkeynu*. The last one of those pleas very appropriately and with great humility, asks, "Our Father, our King, be gracious to us and answer us, though we have no worthy deeds; act with us in charity and loving-kindness and save us."

But our Father ignored our prayers and confessionals. Quite possibly there was not sufficient time for the prayers to reach the heavenly heights. Each one of those prayers was delivered with tears and supplication, not only by the *bal tfile*, but the entire congregation — men, women and even children. As it turned out, He still did not listen. One of the pleas, the most appropriate for the moment and deeply felt, was delivered with tremors and quivering of limbs, bones and tissue. I still vividly remember my uncle Yerakhmiel's heart-wrenching scream of that final prayer, and it still rings clearly in my ears, the sound of my uncle's voice coming to me as if I heard it only yesterday: "Ovinu malkeynu, KRAAA roye g'zar dineynu!"—*Our Father, our King,* TEARRR UP *the evil decree against us*! But it never happened. The evil decree against us was executed, and my uncle Yerakhmiel was the first victim.

In the synagogue that year, I particularly noticed one of the visitors from Brest-Litovsk, my zeyde Berchik's brother-in-law, Kagan. He cried the loudest throughout the entire services. I later learned the reason for his crying: ironically, he was not especially worried about himself and his family in Brest-Litovsk living under German occupation but about his two young boys living in Palestine. As my uncle Yerakhmiel cried and pleaded "KRAAA roye g'zar dineynu," he too believed that the prayer would help to avert all evil decrees, even the ones in Palestine.

~

The Germans didn't even show up in Kortelisy until one frosty morning, probably in December 1941 or early winter 1942, when it got very cold in Kortelisy. From inside our warm house, through the sole window facing the old cemetery on the green hill, we saw for the first time a German soldier; his rifle was on his left shoulder, and he was standing in the middle of the road. It was terrifying just to peek at him through the window, but he looked like an ordinary man. He was obviously cold and uncomfortable and was jumping up and down, thumping his feet, waving his arms at his sides and rubbing his ears. Inviting him into the house to warm up was clearly out of the question. We were not bold enough to approach a German soldier, even though for a killer he looked perfectly human.

My father looked at the freezing soldier through the window, turned to his family and made a firm pronouncement on the final outcome of the war and success of the German army. "They can't win the war," he predicted triumphantly. It was as if my father was privy to the military strategy of the Soviet generals and could see the eventual defeat, with the assistance of the weather and Grandfather Frost, of the Germans at the gates of Stalingrad in February 1943 and then Leningrad in January 1944.

REHEARSAL FOR THE FINAL DESTRUCTION

We did not see another German soldier in Kortelisy for quite a while, until one Shabbos morning in the early spring of 1942. My parents were up, but my brother and I were still sleeping when the soldiers walked into the house. I was awakened by a blow to my neck with a truncheon. German soldiers in brown uniforms were picking up items from around the house and throwing them on the floor. My parents were just standing there; they were not in a position to object. This appeared to be more serious, not just the usual terrorizing we had been experiencing at the hands of the Ukrainian collaborators. However, my father did protest when the soldiers picked up his pouch of fine tobacco and started spreading it all over the floor. This was not just ordinary tobacco; it was the prescription tobacco he smoked to provide relief from his asthma. When my mother used to dust the furniture and sweep the floor, my father would have to leave the house, as he would have difficulty breathing. When my father protested, one of the soldiers just threw the pouch at my father with whatever tobacco was still left in it.

For some reason this act of returning the tobacco pouch had a calming effect on us children and our parents. Returning the tobacco was like giving life. It was obvious to us that it was a humanitarian gesture on the part of the German soldier, and it turned the soldiers from vicious killers into rational and reasonable people in our minds.

We no longer thought about being shot. Surely, we thought, if they intended to kill us, they would not give the tobacco back to Father. Like everybody else, my parents believed what they hoped for. And, after all, the Germans were a civilized people who had given the world Bach and Goethe, among others — and the German soldiers of World War I my grandparents and my father had known were not scary, were maybe even friendly.

The soldiers took my parents away but left us children behind. They brought the entire adult Jewish population to the square in front of the church. There was one German soldier left standing in front of our neighbour's house wearing a blue-grey uniform. At this point, I didn't see any danger or expect anything bad to happen. There was no breakfast that morning, so my brother and I got dressed, went outside and walked over to the soldier in the blue-grey uniform. We bonded immediately. He was friendly and smiled at us. I even expected to receive chocolate or candy from him, but we did not get any. I remember conversing with him, though I don't remember what was said and in what language. Most likely, I spoke to him in Yiddish and he spoke in German. I may have asked him about my parents and he may have assured me of their safe return. It's also quite possible that he considered us to be friendly human children. Maybe we even reminded him of his own children at home, in Berlin, Munich or a small German village not unlike my own. After this brief but warm exchange, he pointed with his rifle toward the Sheftels' door and ushered us in. There, together with the two Sheftel boys, we awaited our parents' return, by now quite hungry. The thought that my parents might never return did not enter my mind.

This time everyone returned home safely. But before the German soldiers let everyone go, the Jews who were assembled in front of the church were given a long harangue about the need to wash more often, not be lazy and work much harder. Words like *Scheisse* (shit) and *Entlausung* (delousing) were repeated again and again. In truth, the Jews of Kortelisy worked hard and washed on a daily basis. Some days we even washed more than once, and we recited blessings with every washing. We even had our own ritual bath out in the field. Washing was a religious habit; our sacred books commanded us to wash. As for working hard, we had no choice in the matter. We had been working hard since Adam was cursed by the Almighty's pronouncement, "B'zeas apekho toykhal lekhem"—*By the sweat of your brow shall you get bread to eat.* As for me, I didn't work hard, but I did wash many times a day and make a blessing each time I washed.

When the final words were shouted by the officer in charge — *Juden*! *Laufen*! *Schnell*! — everyone started running as instructed, probably expecting to be shot in the back. But nobody was shot this time. Except for the screaming of orders, the Germans were quite polite and considerate of the welfare of the Jews and the entire village. In fact, they were so terribly polite that when one elderly Jew fell while running, one of the soldiers ran over to him and helped him up. The crowd was thrilled and terribly impressed by this courteous gesture and were assured by this act that the Germans were very civilized, maybe even more civilized than the Soviets, or even the Poles. Rumour had it that even the Ukrainian police were giving the Germans a favourable report about the Kortelisy Jews. We were now reassured that nobody would be hurt and that we would have a peaceful life.

Jews said comforting words to one another: "We shall live quietly. We won't bother them and they won't bother us. We will just have to be careful not to provoke them, not to give them any reason to bother us or hurt us. Just give them what they want, without argument." It even turned into a joke: "We will just have to work harder and wash more often. Easy." And words of even greater comfort: "We are in *goles* and must live in fear, always reminding ourselves of the greater sufferings of our ancestors at the hands of the Babylonians and Romans, Haman, Torquemada, the Crusades, Cossacks and Khmelnytsky, *yimakh shmoy*, may his name be erased. And there was the destruction of the temples and being chased out of our ancestral lands. We have survived all those evils and we shall, with God's help, survive Hitler, *yimakh shmoy* and, eventually, not unlike every other *gzeyre*, this cruel edict shall pass too, as we prayed it would with the words 'KRAAA roye g'zar dineynu' on Rosh Hashanah and Yom Kippur."

In our attempt to rationalize our new reality, these events were designated as true *meshiekh's tsaytn*, signs of the arrival of the Messiah. And while this roundup in the square in front of the church was a disturbing event, considering the results, it was viewed as quite encouraging and hopeful. We had expected to die but our lives were spared. We concluded that we would just have to suffer through the war until it ended. All we had to do was not lose hope and our faith in the Creator, who would surely protect us from all evil.

Still, Kortelisy Jews continued to look for an explanation for the cruel visit sprung on Kortelisy by the German soldiers that Shabbos morning. One explanation that gained currency among a number of Kortelisy Jews was presented by Tulier, the wisest and richest Jew in Kortelisy. Tulier had told the prospective killers that they wouldn't win the war if they continued killing Jews. Apparently, the Germans had been so impressed and swayed by this argument that they decided not to kill anyone and told everyone to go home. There were some sceptics who didn't believe this explanation.

Around this time, a German officer suddenly appeared in front of my paternal grandparents' door with some goodies. At first, it was a frightening sight, but it turned out that this German colonel had been a simple soldier during World War I, one of those my father had helped with translations and who had spent time in my grandparents' house. News of this encounter spread like wildfire throughout the village. We have a friend in the German army, people said.

ESCAPE BY THE BACK DOOR

The next time the Germans came to Kortelisy there was a completely different ending, and all hope of survival was shattered. It was Sunday, July 12, 1942, a week before my tenth or eleventh birthday. My parents had decided that we would stay overnight with my paternal grandparents; for some reason, they felt a little bit safer at the other end of the village, next to the church square.

Early that Sunday morning, while it was still dark and we were all sleeping, there was a powerful pounding on the front door and roaring in German — *Aufmachen*! Open up! This was not a *gemütlich* sound of invited guests arriving for breakfast. The Germans had come to kill us, and the pounding and roaring put the fear of God into us. I was not ready to die. I can still hear the sound of it, and it still frightens me and gives me the shivers; I still have the urge to run and hide. We all woke up. Anticipating danger, we ran out through the back door, straight into the fields of tall rye that grew at the edge of my grandparents' house. Somehow we were calm and accepted the situation as part of being Jewish, running away from the Hamans and the pogroms, as our ancestors did. Once inside the dense rye fields, we ran in different directions. But my mother, as usual, held on to me and my brother. Sonia, a young schoolteacher who had arrived with the Soviets in 1939 from Kyiv to teach in the local school and was a colleague and girlfriend of my uncle Ben-Tsion, was holding on to my mother. Sonia was dark and beautiful, with deep black eyes; the Russian song "Ochi Cherney" (Dark Eyes) could have been written about her. She proudly insisted that she was a true *yevreyka,* Jewess, even when the Germans arrived.

The four of us stayed together, tucked inside a furrow in a rye field without moving a muscle the whole day, afraid of disturbing the rye and giving away our hiding place. We didn't know what was happening to the Jews in the village. We had no food or water all day and emerged in the evening and returned to my grandparents' house, where we reunited with our father, paternal grandparents, Ben-Tsion and my mother's parents, who had also managed to escape.

Not everyone was that lucky. Some twenty innocent Jewish men, women and children — entire families of Kortelisy — were rounded up, murdered in cold blood and buried in the green grazing fields outside Kortelisy, in a flat, unmarked communal grave. Among the murdered was a family of four, whom I still remember. The father's name was Binyomin, and one of the boys, who'd had his bar mitzvah two or three years earlier, was called Bentse.

Later in the evening, when we returned to our own home and walked through the open door and saw everything in disarray, we realized how close we had been to being included among the victims. Father immediately pronounced that our staying over with Zeyde and Bobeh was nothing short of a miracle. Being the first house as one enters the village from the west, we would have most certainly been caught in our sleep and killed. We had no back door to escape from even if we had been awake.

MASSACRE IN THE MARSHES

After this event, those who survived abandoned their homes and hid in the marshes next to the lake. But many of the survivors soon left their hiding places in the marshes and returned to their village and homes, as if nothing had happened. They gave up trying and planning and instead relied on fate, expecting the worst and hoping for the best. There, in the village, life continued as usual except for some unhappy interruptions: beatings, threats, attacks and robberies of Jewish homes by the police and civilians from neighbouring villages. These acts were uncomfortable, highly humiliating, but tolerable under the circumstances, providing the Germans did not continue killing Jews. Some families, including my own, continued to live in the marshes. Even though we blamed our misfortune on "our sins and the sins of our fathers," still, comforting and consoling words came from Yisroel, the communal matzo baker, yeshiva graduate and teacher. He pronounced in a thundering voice that we were in God's hands and were living in *meshiekh's tsaytn*; the Messiah would soon arrive. The signs were visible to the eye, to whoever wanted to see them: "We must continue in our faith in the Almighty God and our deliverance will surely come! The Almighty has helped us before and He will do it again. Let us remember that He brought us forth from the land of Egypt!"

The marshes could be very dangerous. One could easily drown by breaking through the floating layer of earth and prickly grass. But this was the best possible hiding place, especially if one was able to find one of those solid little islands with shrubs, a piece of ground formed in the middle of the marsh that was quite secure from sinking.

Sitting in the marsh, my father recited Psalms: "Mimaamakim krosikho adoynoy" and "Min hameytzar korosi yoh"—*From the depths* and *from the straits did I call upon God, and God answered me with great magnanimousness.* Father was persistent: "We must not lose our hope and faith in the Almighty." And here we were, in the marshes for safety — my parents, my brother and I, one Friday evening, sitting together on a piece of relatively solid ground in the middle of the marsh, "in the depths," as described by the Psalmist, receiving and celebrating the arrival of the Sabbath. My mother said the usual prayer and lit the Sabbath candles. My father recited the complete Friday night prayers, making the proper bows and turns, with particular emphasis on "L'kho doydi likras kalo!"—*Come, my Beloved, to greet the bride; let us welcome the Sabbath*!

While he was reciting L'kho Doydi in that old traditional tune, the *nusekh* of Volyn, Father, in his exuberance, completely forgot where he was. In his mind, he was no longer in the marshes, hiding from the Germans. He was surrounded by beautiful green fields, walking toward the bright orange setting sun, joyously welcoming the Sabbath, not unlike the sixteenth-century poet and composer of this inspiring song, Rabbi Shlomo HaLevi Alkabetz, and the following generations of kabbalists in that ancient and mystical city of Safed. He then recited the Sholem Aleichem, a greeting sung to the angels who escorted him home from the synagogue — as if he had just returned from the synagogue to his warm Sabbath home to be surrounded by his happy wife and children. Father then recited the Kiddush, but not having wine or any other liquid over which one may make the blessing, he was careful not to recite the blessing over wine, which would have been a *brokhe l'vatole*, a blessing said in vain. Not seeing the irony, we recited blessings and prayers and sang the *zmires*, as if there was in front of us a bounty of all sorts of sumptuous Sabbath dishes.

We had no food in front of us of any kind. Not even a piece of fresh rye bread. Yes, we did have *sukhares*, a sliced black rye bread that was dried by toasting in the oven so that it would never get mouldy or spoiled. But this bread was as hard as a rock. It was among the foods especially prepared to take with us quickly in case we had to leave in haste. We had brought no other food with us to the marshes. But we did bring a pair of Sabbath candles and our voices with which to praise God for all the grace and the good blessings bestowed upon us. And from the depths of the marshes we sang and we prayed, just to please the Almighty and give Him thanks. We were hungry and uncomfortable, but we felt safe enough to raise our voices in songs and prayers.

On the Sabbath day, Father recited all the prayers of the day: Shacharis and Musef, the morning prayers; Minchah, the afternoon prayer; and Maariv, the evening prayer. With sunset on Saturday night, my mother recited the prayer of Got fun Avrohom (God of Abraham) in Yiddish, and Father made the Havdalah. But, again, not having any wine or any other appropriate liquid with which to make the blessing, he carefully omitted the blessing over wine to avoid a *brokhe l'vatole*. He also recited all the additional prayers usually recited before and after the departure of the holy Sabbath. My father was fully comfortable and satisfied that he had pleased the Almighty. Throughout the holy Sabbath, my father was totally engrossed and preoccupied in prayer and in praise of the Almighty, even though he and his family were hungry, cold and lived in fear, and God did nothing about it — like, for instance, sending a plague to afflict the Germans and the Ukrainian police, as He had done to the enemies of Israel in biblical days.

It did not take long for the Germans to return. Only nine days after the first massacre in Kortelisy proper, on a Tuesday morning, July 21,

1942, they came back, only two days after my tenth or eleventh birthday, which obviously was not celebrated. But this time they entered the marshes where we were hiding with some other families. At one point in the early morning, we could hear the sound of male voices a distance away. We were unable to see the speakers, but the voices were getting closer and closer, moving toward us. It was two people, dressed like Ukrainian women, their heads covered with kerchiefs. One of my relatives, Hershl Blitt, who like us had left the village to hide in the marshes, started talking to them in Ukrainian. He was actually flirting with them and making jokes. But instead of listening to his jokes, the two people opened fire and killed him and his small son in his arms. They fell together to the ground, dead, still in an embrace. The voices we had heard belonged to two German soldiers disguised as Ukrainian women.

As the Germans started shooting, the other Jews in Hershl's group scattered. Some were killed as they ran, while others managed to escape and save themselves by running deeper into the marshes. A few ran past us, as we lay low nearby, flattened against the moss to avoid detection. We could see the carnage in front of us and hear the crying and wailing of adults and children, many of them reciting the Shema Yisroel, Hear O Israel, making peace with the Almighty, acknowledging Him as the one and only creator of the universe. The screams and supplications of Shema Yisroel and the shouted words from the Viduy, the confessional prayer asking for atonement for one's sins, were only interrupted and silenced by the sound of the guns. Mothers were shot, falling to the ground with babies in their arms. Some babies fell dead with their mothers, while others survived and walked aimlessly, crying "Mameh!" They were silenced by a single shot.

Some eighteen Jewish men, women and children were murdered in the marshes in front of our eyes, including Hershl and his baby boy. Hershl's pregnant wife had stayed behind in the village because of her pregnancy, but she had insisted that her husband and son leave the village and go into hiding in the marshes. She suffered because of this for the rest of her life, blaming herself for their deaths. Women who tried to comfort her reported that "Zi filt zikh nebekh shuldig"—*Poor thing; she feels guilty.*

Another family who perished in the marshes on that day were our neighbours who shared our water well, Hershl and Zlate Sheftel and their two boys, who were the same age as my brother and me. Now it seemed that not even the marshes could provide a safe and secure hiding place.

After the slaughter, a few other Jewish families who had survived joined us. We remained together in the marshes, all of us cold and wet from lying flat on the wet ground to conceal ourselves. We were hungry and shivering, afraid to leave and terrified to stay. Yisroel, as usual, refused to give up hope and faith in the Almighty. He returned to the village and ran up and down the street, pronouncing his message of hope and faith. Instead of screaming "Hide!" or "Run, save yourself!" to those remaining in the village, he screamed his message of belief in the coming salvation: "S'iz meshiekh's tsaytn!"—*It's the coming of the Messiah*! According to Yisroel, the greater the atrocities, the closer we were to redemption. All we had to do was not lose our faith, and salvation would come. "We are being tested in our faith!" he cried. The Jews in the village seemed to accept Yisroel's message, perhaps because all hope had been lost in the face of the executions carried out in the marshes in plain sight of God and man.

It was late in the evening, getting dark, and the disguised Germans were still around, snuffing out the little bit of life left in the bodies of the wounded. Their cries of pain echoed throughout the marsh, until they were silenced. As the two disguised Germans searched for more victims to kill, including crying babies, they came pretty close to our hiding place. Luckily, they never spotted us. We were probably well concealed, hidden by tall grasses and shrubs. Then, later in the evening, there was silence — no more crying, not even a whimper. There was only the sound of croaking frogs, buzzing flies and chirping crickets — and over that, the voices of the two Germans singing. The first several lines of one of the songs they sang — a sad and haunting tune that I completely understood, as it sounded like Yiddish — remain stuck in my mind. As I learned after the war, the song was popular even in Nazi Germany, though it was written by Heinrich Heine, *der Jude vom Rhein*, the Jew from the Rhine, who had converted to Christianity. Obviously, if he had still been alive, he too would have been forced to hide in the marshes to save his life, while his prospective killers sang his song.

The song begins with the words, "Ich weiss nicht, was soll es bedeuten, dass ich so traurig bin"—*I don't know what it means that I am so sad.* Maybe the reason for their sadness came later on in the song, but I didn't understand why they were so *traurig*. Did they have regrets about killing all those men, women, children and babies? Were they asking for God's forgiveness by singing this song? It appeared that God listened more to their song than to my father's prayers and the Shema Yisroels of their victims, the hunted and murdered. Did God listen to the crying babies who fell out of their mothers' arms as their mothers were shot dead?

The soldiers didn't have to hide. They didn't live in fear. They were not afraid for their lives. They were not hungry. They were sated, dizzy with their cruel achievement. They were the killers. They had guns and loved to use them on Jews, no matter what age. We didn't have guns; we didn't know how to use guns. We didn't even want guns. It was obvious that God listened to the soldiers and respected the subhumans with the guns who were ready to massacre for the sake of their fatherland and their evil leader. It would appear that the Psalmist was singing about the killers when he said: "Adoynoy li, lo yiro"—*God is with me, I have no fear.*

After several days, my parents and some other surviving Jews, no longer feeling safe in the marshes, decided to return to the village and let fate take its course. The day after we returned to the village, my father and a few others went back to the marshes in the middle of the night to look for the bodies of the victims and for possible survivors. They found only the dead, lying wherever they had been shot while running. Bodies of men, women and children were scattered all over the place.

When my father returned from the marshes, he told us more about the gruesome massacre, who was dead and how they had buried all the dead — eighteen men, women and children — near the lake, in separate graves, by working throughout the night. Among the dead, besides the Sheftel family and Hershl and his baby, was Rabbi Shmerl Romanowski and his wife, whom I remember fondly. Rabbi Romanowski was the rebbe, the *shoykhet* and the spiritual leader of the Jewish community in Kortelisy. He was an inspiration, and always had a cheerful disposition and a smile on his face. He regularly visited the sick and ensured that the poor, of whom there were quite a few in my village, were helped with food and money; and during certain holidays he would, not unlike Elijah the Prophet at the Passover seder, visit every Jewish home in Kortelisy to sample the holiday delicacies, whether it was *blintses* on Shavuos, *kreplakh* on Simchas Torah or potato latkes on Chanukah. He would always express his approval and give his thanks and generous compliments to the *baleboste*, the mistress of the house.

I remember an incident involving Rabbi Romanowski that must have occurred when I was six or seven years old and still attending cheder under his supervision. Like every child in the village, I was supervised by every adult in Kortelisy. One Shabbos, in the late afternoon while I was in the synagogue, Rabbi Romanowski asked me, as was his right and duty, whether I had recited Psalm 104, the Borchi Nafshi, which was recited every Shabbos after Minchah, beginning with the Shabbos after Simchas Torah and ending with the Shabbos before Passover. I most certainly would not admit that I had skipped this special and most important prayer and the opportunity to connect with God that was given only during this specific period of the year. It would be sinful to miss this opportunity and the advantage of a temporary open window through which to reach the Almighty. To avoid serious trouble, I decided it was best to lie. With a straight face

I gave Rabbi Romanowski my halting answer: "Yes, I did recite the Borchi Nafshi." But Rabbi Romanowski very kindly informed me that he could read my mind and see in my face that I had not recited the Borchi Nafshi. Naturally, I fully believed that, being a rabbi, he could read my mind and see in my face that I was lying about such an important matter. Unfortunately, when I lied, I had not anticipated the rabbi's ability to read faces. Not wanting to get deeper into trouble, I promptly admitted that I had not recited the Borchi Nafshi. I expected a good smack on my face for not saying the Borchi Nafshi and for lying about it. But instead of hitting me, the rabbi, much to my surprise and joy, started lecturing me: "You know that the Messiah will come only when all the Jews in the entire world observe, fully and completely, at least one Shabbos and observe all the mitzvahs connected to the observance of Shabbos." Of course, I knew that. And he continued: "One of those commandments is to recite the Borchi Nafshi, as prescribed by law and tradition. You sinned. You failed to observe Shabbos fully and lied about it."

I began to understand what I had done, and I became frightened as I realized that I might be, at least in part, responsible for impeding the Messiah, whose arrival we prayed for every day. I expected the severest punishment, but much to my surprise, the rabbi continued talking, now even more softly. "You are a very lucky little boy. You are saved from a good smacking because it's Shabbos, even though you are a liar and a sinner to boot and well deserve to be punished. It is not permissible to smack someone on the face on the Sabbath because the cheeks would turn red and it would be like painting, which is certainly an activity not allowed on the Sabbath. So, you are lucky it is Shabbos." I expected him to end this lecture by telling me to return when Sabbath ended, with the appearance of at least three stars, or on Sunday, to receive my punishment. But he did not ask me to return and I was truly saved by the Sabbath. My punishment was not only temporarily suspended, it was probably forever stayed. But my guilt for my contribution to impeding the arrival of the Messiah would last for a long time.

After this event, I was lucky not to have turned into a regular Shabbos criminal, as it appeared to me that Shabbos was the only day of the week you could commit an offence without being punished, even if you were caught. However, not wanting in any way to further impede the arrival of the Messiah, I instead became very careful in the observance of the Sabbath and always made sure not to break any of the Sabbath commandments.

Now, knowing that Rabbi Romanowski was dead, I concluded that I would never be punished. However, I felt miserable; I was ready to take my punishment, if only I could bring the rabbi back to life. But I could not do it. I wanted to confess, but I didn't know to whom. I was consoled by one thing: I knew that one day when all of God's commandments would be observed by all, or at least one Sabbath would be observed by all Jews, the Messiah would come and I would have to face Rabbi Romanowski again and receive my deserved punishment for my failure to say Borchi Nafshi and, worse, for having lied.

The Romanowskis were not from Kortelisy and had come to the village from one of the big cities of Poland. They had one daughter named Itke. Itke was a beautiful young lady with thick, long, blond braids. She was tall and sweet, and she always had a warm smile on her face. On that fateful day of the massacre, Itke was with her parents, hiding in the marshes next to the lake. She was probably separated from her parents when the shooting began and started to run as everyone else did. She managed to survive the shooting and ran home, hoping to find her parents there. By then her parents were probably dead, and when she walked into her house, instead of finding her parents, she found strangers, some local farmers robbing the house. She was gang-raped by these robbers, still in her complete innocence, and murdered at the young age of sixteen or seventeen — the rapists and murderers bragging about it, as if they had accomplished a great deed.

DEATH AFTER HAVDALAH

After the massacre in the marshes and our return to the village, my family began to stay at home during the day and sleep on the farm of a Christian family friend outside Kortelisy at night. There was a time when my father and I had worked for the farmer, threshing rye. And once, when we had been served some boiled rice in one bowl with two spoons, I had been admonished by the farmer for eating faster than my father. He kept saying, "Otets' odyn, syn dva"—*Father takes one spoonful, and the son takes two.* I suspect it was true; my father let me have two spoonfuls to his one.

The Germans returned to Kortelisy, this time in uniform, on Wednesday, July 29, 1942. They killed fifteen Jews, including Zalmen der siver, my grandfather Meyer's neighbour. I believe this was when Dvoyre di alte and her family were murdered as well. She was buried, without her shrouds, in an unmarked grave with the other murder victims. I hope the Almighty received Dvoyre's bullet-riddled body in her modest and torn street clothing, accepted her spirit and recognized her good and generous soul, even without proper shrouds. She had spent more money, time and effort on her shrouds and preparations for the world to come than she had on this world, her worldly clothing and worldly needs. And she had loved her young patients and always wanted to make them happy, sharing the very little she had. Hopefully, the Almighty understood that she had done everything in her power to make a dignified entrance and not to be an embarrassment when appearing before Him.

At this point, my parents decided that we would stay away from the village altogether, even during the day. We completely abandoned the house and stayed with some Christian Ukrainian farmers and friends outside the village. One Friday afternoon, we said goodbye to both sets of grandparents and our two uncles, Shmilke and Ben-Tsion, and we went to one of these farms. We brought some food for the Sabbath and settled in the hayloft in the dark stables. It was much more comfortable than the marshes — maybe even safer than the marshes or the village. At least we had some food to eat and were not sitting on the cold, wet ground that could tear open and swallow us up. Father conducted the usual Friday night services as if we were in our own home and not in dark stables shared with domestic animals. Father always said that one should never ruin the peace and tranquility of Shabbos no matter what. After the meal, followed by the chanting of the Grace After Meals, we all curled up in the hay and went to sleep, the aroma of the stable, a combination of manure and hay, in the air.

The next morning, August 1, 1942, we got some water to wash, then said the morning prayers and had some cold food. We stayed in the stables the whole day. In the evening, after the Sabbath was gone, we sat down to eat. As we did, the farmer walked into the stables with a sad face and told us that my maternal grandparents and another fifteen Jews had just been killed in their homes in Kortelisy. This time, the killing had been done not by the Germans, but by Ukrainian collaborators, the Bulbovtsi or Banderivtsi — members of nationalist groups named after Ukrainian national leaders and heroes. Or possibly they were killed by God-fearing Christian neighbours who hated Jews and felt that it was their Christian duty to kill and exterminate them. We could not finish our meal. My mother's face turned ashen and she was crying and screaming in pain. She choked on the food and stopped eating. But, she still felt she had to recite the prayer after the meal, and she completed it with bitter tears but left out the words with which one asks the Almighty, "May the Compassionate One bless — me…my father, my teacher / my mother, my teacher…." Her parents — my sweet grandparents — were now dead and did not require any blessings.

Mother never laughed again and was in mourning for the rest of her life. She lost her will to live. She felt guilty, as if she herself had pulled the trigger and released the bullets that killed them, and she always thought about what she could have or should have done to save them.

I can still picture the scene that would have unfolded in my grandparents' home that Shabbos. The sun was setting, and as was customary, everything was being done to slow down the departure of the Sabbath. Slowly, meticulously and with great leisure, as if holding back a departing dear guest, my grandmother Frumeh would have looked at the dark sky for at least three stars. When she found them, she would announce, "It's already time." She would then brush her hands against the moist glass windowpane and walk in the dark to a chair in the corner, sit down and begin reciting the Yiddish prayer Got fun Avrohom, as was the custom of women to recite before Havdalah, to pray for a good, healthy and prosperous week. She would say the prayer very slowly, just to impede the departure of the Sabbath, counting every word in that sorrowful ancient tune, begging the Almighty, practically in tears, "God of Abraham, of Isaac and of Jacob, protect Your beloved people, Israel, from all evils…as the beloved holy Sabbath takes leave — that the coming week…may it arrive to bring perfect faith…love of good friends." She would then recite, even more slowly and with supplications and tears, the final passage. "May this week…arrive for mercy, for good health, for good fortune, for success, for blessing, for kindness, for children, life and sustenance, with the help of Heaven, for us and for all Israel. And let us say, Amen."

The Sabbath would then be over and Bobeh would light a candle and move to the dining room table, where Zeyde Berchik was standing, as he did every Saturday night after Bobeh Frumeh recited Got fun Avrohom, preparing to make Havdalah — setting out the spices, braided candle, wine, the Havdalah cup and matches. Zeyde Berchik would fill the wine cup, holding the lit candle high, with my tall, beautiful, graceful, statuesque and most generous grandmother Frumeh standing by, listening to Zeyde pronounce boldly and loudly the words of the Havdalah. "Behold, God is my salvation. I will trust and not be afraid. The Lord, the Lord, is my strength and my song. He has become my salvation. With joy you will draw water from the springs of salvation." Then, after the blessing over the wine, he would drink from the cup and pass it to Bobeh Frumeh, followed by the smelling of the spices to recover from the weakened state created by the departure of the *neshome yeseyre*, the additional Sabbath soul, which leaves the body with the departure of the Sabbath.

After Havdalah, my grandmother would have left the house and gone into the garden to pick vegetables for supper. And this is when vicious killers broke into the house and shot my grandfather dead. My grandmother, instead of saving herself, left the garden and walked into the house, confronting the killers, and was also murdered.

The Jews of Kortelisy who were killed that Saturday evening were buried in the green grazing fields outside the village in an unmarked grave, in the same field where the first victims had been buried. The prayers for hope, dignity, love, life, salvation, friendship and confidence in the Lord that were recited by my grandparents as the Sabbath was departing did not help. God did not listen. Instead, He sent brutal killers, and my grandparents, like the other Jews in the village, lost not only the additional Sabbath soul, but also the permanent soul, which sustains life during the week and is presumed to reside inside all human beings as long as they are alive.

OASIS OF SABBATH TRANQUILITY

By now, very few Kortelisy Jews were left. Most of them, including all the children and infants, had been murdered. As for our relatives, only my grandparents Meyer and Freyde and my uncles Shmilke and Ben-Tsion were still alive. Life in Kortelisy became impossible and dangerous, not only because of the Germans. Jews were also at the mercy of the Bulbovtsi and Banderivtsi, the Ukrainian police and even ordinary citizens. It was open season on Jews. Nothing was left of the Jewish community in Kortelisy. It had been decimated. At one point my parents decided to leave our hiding place on the farm and move to Ratno, where the Jewish community was still relatively intact. Our family and a few other surviving Kortelisy Jews, all adults, started late at night on a dangerous trek toward Ratno — a distance, if taking the regular route, of some twenty-five to thirty kilometres. We travelled only at night so that we wouldn't be detected. My brother and I, the only children in the group, slowed down the pace. Eventually, the others walked ahead and abandoned us and our grandparents and uncles.

My father carried my brother piggyback, but I had to walk on my own two feet, barefoot, having left my boots in the safety of our home because I was afraid of spoiling the leather in the marshes. We walked through the fields at night. By now, the harvest had been completed and the rye cut, leaving razor-sharp stubble and prickly grasses on the ground. Walking barefoot over this surface, especially when the stubble was covered with the chilling early morning dew, was very painful. I cut my feet so badly that they bled profusely. Because of my crying with pain all the time — the others called it kvetching — we didn't walk very fast and we made little progress toward Ratno. We had to stop quite often to examine my feet and give me some relief. We would stop walking at sunrise and rest in the forest or in the furrows of harvested rye or potato fields. When we stopped for the day, the punishment to my feet was suspended, giving them time to heal. I also discovered that I could get some relief by digging a hole in the soft ground, burying my feet tightly inside the hole and covering them with the warm earth.

One Friday morning, after wandering for a good week on the way to Ratno, we reached a little hamlet, a *khutor*, where a Jewish family lived. By then we were alone; only my parents, my brother and I arrived at that hamlet. All the others, including my grandparents and uncles, had moved ahead. As we entered the house, the first thing Mother told us was that we had to behave. She sternly warned us not to touch anything. Of course we would behave and wouldn't touch anything. We were afraid of our own shadows, totally traumatized by what we had heard and seen, particularly the killings in the marshes. We walked gingerly around the house for fear of touching any furniture or bumping into the other people in the house. I do not recall any of the names of the members of that family or the name of the hamlet, but it was wonderfully refreshing and exciting to be in a real house again, to have real food and be able to drink a glass of clean water that did not smell of marshes and taste like swamp.

Besides the adults, there were also children in the house, but we did not play with them; we were simply afraid to approach them or even their toys. I had not seen any children, except for my younger brother, in quite a while. All the Kortelisy children, our playmates, were dead by now; they had all been murdered. We could not warm up to these new children, even though we wanted to be friends and play with them. All we did was watch from a distance, always remembering Mother's instructions as we had walked into the house. Unlike my brother and me, these children were not afraid. They were free and happy children. They laughed, they jumped, they made mischief and they sang. And they had many, many toys. I was especially impressed with their four-wheeled wagon, which was controlled by a handle. You could roll down the hill in that wagon with as many as three or even four children inside. The wagon reminded me of the one I tried to steal from that little boy in the village I had visited with my grandmother Frumeh before the war. This time I made no plans to steal the wagon. It didn't even enter my mind.

After staying a while at this house, an illusion of safety was created in our minds, and we slowly started feeling some warmth and comfort. My brother was probably too young to comprehend the events, but even I, who was older and knew that we were being hunted, began to feel secure in the house, thinking that the worst was over and no harm could come to us as long as we were there. So I tried as hard as I could not to give our hosts a reason to throw us out of the house; I made myself as invisible as I could.

Everything in the house was so normal and calm; the family acted like there were no bad Germans or Ukrainian policemen, as if nothing bad was happening. As if Kortelisy and all the Jews of Kortelisy including the children were still alive. As if my grandfather Berchik, my grandmother Frumeh and my uncle Yerakhmiel were still alive. As if there had been no killings. The man of the house was particularly relaxed. He was a tall attractive man with a big head and a huge chest and shoulders. When both of us were standing, I had to stretch my neck to see his face. He had a long charcoal-black beard and the bushiest eyebrows I had ever seen and long, protruding nose hairs that overlapped with the top of his moustache. He was always content and was usually humming a synagogue tune. He loved to pinch my cheeks — my parents told me it was out of affection — which I didn't like. But, like with Ligutka, there was nothing I could do about it. I had to suffer through what appeared to me to be a strange way of showing affection. And he always smiled when pinching my cheeks and asked questions. "Vi ruft men dikh, yingele, un vi alt bistu?"—*What is your name, little boy, and how old are you*? He knew my name — Pinchas Elye. But he never waited for an answer and always continued asking more questions, examining my knowledge of the Chumash, asking if I remembered to say the Modeh Ani prayer in the morning and Shema before going to bed and, again, never waiting for an answer. As soon as I would open my mouth, he would come up with another question.

The entire aura of the house created fear on the one hand and security on the other — fear of being evicted, and security because, after what we had been through, everything was so comfortable. Seeing the adults, including my parents, praying, eating, singing and telling stories gave me a sense of permanence and safety, which we had not had for almost a month. All my brother and I had to do was remember Mother's instructions not to touch anything and everything was going to be fine.

As the sun was setting on Friday, my mother, the lady of the house and her mother all lit the Sabbath candles and recited the appropriate blessing. The men — my father, the owner of the house with the big black beard and bushy eyebrows, and his father — recited the Friday night prayers, and after the appropriate exchange of Shabbos greetings and hugs and blessings bestowed on the heads of the children, the men recited Sholem Aleichem, which was usually done upon returning from the synagogue. This family, living in a little hamlet and being the only Jewish family, did not have a synagogue and attended synagogue only on the High Holidays, probably in Ratno, or maybe even in Kortelisy.

After the prayers and Kiddush — this time over real wine — we all sat down for the Sabbath meal. It was a genuine feast. There was the proverbial gefilte fish and challah followed by chicken soup and *farfl* noodles and a choice of either roasted or boiled chicken along with *lokshn kugl* (noodle pudding) and all sorts of vegetable trimmings, including *tsimes* (a sweet vegetable stew).

Zmires were sung after every course with great gusto. My dear father showed off his great singing talent to the delight of all the others. For dessert, which as far as I was concerned was the best part of the meal, we ate a delicious sponge cake and a compote of the sweetest boiled plums. Unfortunately, the compote was served in tiny bowls that could hold, according to my count, only three plums. I was too shy to ask for more for fear of being evicted and sent into the arms of the Germans. After dessert, the women brought out the *mayim akhroynim*, the finger bowls in which the men dipped the tips of their fingers. Then we recited a very hearty Grace After Meals with a *mezumen*, an invitation to bless that was recited when at least three men who had already had their bar mitzvahs participated in the meal. I couldn't help but notice that during the recital of the blessing Mother was wiping tears from her eyes; ever since the death of her parents, she would cry during this blessing, in which she no longer had to mention her parents to ask the Almighty to bless them.

In spite of the joy and serenity of the occasion, I saw sadness in the faces of my parents, and I found it difficult to participate fully even though we were happy to finally get some rest and fill our bellies with delicious food. Looking back at this time, I still don't understand the frivolity of the people present at this Friday night dinner, including that of my own parents, who through their sadness and with halting joy, actually smiled. I ask myself, how were they able to laugh, eat, sing or even sit still? How were they able to relax, even for a moment? Where was their rage?

It had not even been a year since the brutal massacre in Babi Yar which, if the family or my parents had heard about at all, was probably nothing but a horrible rumour to them. Nothing was said about the murder and destruction of Jewish Kowel and Kortelisy or about the first victims of Ratno, murder that had happened close by and was not just a rumour. Years later, I still think that maybe this sole

Jewish family in this little hamlet lived in an illusion and considered themselves immune to German brutality. Or was it fatalism or total helplessness that formed the thoughts and actions of the Jewish family in that hamlet, as well as the thoughts and actions of the Jews in the other villages and even in the big cities? Or maybe it was complete surrender to faith and the will of God, a faith and trust in the Almighty so strong that they left it completely up to Him. Was death no longer a consideration because, notwithstanding all the massacres, God was with them and not with the killers? Or, were they all in a state of denial, knew nothing about what had happened and what was coming and didn't want to know? In any case, it seemed that no one at this Friday night dinner table expected to meet the same fate as the Jews of Babi Yar, Kowel or Kortelisy.

As for me, I had most certainly discovered death, and it was very frightening. I didn't want to die. I decided never to stand still and wait to be shot. Instead, whenever there was danger, I instinctively remembered the words of my grandmother Frumeh, to hide behind the stables. If I could not find stables, I was to run and hide anywhere else, but never stand still and wait to be shot. This instinctive reaction had already taken hold of me. On one occasion, immediately upon the arrival of the Germans in Kortelisy, but before the killings started, Ukrainian police and some of our neighbours invaded Jewish homes to harass and beat up Jews. We stayed in our homes but trembled in fear. My zeyde Berchik's home was the target of one of these raids while my brother and I were there with my parents one night. A gang broke into the house and started with their usual horrible threats and abuse, pushing and shoving my parents and grandparents and pointing their guns at them with the click of rifle chambers loading, a sound that was particularly scary. Without speaking to my parents, without a single word, I jumped through the open window into the night, abandoning my brother, my parents and my grandparents. I spent the night freezing and shivering in the cold in the furrows of the field.

In the morning, a bit warmed up by the rising sun, I carefully left the furrows and returned to my zeyde Berchik's house. The house was empty, the furniture scattered and broken, the pillows and coverings torn and the kitchen utensils in disarray. I finally found my parents, my brother and my grandparents, not behind stables, but inside the stables of a neighbour, sitting with other Jews, crying and gloomy. Everyone was totally stunned, hopeless and helpless, just waiting there, waiting for whatever would come, maybe the Messiah. In their distress, my parents hadn't even looked for me. And there was hardly any reaction when I walked into the stables, as if I had never left. They were dehumanized; there were no mothers, fathers, brothers and sisters, relatives and friends. Parents couldn't help children and children couldn't help parents. Everyone was on their own. We had turned into stone, were sitting in perpetual mourning, sitting shiva for the living dead. And that was only the beginning.

After Havdalah that Saturday night, my parents told us to start packing; we were leaving. This was very upsetting to me, and I became hysterical. But in spite of my hysteria, begging and tears, the decision had been made. Remembering the danger and the painful ordeal of walking through the fields barefoot, my parents' decision to leave seemed totally irrational to me. I kept asking if we had done something wrong, not realizing that our stay was only temporary, merely a stopover on the way to Ratno. We had to say our goodbyes and walk into the cold dark night, maybe to meet our deaths at the hands of the Germans or the Ukrainian police. Our parents tried to comfort us and assure us that it would be much better in Ratno, and we left the comfort of the house in the hamlet to continue on our journey, walking all night through the harsh and empty fields.

My feet, which had almost healed, started to bleed again. After a night of walking, we arrived at dawn in the village of Samary, called by Jews Samarvitch. There was still a Jewish community there, untouched and intact. My parents knew the Samary Jews, and we ended up in one of their homes. They knew all about what had happened in Kortelisy, and they received us with tears and open arms, as if we were survivors of a fire or some other calamity, which we were. They questioned us about their relatives in Kortelisy, and my parents had the unfortunate job of reporting that they were dead. They fed us and gave us a place to sleep. There was a great deal of crying in Samary, especially when we met with other Kortelisy survivors who were also on their way to Ratno. In particular, it was heart-wrenching when we encountered the pregnant wife of Hershl Blitt, who had been murdered with his little son in the marshes by the German soldiers disguised as Ukrainian women. She was still tortured and blamed herself for the death of her husband and baby; she was now praying for a successful delivery, expecting, based on her size, possible twin boys to name after her murdered husband and child.

ONLY THE LUCKY ONES DIE

In Samary, I encountered for the first time a Yiddish-speaking Ukrainian Christian. I later learned that this individual had been born Jewish, but that he and his two beautiful daughters had converted to Christianity. There was no mention of a wife or mother. I had never met converts or Yiddish-speaking Christians before. He and his two daughters had converted years before the Germans arrived, while western Ukraine was still part of Poland. He and his two grown daughters, who wore colourful kerchiefs and were beautifully dressed like city people, would visit the Jewish home where we had settled, even though the Jews openly cursed them and mocked them, though mostly in jest. The convert would argue that it was a wise decision on his part to convert because this would save his life and the lives of his daughters. Unfortunately, as he would discover, conversion to Christianity was not a passport to life.

Also in Samary, I learned, in a tragic way, where babies come from, though still without understanding the mechanics required to achieve pregnancy. I already knew where calves and colts came from. I had even "helped," or rather interfered, hanging around during their delivery. I had witnessed puppies and kittens being born, and I had helped chicks extricate themselves from their eggs by gently breaking the shells. I had seen the birth of animals with my own eyes many times. These childhood experiences, however, did not inform my knowledge of human birth until I saw the late Hershl's widow give birth to triplets. The very same day that we arrived in Samary, I learned that babies are not delivered by angels or storks. I was introduced to childbirth with a terribly harsh and painful experience that still haunts me, even in my old age.

First, I overheard murmurings that the pregnant woman's situation was very serious. Then, I heard talk about the size of her belly and that she was about to give birth to more than one baby. Maybe God had regrets for allowing the death of her first-born and He was about to bless her and reward her with twins to replace the terrible loss of her first child. But, it seemed that God was a trickster. He played a cruel game with the widowed mother that did not result in a happy and joyous ending. The woman lay in a bed, screaming horribly, completely uncovered. Four or five women surrounded her, trying to help her, I presumed. At first, I wasn't quite sure what was going on, and I thought that she was just sick and in pain because of her sickness. But soon the women around her started talking not only about the size of her belly but also about babies, and they began pulling not one but three babies out of her. As each baby was picked up, one of the ladies would slap its bottom, which I thought was strange; the babies did nothing to deserve a spanking — why slap the baby? The woman kept on slapping the babies, but nothing was happening. The babies were silent and, after a while, the mother too stopped screaming. They were all silent, dead. Everyone stood around stunned, helpless, stricken by grief. The men murmured silent prayers.

Then I overheard conversations among the adults. They were saying how lucky the woman and her triplets were to die and avoid being murdered by the Germans. In the spirit of Nachum Ish Gamzu, the consensus was that perhaps the death of the mother and her triplets was for the best. The consensus was that only the lucky ones die.

The following day there was a naming and funeral. At the burial site, the women were crying and the men were arguing. I later learned from my father that the argument was about Jewish law and tradition: how to deal with stillborn baby boys or baby boys who die before their bris. Different schools of thought were pronounced and advanced. Finally, in view of the urgency, a quick compromise was reached. The circumcisions were performed at the graveside, and the three babies were given proper Jewish names: one was called Yisroel, and the other two were named after their murdered father and older brother. Part of the compromise, however, was that no *brokhe* was said during the bris ceremony. Curiosity led me to read the blessing: "The Lord spoke to Moses, saying: Pinehas the son of Elazar, the son of Aaron the priest, turned back My rage from the children of Israel, when he was zealous for Me among them, and I did not annihilate the children of Israel in My own zeal. And so tell him, that I now give him My covenant for peace." After reading this prayer, I surmised that there may have been another reason the circumcision prayer was not recited. It would appear that the very jealous God of Israel was on the path of annihilation again, in our own time, and the Samary Jews, facing destruction themselves, didn't want to hear about a cruel God at the gravesite.

The mother and her three babies were buried together in the same grave. The funeral was attended by the village's entire Jewish community. The Kaddish, the prayer for the dead, was recited by my father. There was no family to mourn their death. Still, everyone attending the funeral cried bitterly, as if the dead were their own, even though many considered Hershl's widow and her triplets lucky.

We decided to leave Samary shortly after the funeral and continue on our way to Ratno. The woman of the house put together some food for us and wished us well, and we left as soon as it got dark. This time, however, to my great delight, I had been given a pair of old, slightly torn and oversized boots. I was also given two pairs of socks, which I wore on top of each other to help make the boots fit. With boots on my injured feet, I actually enjoyed the walk, at times even playfully jumping over puddles, cracks and crevices on the ground. And in the harvested rye fields, I jumped with great delight over the sharp rye stubs, as if in revenge for what they had done to my naked feet when I walked shoeless.

I continued to think about the poor lady and her dead babies and the talk of their death being a blessing and how God did her a favour by making her and her babies die. I certainly did not agree with that idea; I thought God had done the wrong thing. I didn't think that it was better for them to die. I thought it was always better to be alive, no matter what and whatever the circumstances may be. I certainly didn't want anyone to say "gam zu l'toyve"—*this too is for the best*—upon my own death, which I could not envision, even when I was facing it head on.

MY ONLY FRIENDS AND COMPANIONS

We arrived safely in Ratno and joined the rest of our family. We had no money and no income and Father had no job. Of course, there was no such thing as having a job at that point. But somehow, with the help of the Jewish community, we settled in the town, in a house with several other families, sharing whatever meagre food we could find.

While Jewish Kortelisy was destroyed, Ratno still had most of its Jewish population intact. A number of Jews had been killed, some of them immediately after the German forces arrived, when the entire Jewish population was paraded before the killers and thirty young men were picked out to be executed. The claim was that the Jews had attacked the German forces. It is true that on that day the Germans arrived, a day as black as coal, the Jewish population would have been very happy to resist and attack the German army. Unfortunately, not one among them had a rifle or shotgun. To fortify their message, the Germans added the same number of Soviet prisoners of war to be shot together with the Jewish young men.

And here we were in Ratno, just waiting, still unable to believe what was happening but waiting for the inevitable. Though the murder and killing of Jews was all around us, the remnants somehow maintained a ray of hope that they would survive, even though no one had a serious plan to ensure that survival. At most, people prepared a hiding place in an attic or cellar or inside the walls of their residences. There was no real panic, and Jews continued to live as if nothing bad was happening, even rationalizing the killings, thinking that it would never happen to them. At the same time, parents were worried about their children and sought ways and means to save them. One plan that was quite popular but turned out to be tragic in most cases was to hand children over to Christian families. Parents hoped that, even if they did not survive, their children would continue to live in gentile homes and maybe even survive the war. My parents too thought that this was a wise idea.

So, with heavy hearts, my parents decided to send me to a farm, hoping to save my life. (Lucky for my brother, he was much too young for the deal.) Within days of arriving in Ratno, they found a Christian family for me to live with on a farm in a neighbouring hamlet. The idea of leaving my parents to live with a strange family did not appeal to me but, like a good little boy, I did not object to the project of keeping me alive in the event of my parents' death, and I complied without protest. In fact, I too thought that this move would ensure my survival. Considering my great fear of dying, I was ready to do anything so as not to be shot, even leave my parents. At the same time, the thought of my parents dying was bizarre, and I could not imagine it.

The Ukrainian Christian family my parents found for me had a farm in a hamlet about ten or fifteen kilometres east of Ratno, on the east side of the Pripet River. The owner of the farm was a widow, and she had a daughter in her early twenties who was dark and attractive and would bring bread and milk to the stables where I lived and slept. There was also a son, probably about eighteen years old, who thought it was his duty to threaten me with death and give me regular beatings. Not a day would pass without him reminding me that I was there only temporarily, by his grace, and that as soon as they started killing the Jews in Ratno, he would personally deliver me to the Germans for proper and just treatment. It was frightening to hear him talk like this, but he thought it was funny. He would repeat it again and again and always finished by pointing his finger at me as if it were a gun or a pistol and making the sound of a discharged bullet — *pough, pough.* Or he would make a choking sound and move his hand across his throat, indicating another way I could die. His threats made me feel less than human, like an earthworm. I completely lost my pride and lived in constant fear of him and submitted to his threats and beatings. But the more fear I showed, the more aggressive and threatening he was.

The widow herself would bemoan my misfortune by telling me that even if I survived the war there would be no Jewish girls for me to marry, and no decent Christian girl would ever marry me. Actually, I was not thinking of marriage then, but it was still hurtful and frightening to hear her talk like this because the way I understood what she was saying was that all Jews, and therefore all Jewish girls, would be dead, even if I survived. And whatever an adult said I firmly believed to be the honest truth.

I was only about ten years old, but I worked hard and with great diligence, doing my very best to please the widow and, in particular, to please her nasty son — or maybe just to avoid the threats and beatings. I slept in the hayloft in the stables with the cattle, horses and other animals. I would wake up at around five in the morning with the mooing and lowing of the cows and the gentle, sweet whinnying and neighing of the horses. I would say the Modeh Ani and my morning prayers and take care of my chores around the stables, have my breakfast of stale black rye bread and milk, and then take my flock of two horses, several cows and about a dozen sheep into the grazing fields. I would return at around five o'clock in the evening, in time for the milking of the cows. As for my lunch, it was usually black rye bread and milk. Occasionally, I would also have a hard-boiled egg or a cold boiled or baked potato. And I would have the same food again for supper.

As I fell into this routine, the hard work and the lack of food, and even the regular beatings, ceased to bother me. I adjusted, and my mind and body became numb and acclimated to the abuse of the widow's cruel son. I wasn't even frightened by his threats to take me to the Germans. I stopped thinking about Germans. I even thought about how if he took me to Ratno, at least I would see my parents again. I stopped thinking about survival and dying because within days of my arrival I began to miss my parents. Even though I understood what was going on and the reasons for my situation, I started feeling sorry for myself, motherless and fatherless, totally abandoned, without love and without anyone to care for me. Instead, I was now the caregiver to a bunch of animals, while I was neglected and unloved.

When I wanted to recite prayers from my tiny prayer book, I would conceal myself in a furrow so as not to be spotted by the neighbours and the other shepherds. With one eye on my pocket-size prayer book, which had been partly handwritten by my uncle Ben-Tsion, I kept the other eye on the flock of sheep, which tended to react to any sound by spreading out and running in all directions. The horses had their front legs tied, so they stayed put, and the cows would usually move slowly, grazing in a small area.

"The Lord is my light and my salvation — whom then shall I fear?" I would regularly read chapter 27 of Psalms, which is recited daily from the beginning of the Hebrew month of Elul until Shemini Atzeres, the last day of the Jewish High Holiday season. But I feared everyone and everything, including God. With the arrival of the Germans, every Jew, including me, lived in a state of unrelenting, debilitating fear. What kept me going were the messages I had received from my grandmother Frumeh: "It is our fate to fear and deal with life the best we can and never lose hope and our faith in the Almighty. We are in *goles*," and "Vayl mir zaynen yidn." And, of course, there was her advice when facing Cossacks: run, and hide behind the stables. In truth, I had been raised on and lived in fear even before the Germans arrived. I must have been born with an innate mental and physical ability to live in constant fear, as if it was just a part of life.

However, my grandmother could not help me when I reached

verse 10 of chapter 27 of the Psalms: "Although my father and my mother have forsaken me, the Lord will gather me in." When I would reach this point in the Psalm, I would break down and cry bitterly, totally lost in self-pity and fear. The Psalmist was telling me that I was abandoned by my parents, and now even by God, who would "gather me in" only after I was dead. I would extricate myself from the furrow and stumble along in the midst of my flock and continue to cry, completely deranged, out of control, lifting and waving my arms to the sky, as if in prayer. At times, holding my head in my hands, I would get terribly agitated, not knowing what to do with myself. I would begin to panic and start screaming, out of control. I was angry with God, and it seemed like the feelings of anger and mistrust were mutual and reciprocal. I felt like leaving my flock and running across the Pripet River to my parents in Ratno. Eventually, I would gather my strength and try not to lose all my senses.

I could not leave the flock; I had grown attached to it. I spent twenty-four hours a day with these animals, during the day in the field and at night in the stables. I slept when they slept and I ate when they ate. The cows and horses were my only friends and companions. They were the only ones around I could speak to; they stood still and appeared to listen to me. And there was no one else to hug or be hugged by. To help calm myself, I would pull down on a horse's muzzle and squeeze its head, hugging it to my chest and hanging onto its neck like it was an old relative or friend.

SURPRISE VISIT AND THE SOUND OF GUNS FROM RATNO

My parents were obviously anxious about me, and I had been on the farm for only about a week or ten days when I was treated to a surprise visit by my mother and brother one evening. I was very happy to see them and jumped up and down with joy. I hoped that my parents had decided to take me back home. We went into the stables and sat down in the hayloft, and I showed my mother where I slept, where and what I ate, and the animals I took care of. My mother asked me how I was doing. Was I happy and did I get enough food to eat? I lied. I told her I was happy and treated well but that I would still like to go home. It was out of the question. Ratno was not safe for Jews and was no place for children. My chances of survival were much better on the farm, my mother insisted. But my parents, in their anxiety to save me, did not consider how I would survive if they were gone. I guess none of the parents who gave their children to Christian farmers, hoping for their survival, asked this question.

We all slept in the stables that night. In the morning we were awakened by loud shooting coming from the direction of Ratno, across the Pripet River. My mother started telling me that before she left there had been rumours — nothing unusual, there were always rumours — that Jewish Ratno was to be liquidated. But there had been another bad sign. On the road on the way to the farm, Mother had seen many military vehicles moving in the direction of Ratno.

We realized what was happening there. On Wednesday, August 26, 1942, the Jewish population of Ratno was murdered, including my paternal grandfather, Meyer; my uncle Shmilke, my father's younger brother; my uncle Ben-Tsion, my mother's younger brother; and Ben-Tsion's girlfriend and colleague, Sonia. We would find out later that my grandmother Freyde, who had managed to survive previous pogroms, also survived this one.

I thought about my uncle Shmilke, who had tried to teach me how to ride a bike when I was six or seven years old. He had picked me up and placed me on the bike seat, but my legs were too short to reach the pedals. He told me that I would have to wait, maybe another year or two, for my legs to grow longer, and then he would teach me how to ride the bike. But before my legs grew longer, the beastly Germans arrived, and his bike was confiscated by the Ukrainian police. And now, most agonizingly, with his murder in Ratno, I knew he would never be able to teach me how to ride a bike.

Sonia, even in the face of death, refused to deny her Jewishness. She didn't know the Hebrew *alefbeys*, she didn't speak Yiddish, and she knew nothing about the Jewish holidays. But she always insisted that she was a *yevreyka*, and eventually she died because of it. I thought of the last time I had seen Sonia. It was in Ratno, and we were all sitting under a tree with thick branches. She was there together with my parents and brother and my uncles Ben-Tsion and Shmilke and my paternal grandparents. Looking at the tree, Sonia had remarked, "The top of the tree would be a great place to hide." I fully understood what she meant; we were always thinking of hiding places and survival. The tree might have been an even better place than behind the stables. By then everyone expected the worst, but nothing useful was done about it. We were unprepared. We were doomed.

Considering the threats of the widow's menacing son, I told my mother that if Ratno was being liquidated, and there was no doubt about it, we had to leave the farm. It was too dangerous to continue staying here, even though the widow was prepared to let us stay, risking death for herself and her family. We presumed that my father, who had stayed in Ratno, was dead. We cried, and we missed him, but we had neither the time nor the luxury to mourn; numbness set in and we were too busy with self-preservation. Mother was now alone, facing a terrible and insurmountable task and struggle: how to feed and save herself and her children.

We left the widow's farm the very same day and fled into the surrounding forest. There were other Jews in the forest who had managed to escape death or who happened to be away from Ratno at the time, like my mother and brother. But the most horrible sight for me was that of the young Jewish children whose parents had entrusted them to local farmers for survival. These children were now orphaned and had been thrown out by the farmers who were supposed to be their protectors. It was heart-wrenching to see these children suffer, trying to take care of themselves. Alone, they had no chance of survival. They eventually perished in the green fields and huge forests of the area — captured and shot to death by the Germans or Ukrainian police, or beaten to death by some locals, or they starved to death.

None of the other adult survivors were willing to help and accept those children. They did not want us either and told us to stay away. One man in a white suit and a white fedora pointed a small silver pistol at us. "If you follow us, I will shoot!" he shouted. Even though we no longer had our father, unlike the orphaned children, my brother and I had our very heroic mother, who mustered her strength and stood up to the man with the pistol and the others who refused to accept us. Even though we were in constant danger of being killed, I felt safe with my mother and I had no fear of being abandoned. I was a child again and fully recovered from my loneliness. Mother was there, the strong and powerful rock on whom I was able to lean.

But, of course, I was still not prepared to be shot, and we all continued to live in constant fear of death. Our mother would console us with her usual words of comfort. "Don't be afraid. Dying is not so bad. And, don't forget, should we die, we will all meet again and be in heaven together with Zeyde and Bobeh and all the uncles and Tateh." Even though I loved my father, my grandparents and uncles dearly, the idea of dying so that I could see them again, even in heaven, did not appeal to me. By then I had seen killings and shootings, and it wasn't a pleasant sight. Just thinking about it put me in a panic and made me ready to run. But listening to my mother and her consoling words, I always showed a brave face and an expression of complete confidence in what she was saying, pretending to be happy, as if I could no longer wait to be shot to be in heaven with all my relatives. She meant well.

The three of us continued wandering in the forest, moving from hamlet to hamlet. At night we would sleep in the fields, inside the haystacks, where it was warm and considered safe. The haystacks were quite comfortable and, for a young child, even pretty exciting. In any event, by now I had grown accustomed to sleeping in hay, and the smell of hay was pleasant to me. It must have had a relaxing effect on us, because we would wake up feeling well rested. However, we had to stop sleeping in the haystacks when the Germans discovered that Jews were hiding in them and they started shooting into them.

We also had to leave the forest and go to the hamlets to search and beg for food. The farmers were not always generous. Some were even dangerous and hostile, not necessarily because they were wicked, but because they were afraid for their own lives and the lives of their families. As soon as they saw us coming, they would run out of their houses and shoo us away and threaten us. They were truly afraid of retribution from the Germans for helping Jews in any way, as the Germans and Ukrainian police were executing entire Ukrainian Christian families as a punishment for hiding Jews. Some would take risks and help us out with food and shelter. Others were motivated to take such risks when it was combined with bartering or monetary benefit.

Despite my lack of expertise in ladies' styles and apparel, I could not help but notice that my thin mother was somehow on the fat and heavy side when she arrived at the farm with my brother. I could not explain the change until I realized that my mother was trading with some of the farmers. In exchange for food, she was bartering her dresses, which she wore one on top of the other, giving her this heavy appearance. When she had left Ratno, not knowing what to expect, she put on about a dozen dresses, and from time to time she would take off a dress and exchange it for food. She continued doing this until she was left with only one dress.

Some farmers tried to help out of the goodness of their hearts. I remember one such farmer in particular. He was tall, and his attire did not resemble that of a regular farmer, like the ones in my village with their homespun clothes. He wore a regular dark suit and a white shirt with an open collar. He also wore regular dark shoes. After seeing that farmer, I began to realize that not all of Ukraine was like my village. Like most Ukrainian men though, he sported a huge moustache. As we were wandering in the village, begging for food and getting waved away by the frightened farmers we approached, this man called us over. He was looking around in all directions for a place where he could talk to us in secret. We finally ended up inside his barn. "Listen," he told us, "if you wish, you can walk into the stables and sleep there at night. I will even leave some food for you to eat. But you must leave before sunrise. And if you are found in my stables and barns by the Germans, I will deny ever giving you permission to stay or even knowing you." We thankfully accepted his generous offer.

It was quite pleasant to sleep in the hayloft amid the familiar scents of animal, manure and hay. Sometimes a horse would decide to neigh or a cow belch or low in the middle of the night, and that would wake us. But it was always warm inside the stables, whatever the weather was outside. I still enjoy the smell of manure and hay. I associate these odours with the best and most expensive perfumes, with warmth and comfort.

We continued to sleep in the kind farmer's stables, and he would leave us some food, mainly hard cheese and bread. For our part, we would always leave the stables before sunrise. My mother offered him a dress for his wife, and he politely refused. "You will need it for yourself," he said. "You can't walk naked, especially in the winter. You will have to be dressed warmly." When we were arriving or departing, late at night or in the early morning, he would always suddenly appear and bless us with a "dhay bozse zdorovya"—*may God grant us health.*

With our night accommodation assured, save for the constant fear of being captured, the rest of the day was relatively easy. Most of the day would be spent picking and eating blueberries and cranberries in the forest, which were plentiful at this time of the year. We even picked some of these berries and wild mushrooms for the farmer, presenting them to him on our return to the stables for the night. He would always graciously accept this small token of our appreciation and thank us profusely, blessing us and wishing us good fortune and health.

A GOOD MESSENGER

While in the forest, we continued meeting other survivors. Some of them had managed to escape the Ratno liquidation, and we began to hope that Father too might have saved himself. My mother thought that we would be safer in numbers, but the other adults still did not want us. They thought that their safety would be compromised by having children around. The man in the white fedora and suit was always there to threaten us with his little silver-coloured pistol. He warned us that if we followed the group that he was supposedly leading, he would kill us. My mother was brave and argued with him. She told him, in a loud voice, that if he wanted to kill, he should kill Germans; there were plenty of others to kill Jewish mothers and their children. After calming herself, she softly assured the fellow with the pistol that her kids were well-behaved and that we understood the situation and would be quiet and cause no trouble. Pointing at us she said, "Look, they are practically adults." We nodded in agreement.

Somehow the man in the white fedora and his group of survivors had pity on us and agreed to accept us. During the day we would stay with this group, picking berries and mushrooms like all the others. At night, we would sneak away into the stables. One warm summer night, Mother decided that we would stay with the group overnight. As we walked through the forest, looking for an appropriate sleeping place, we saw through the trees a small fire with some men sitting around it. We all stopped, contemplating the situation. Could they be German soldiers or Ukrainian policemen? Either would be deadly. Maybe they were surviving Jews? It would be good to increase and strengthen our group with adult men. But someone would have to take the risk and move in closer to the fire and investigate. Wishing to show that she was capable of contributing and being helpful to the group, Mother volunteered. Her mantra was always, "I have nothing to lose, I can take the risks." She would say it but didn't actually mean it. She wanted to live and save her children, and she fought like a lioness to protect us. But she also wanted to convince the others that she was as capable as any man.

So Mother carefully walked toward the men around the fire and, sure enough, she recognized one of them. She knew this man from way back when she was still single. He was from a village that neighboured Kortelisy. The man recognized my mother as well, and as soon as he saw her, he asked, "Eydl, vu iz dayn man?"—*Adele, where is your husband*? Tears running down her cheeks, she replied, "Where all the husbands are." The man exclaimed, "What are you talking about?" And then, taking credit for something we later learned he did not do, he said, "I took him across the river in a boat. He escaped from Ratno. Your husband is alive."

Our father was alive! Our joy was beyond all description; the event was beyond belief. We were jumping, clapping our hands and crying out of happiness. The Almighty had returned our father to us — alive. Mother hugged both of us and mumbled a prayer. I even made peace with God. It seemed that Father, true to his nature, was determined to live and had done everything he could to be reunited with his family. The entire group was excited and happy for us. We did not, however, know where our father was and what he was doing. How had he survived the liquidation? Was he looking for us? It made no sense for us to return to the widow's farm because Father didn't even know where it was. It was at this point that Mother decided to leave the group and this area of the forest and start looking for her husband and our father around the vicinity of Kortelisy. So, the great search began in the forest, villages and hamlets near Kortelisy.

My mother exchanged her remaining extra dress for food. Now we spent most of our time moving around, searching for my father. Some of the survivors who had escaped from Ratno had seen my father in the forest, but they told us that he had taken off quickly and did not stay with them. We asked farmers who knew my father if they had seen him. Some of them said that they had but that he was acting crazy: "Leiba z'durev"—*Leiba is crazy*. From these reports, it seemed Father was confused and running around as if on the verge of insanity. On several occasions, we came to a village and were told that he had been there an hour or two earlier, or was just around the corner but had vanished. This happened again and again, as if he was trying to avoid us. The thought may have crossed my mother's mind because husbands did abandon their families, thinking that it would be easier to survive without being burdened by a wife and children.

One of the Ukrainian Christian villagers from Kortelisy ultimately reunited us with our father. He had seen him in the forest. This man told us exactly where Father was — sitting under a specific tree — and that he had seen him there about half an hour earlier. Sure enough we found Father, under the tree, asleep. After searching for him for over a month, there he was, as though he was waiting for us. Mother woke him, and he was startled and in shock, seeing her there. Of course, finding Father alive and well was, in our eyes, a miracle of biblical proportions. Father hugged us and kissed us and kept on reciting the blessing in Aramaic from his *siderl*, his little prayer book, of "B'rikh rakhmono diy'hovokh niholon, v'lo y'hovokh l'afro"—*Blessed is the Merciful One Who has given you to us, and has not given you to the dust* — as if he just returned from the dead and we were still among the living.

It is difficult, truly impossible, to describe the emotions we had on seeing our father alive. Even the words of the wonderful Aramaic poem of Akdomus, composed in praise of the Almighty, could not describe our feelings: "Were the skies parchment, Were all the reeds quills, Were the seas and all waters made of ink, Were all the world's inhabitants made scribes" it would still be insufficient to describe our wonderful and exalted feelings on finding Father alive. We were totally overwhelmed, body and soul, by this great emotional experience. Nevertheless, at the same time, I felt strangely ambivalent; something was gnawing at my brain. I was angry with him. My father, my hero, who had always provided safety and comfort, had failed me this time. The thought spawned in my mind that Father was trying to abandon us. I was still angry with him for sending me to work on the farm, even though that may have saved us all. I also blamed him for not being with us and for staying behind in Ratno. And so I was aloof and kept my distance, and I pulled away from his hugs and kisses. It took several weeks for me to get close to him again.

When Mother had left Ratno with my brother to visit me and my father stayed behind, no one, including my father, expected what would happen. There were always rumours of liquidation and murder. In the minds of the victims, there was no valid reason to run; this is what they wanted to believe. And yet, the place became deadly and escape miraculous, as my father used to relate, with much gusto and in great detail, to anyone who would listen.

FATHER'S ESCAPE

On that fateful day in Ratno, the Ukrainian police had rounded up my father together with three or four other Jews and lined them up to be shot on the streets of the town. One of the Jews was Tulier, originally from Kortelisy, who had survived the killings there but was now facing the guns of the Ukrainian police with my father. Tulier, who had the liquor monopoly in Kortelisy and surrounding areas, was a very generous man. His contributions had helped the rather poor Jewish population of Kortelisy build a synagogue and a mikveh, and support a *melamed* for the school as well as a rabbi and a *shoykhet.* In Kortelisy, he was called the Ba'al Shem after a saintly rabbi, the Ba'al Shem Tov, the founder of the chassidic movement.

My father, who was always calm and collected and approached everything with humour, thought to himself that the killers were just ordinary people with guns and that developing a relationship, a sense of belonging, friendship and brotherhood, even with people who were about to murder him, would save his life and the lives of the others rounded up with him. Father knew these people; he had dealt with such people before. He spoke and understood their language and knew how to talk to them. He thought that, under the circumstances, just a simple conversation, man to man, would convince the killers that all people are brothers, would provide them with a moment of reflection that would change their minds about killing innocent people, convince them that even Jews are human beings.

Father turned to the killers as if they were his best friends and buddies, expressing his willingness to be of assistance in his own execution. “Look here, my little brothers,” he said to them in colloquial and folksy Ukrainian. “I have nothing against you. You are only fulfilling your duty. Be practical. It makes no sense for you to kill us here on the street and then have to drag our bodies for burial. Let us walk to the burial place together, like friends and brothers, and it will save you from a messy job.” Of course, these killers were trained to kill Jews and had already amassed a great deal of practice in this area; they had no sense of humour and were not amused or swayed by my father's suggestion. They had no interest in conversations or compromise of any kind. As my father talked, one of them aimed and fired at Tulier, who fell with an agonized yelp. It was then that my father realized that to continue ingratiating himself to the killers would not save his life. He began to run in the direction of the Pripet River. The police started shooting after him.

At this point, my father recalled a story that had been told to him by a local farmer, how during World War I, German soldiers were shooting after the farmer and, while running away from them, he ran in a zig-zag pattern and they missed him. So, my father started zig-zag running. The only difference running zig-zag this time was that they were also shooting at my father with machine guns and not just single-shot rifles, as had been used to shoot after the farmer during World War I. But the killers missed my father completely, and he ran into the river fully clothed. He reached about the middle of the river and was up to his neck in water.

Unfortunately, like all Kortelisy Jews, my father had never learned how to swim. He was thus faced with the terrible dilemma of choosing a method of death: Should he continue crossing the river and drown in the process or return to the town and be shot? There was no preferred choice, but my father was a fighter. The greater the challenge, the more determined he was to fight back and survive. He wasn't about to return to Ratno to be shot after having escaped that particular death. He decided he would rather drown than surrender to his killers, but as he waded deeper into the water, which now reached his chin, he discovered that it was not easy to drown. His head was under water several times, and each time he popped up like a balloon, out of breath. Then he began to realize that what he was doing might be an attempt at suicide and that he was failing miserably. Then, the more serious question of suicide popped up: it was against the Jewish religion. There was a specific prohibition against suicide from the Almighty Himself. Father's options were more clarified in his mind now that religion became a factor. Now he had to choose whether in his death he wanted to go to heaven or to hell. He was faced with a theological dilemma: if he surrendered and was killed as an innocent, he would most definitely go to heaven, but if he took his own life, the likelihood of his going to heaven would be very slim and he would most likely end up in hell.

If Father could neither return to the Germans nor deliberately drown, the remaining option was to just stand in the water until he died of hunger or exhaustion. However, my father was determined to live. After all, he had to find and take care of his family. In the end, his will and desire to live and survive his ordeal, even while standing up to his chin in water, facing death, became more important than hell or heaven. As sure as there was a God, which to my father was a certainty, even as he was being hunted like a wild animal, he felt that he would not be forsaken in this horrible predicament. And in a miracle just short of splitting the Red Sea, He did save him. The messenger came in the form of a little boat carrying a large peasant, a big dog and a long cane.

As the killing in Ratno was going on and the unfortunate victims were being buried in the sand dunes of the nearby village of Prokhid, northwest of Ratno, life was going on at a normal pace for the rest of the population, the non-Jews. In the middle of hell, the circles of torment in Dante's *Inferno*, regular, non-Jewish people were getting up, washing, getting dressed, having breakfast and even going to work.

Some, I surmise, were saying their morning prayers, maybe even thanking Jesus for not being Jewish. Christian children were playing in the streets under the watchful eyes of their parents, who made sure they were not confused with the Jewish children, who were being killed. One of these ordinary people, doing his daily chores on the river, was rowing his boat in the direction of my father. The man was huge, and he rowed his boat quickly and with great strength. He was wearing a grey *kutchme*, a fur hat, over his head even though it was still summer, and his shoulder-length hair protruded from under his headgear. A huge moustache covered his upper lip and spread to both sides of his cheeks. He was dressed in a homemade peasant's coat tied up with a traditional flowery sash of many colours. No doubt, on his feet he wore the usual *postoly*, made from the bark of the birch tree and worn over boot rags, tied up to his knees with fine, colourful strings.

At first, my father was worried. The peasant could be a policeman out of uniform or a farmer who might or might not be sympathetic to a drowning Jew. My father tried to hide, but the only way to hide was to go under the water. My father finally decided to just stand there and rely on fate. As the little boat came closer, my father yelled out to the approaching farmer: "Ho, ho *batyushka*, little father, would you be so kind and help me out here? Please, *batyushka*, help me to the shore. I am stuck. And God will reward you for your kindness."

"A chtoh tebe tut v'perlo?"—*What dragged you into here*? the peasant asked. He continued questioning my father in a gruff voice, and using coarse and colourful language, implied that since my father had crawled into the river like a total imbecile, fully clothed, he must be an early morning drunkard.

My father, still concerned about the man's intentions, would not tell him the real reason for his predicament. It appeared that the peasant did not suspect that Jews were being killed in Ratno, even though one could clearly hear the shootings. He most definitely did not connect the two events. There was also the risk that if he told the man that he was running away from the Germans, the man would be afraid to even touch him. Even if he were a good and honest man, he would be afraid of German reprisals for helping a Jew escape. So, with a straight face, my father, in his very pleasing voice, spoke man to man with the farmer in the local accent and told him, "May all of God's blessings be upon you, little father. You see, little father, this is the time of the year when we Jews, to serve God, dunk ourselves in the water. Unfortunately, I got stuck. I am tired and I am having a hard time untangling myself and getting to the shore. Will you, therefore, for the love of God, little father, be so kind as to help me out? Take me across the river and bring me to the shore and I will pray for you and your kin and God will bless you manyfold."

The man agreed to help and my father climbed into the boat, water dripping from his clothes. The dog barked and growled at my father, but my father had never been afraid of dogs. He was able to pacify them by just looking at them. My father stared at the dog, told him who was boss, and the dog just retreated and rolled up with its tail between its hind legs. The farmer started to row, moving toward Ratno, where the Jews lived, and not in the direction my father wanted to go, away from Ratno, to the other side of the river, where he expected to find his family. My father was still suspicious that the rescue was a horrible, cruel trick and the man was returning him to the Germans, and he readied himself to jump back into the water. But my father gathered his courage and yelled out, "No, no, little father, I want to go to the other side of the river. I have family waiting there for me." The man, without a fuss, just turned his little boat around and brought my father to the east shore of the river. My father thanked him and blessed him sincerely again and again and promised him the blessings and great rewards of the Almighty God, Creator of the Universe.

As my father parted from the man and moved into the fields, away from the shore, he thought to himself, "Surely, this was not an ordinary man." Then it hit my father like a bolt of lightning: this boatman had been sent from heaven to save him. He was none other than

Elijah the Prophet, who visited our Passover seder and who enjoyed doing favours anonymously and helping people in distress, always disguised.

And the man who had been shot right next to my father and fell with an agonized cry was not really Tulier from Kortelisy, the liquor vendor. It was an angel from God; it had been the sound of the shot and Tulier's cry that gave my father the incentive to run. When my father would tell us about being shot at, he would say that he was followed by a hail of gunfire, bullets flying all around him, and that in the middle of that, he saw beautiful angels with wings — in front of him, at his sides and in back of him, protecting him from being hit by any of the bullets. The Almighty and His angels provided protection and security for him, as it is written, "B'sheym adoynoy, elohey yisroel, mimini Mikhoel, umismoyli Gavriel, umilfonay Uriel, ume'akhoyray Refoel, v'al royshi shkhinas eyl"—*In the name of the Lord, God of Israel: may Michael be at my right hand, Gabriel, at my left; in front of me, Uriel, behind me, Raphael; and above my head the Presence of God*. These angels were more powerful and much stronger than hundreds of thousands of garrisons around a fort, providing protection from evildoers and any possible attack.

Short of splitting the Pripet, the Almighty had performed every miracle to save my father from certain death. But why did He send the Germans and the Ukrainian police to begin with? Why did He send them to Ratno? Instead of all this effort, all He had to do was keep the Germans away from Ratno. Then there would have been no killing and no need for Ukrainian policemen. God is a bad planner and poor organizer.

My father was an honest man and all his thinking was guided by his faith. Father believed that he had been saved through God's intervention, but not because he was special in the eyes of the Almighty. And he had a hard time reconciling the good things that had happened to him with the fate of the Jews in Ratno and Kortelisy — with him being saved from death and Jewish Ratno being destroyed. He knew that whatever happened, whether to him or to the Jews of Ratno, whether good or bad, was the will of God. Nothing moves without the will of God. But although he had great faith in God, he was plagued by the contradiction: he had been saved, but there were neither angels nor messengers saving the Jews of Ratno or Kortelisy, or the Jews who were being murdered in other places. At the same time, he believed that, with God's help, everything would turn out alright. "We are in the hands of God and blessed be His name" was his mantra. God giveth and God taketh, blessed be the name of the Lord. *Borukh dayen ho-emes*. Blessed be the true and righteous judge. Even in the face of death, any death, we always bless the Almighty. And in the words of Nachum Ish Gamzu, "This too is for the best." It appears to me that Father, facing difficult situations, and especially during the war, was unable to resolve serious life and death problems, and his reliance on the Almighty gave him a special kind of hope. My father survived because of his strong will to live, by using his wits, humour and great charisma, and also with the help of a great deal of faith and optimism.

A VILLAGE ERASED

On Wednesday, September 23, 1942, the German killers came to that insignificant village of Kortelisy. They surrounded the village before dawn, and when it got bright outside, they ran through the village with the Ukrainian police, ordering everyone to assemble in the square in front of the church. Unfortunately, the Ukrainian Christian population listened and assembled in the same way and in the same place as the Jews had, not long before. They brought with them their newborn babies and their children and the people who could not walk, those who were deaf and those who were blind — all were brought to this inferno, the square of slaughter in front of the church. All the villagers were murdered. Those who hadn't assembled were rounded up, led to ready-made graves and murdered there — men, women and children, including babies.

Like the timid Jews, the presumably strong and fearless *goyim* were disorganized and dehumanized in the face of German authority and scheming. They came to the meeting of doom, carrying their babies to be slaughtered, without protest and without resistance. Only when facing their graves did they realize what was happening, did they attempt to run. They were shot in the back. Most didn't try to escape; they were numbed and resigned to the massacre, helpless. That day, almost three thousand innocents were murdered by the Germans with the assistance of their brothers, the Ukrainian police.

It made no sense to kill the Ukrainian Christian farmers of my village; they had actually welcomed the Germans. Though there was also no rationale for murdering the Jews and Roma, even though they had not run to Mokrany to welcome the Germans. But how can anyone explain truth and logic to brutes who are driven by their reptilian brains, who consider themselves *Übermenschen* and the rest of the world, especially Jews, to be subhuman, pure vermin?

After murdering the entire population of my village — as if these farmers and peasants were an impediment to German victory — the Germans put the village to the torch. It was completely destroyed, burned to the ground. No building remained standing, including the beautiful church with its cupolas and blue-green roof. Including the house that contained our family prayer book with all its inscriptions of events, like my birth; that was destroyed too, and the exact date of my birth was forgotten.

ADAM, NICOTINE AND PSALMS

When we found Father, he had stopped moving around looking for us and was living in the Nebitch Forest with the Ukrainian Christian survivors of Kortelisy, those who had managed to hide and not be discovered. They had moved into the forest with their cattle and livestock and whatever else they were able to save. After finding our father, we continued to live in the forest, together with the surviving Kortelisy farmers and their livestock, but not for long. After several weeks, the survivors began leaving the forest and returning to their erased village and the surrounding hamlets with whatever possessions they had managed to save. Everyone left except for one Ukrainian Christian couple: Adam and his very tiny wife, who never spoke and whose name I never knew — we will call her Eve. Adam, whose seven children had been killed by the Germans, was afraid to return to his home in Hodyn, where he and his family had lived. It was a *khutor* several kilometres as the crow flies from Kortelisy. Adam decided to continue hiding with us. We were the only ones left in the forest.

I knew Adam because he had been a frequent visitor at the home of my maternal grandparents, as well as from the time when my family had also lived in Hodyn. In Hodyn we had lived in a huge wooden house with a high ceiling and large windows, next to a Roma compound. It was a much nicer and more comfortable house than the one we later had in Kortelisy. The windows alone were the size of walls; the sun practically lived inside the house. We were the only Jewish family in Hodyn. I guess it was even less expensive to live in Hodyn than in Kortelisy. I loved Hodyn, and I especially remember the most delicious sugar cookies that Mother used to bake every Friday while we lived there. I still have the taste in my mouth. At one point, Mother became sick and we left Hodyn and moved to Kortelisy to be closer to her parents and in-laws, who were able to help her and us children. Even in Kortelisy, every Friday, Mother would get out of her sick bed to bake sugar cookies for us.

Adam and I went a long way back. We had even shared a near-death experience one wintry night in my very early childhood. It happened like this: When we lived in Hodyn, I would often stay in Kortelisy with my maternal grandparents for Shabbos. I would get to Kortelisy on Friday afternoon and go to the synagogue on Friday night and Saturday morning. I would also visit my other grandparents and would return to Hodyn on Saturday night. It just happened that Adam would always be at my maternal grandparents on Saturday night and give me a lift home. Or, maybe he was there specifically for the purpose of bringing me home.

On one bright wintry Saturday night, a night with millions of stars and a full moon in the sky, while moving along the frozen lake with horse and sleigh, we broke through the ice and fell into the deep, freezing water. The back of the sleigh, where I was sitting, was almost completely in the water, and I began to feel the ice-cold water at my midriff. The horse was struggling to pull the sleigh and tried to extricate itself and jump over the broken ice to reach solid ground. But all it was able to do was break more ice in front of itself and sink deeper into the water. Of course, the horse could swim, but because of the broken ice and the sleigh, it was getting pulled down into the water along with the passengers.

Adam quickly took off his felt coat, jumped into the ice-cold water, grabbed the neighing, frightened horse by its mane and calmed it down, almost lifting the animal, gently leading it through the broken ice to the shore and the safety of solid ground. I was shivering with cold. Adam was shivering too. But, as soon as he jumped into the sleigh, he quickly tore off my wet clothes and wrapped me in his coat. We galloped to the nearest house on the shore, where we warmed up and received fresh, dry clothing. Adam believed in Jesus as his Saviour, but when I looked at Adam, I believed him to be my saviour — and now, in the forest together after the destruction of Kortelisy, even more than then.

In my childish perception, Adam was a very good-looking and pleasant man. He had a fine and substantial moustache and always had a cigarette in his mouth. Unlike his wife, Adam smiled and talked a lot. Adam was able to speak with his cigarette drooping down from his lower lip, somehow managing to keep it balanced in the air. His smoking habits were legendary. He was totally addicted to nicotine. But while we were in the forest together, he had neither tobacco nor proper paper with which to roll his cigarettes. He would smoke any kind of leaf he could dry and crumble, and use fresh leaves or anything else he could roll as paper to create his ersatz cigarettes. To Adam, smoking was more important than food; it was life itself.

One day, my father noticed Hebrew words on the paper Adam was using to roll a cigarette. "Adam!" my father exclaimed. "What kind of paper are you using to roll your cigarettes? Let me look at it." Father grabbed the cigarette out of Adam's mouth and brought it closer to his eyes. My father's face turned ashen. There was the name of the Lord on the paper, the name that pious Jews do not even pronounce, never mind burn as part of a cigarette. Adam, of course, did not understand my father's reaction. From inside his coat, he pulled out an entire book, which turned out to be a *sider* that included the Psalms of King David. My father was trembling and grabbed the holy book from Adam's hands. Adam became furious, and he and my father almost came to blows, each one pulling the *sider* in his direction. Adam fought back to hold onto his property, which to him was as precious as gold. He did not understand why my father was all excited and ready to fight over a silly book with odd writing.

It was strange to see them angry at each other and fighting. They were friends. They struggled together, walked long distances together in search of food, and most of all, they genuinely liked each other. They had never had any arguments before, except for one minor altercation about my father's boots. Unlike Adam, who wore *postoly*, my father wore knee-high leather boots. Adam thought that the footprints of boots in the ground or snow would be a giveaway, as no one except some surviving Jews and partisans wore boots. There was a danger that German trackers would follow the footsteps and discover us. So it was Adam's suggestion that, for the sake of safety, Father discard the comfortable leather boots and start wearing *postoly* to reduce the possibility of detection. In the end, Father understood the danger in wearing boots and switched to *postoly*.

As each man was struggling to hold onto the *sider*, my father yelled, "Adam, do you know what you are doing?!" "Yes," Adam replied, "I'm trying to smoke a cigarette, and you are bothering me." "Adam!" my father cried out, almost in tears, "You are using the pages of a holy book, *Psaltyr*, to roll your cigarettes. You are committing a great sin." Adam was not impressed. He would have burned his own mother for a cigarette. My father begged and pleaded with Adam to give up the *sider* and even promised to save Adam from the tortures of hell. But for a cigarette, Adam was ready to face anything, even hell.

My father, seeing that under no circumstance would Adam give up the *sider*, suggested a compromise: my father would keep the *sider*, but Adam would continue using its pages to roll his cigarettes. Adam trusted my father, even though the pages of the *sider* were most precious to him. And so it would go throughout the day: Adam would ask my father to deliver the holy book so that he could tear off a piece of one of the pages to roll his ersatz tobacco in. As every page and every word on the page was precious to my father, not unlike one of his children, it was heartbreaking to see my father struggle to decide which part of a page to tear off. This continued until Adam took out of my father's hand the last bit of the last page left of the *sider* and rolled it up and smoked it.

My father wanted to know where Adam got the *sider*, but Adam always refused to tell. Finally, when the last piece of paper had turned to smoke, he told my father that he had found the book on the body of a dead man in the forest, obviously a Jewish murder victim holding on to his *sider*, even after his death.

While we were together in the forest, Adam got mad at me only once, when I was doing a poor imitation of a howling wolf. Well, it wasn't the first or the only time that I had been corrected and verbally assaulted by an adult. It had been common practice in Kortelisy, so why not in the forest? Even at the time, I thought that Adam was right in scolding me. First of all, my imitation of a howling wolf was not very authentic. And secondly, making unnecessary human sounds in the forest was not very safe and could disclose our hiding place to unwelcome and dangerous visitors.

Perhaps Adam had some survival skills that were useful in the forest. Unfortunately, my father did not, even though we had lived next to the forest and used to pick berries and mushrooms in the spring and summer. But we had never lived inside the forest. Adam knew that the first thing we had to do was build a shelter, and for that we needed at least a hatchet. And so we managed to secure a hatchet from a farmer before entering deep in the forest, and we built sturdy shelters, one for Adam and his tiny wife and another for our family of five, which included our grandmother Freyde. We had learned from a local farmer that my grandmother had survived the Ratno liquidation and was living with a Ukrainian family, helping to care for the sick in the village. We reunited with Bobeh Freyde, and she came to live with us in the forest.

Building a shelter was a joint effort and family activity. First we cut half a dozen or so thin and pliable saplings. They were then curved into an arc, with the ends of the saplings firmly stuck in the ground, creating a space big enough to accommodate all of us lying down. Then we covered the structure — first with green ferns, and then, on top of the green ferns, with thick spruce and pine branches, so that neither rain nor snow would penetrate, and so that we would even have some protection from the freezing cold and wind in the winter. The layers of ferns under the spruce branches would also prevent the spruce needles from falling into the shelter when the branches would eventually dry up, and the spruce needles would become part of the roof and thick covering. When we had completed it, the shelter had the shape of a low, elongated igloo. We put straw, grasses and all sorts of weeds, of which there were plenty in the forest, on the ground to separate us from the cold earth. It was pretty comfortable, better than sleeping in the open fields. The only concern my father had was that we had no mezuzah to attach to the entrance. However, he found a solution. He would place the entire *sider* in the doorway; it contained all the prayers, including the one contained inside the mezuzah.

We usually slept in our clothing — no pyjamas. And we did not have much to cover ourselves with, only one thick and terribly coarse homespun covering, a poor imitation of a blanket made of rough rope-like strands of cotton. When it was raining, the part of the blanket that was close to the opening of the shelter and exposed to the cold, wind and freezing rain would turn into a sheath of ice and become hard like tin.

And so, together with Adam and his tiny wife, we settled deep in the forest. Slowly, we adjusted to life there. My brother and I busied ourselves exploring, always finding new and fascinating plants and bugs. My mother, while leaning against a tree, cut her beautiful long blond braids and stuck the hair on a tree branch. Watching the expression on my mother's face as she was cutting her hair, I for some reason did not think it was a good sign and it made me sad.

By Miriam Libicki

Within a few days after building our first shelter, we discovered, much to our surprise and annoyance, that we were not alone. Hundreds of very cute and noisy field mice had made their home inside the roof and covering. We had no choice; we lost our squeamishness and got used to their presence, unhappily resigning ourselves to sharing the space and sometimes even our meagre food when we failed to secure it properly and protect it from those rodents. On one occasion, we found two of them, maybe brother and sister or maybe just playmates, drowned inside our only pot, which contained boiled blueberries at the time. We quickly removed and discarded the two unlucky intruders. But much to our distress, we also had to dispose of the boiled blueberries in the pot for fear that they might no longer be kosher. My father also raised the issue of whether the pot itself was still kosher. Considering that this pot was the only one we had, Father decided that it was. But before we were able to use it again, we replaced the piece of rag that was stuffing the hole in the pot, and we boiled pails and pails of water in it, presumably in accordance with the rules and regulations governing the *kashres* of pots with holes that are stuffed with rags. Much to our delight, thanks to Father's ruling, we were able to continue using the pot.

The little rodents were most noisy and active at night when we tried to sleep and dream of happier days gone by and happier days to come. Sleep allowed us to live in our happy dreams instead of in fear. But the loud squeaking and scrambling kept us awake, which left us irritated and grumpy in the morning. The mice showed a total disregard for our property rights and our need for peace and tranquility. They were nasty and inconsiderate neighbours trying to evict us. There was nothing we could do about it except move and abandon our shelter to them. It was a lost battle. There were only five of us, and there were many of them, in the hundreds. We started making plans to move, uncertain, however, that a new place would not attract the same and other rodents.

One morning Father returned from his overnight search for food with a little kitten sticking its head out from under his coat. As soon as he dropped the kitten to the ground, all hell broke loose. The kitten, though tiny, immediately went to work. It jumped all over the place, and the mice started running, possibly triggered by just the smell and appearance of the kitten. It jumped inside and outside our shelter, on top, in the back and on the sides; and the mice, in their hundreds, squeaked and ran in all directions. To see the incredible sight of the tiny kitten jumping all over the little rodents that were scattering, running for their lives, was sweet revenge for all the sleepless nights we had endured. But that tiny kitten must have been an inexperienced mouser and totally confused by the sheer number of mice. Instead of concentrating on one mouse, as I would have done, it ran in all directions trying to catch all of them at the same time. This agile, carnivorous fury of a mammal failed to catch a single mouse. Still, the mice never returned.

The kitten stayed with us for a long time, protecting us from the nasty little rodents. I do not remember ever having to feed the kitten, and it must have eventually learned how to catch mice. That kitten was a true lifesaver. Thanks to its presence, we were able to sleep and dream again at night. Even after the kitten disappeared one day, the mice never returned. When the kitten didn't show up that day, we searched for it but could not find it. Poor kitten. I hope it did not end up as a meal for some hungry wolf or fox and that it left us only because of the poor, inhumane accommodations and was able to find its way back home.

BEAUTIFUL PANTS AND THE SCOURGE OF LICE

One day, I found a pair of nice pants that had been left by their previous owner on a tree branch. I tried them on and I found them to be very comfortable, though a bit oversized. Nevertheless, the pants were a godsend, considering that they were much superior to my old torn shorts, which now left parts of my body exposed. Unfortunately, this was not a lucky find. I should have stuck with my old shorts because within days of putting on those pants, I developed a terrible rash around my entire groin region and my inner thighs. We suspected that the pants were infected and the cause of my misfortune. I developed a strange skin condition, which my mother immediately diagnosed as *krets*, which was prevalent at the time in the region, affecting mainly the area between the fingers. Whatever it was, it was disgusting, repugnant, unpleasant, itchy and painful. I lived in misery and discomfort for about three to four months, until it eventually healed completely on its own, without any treatment or medical assistance; it just disappeared. I was forced to discard those beautiful pants. Lucky for me I was able to find my old shorts, still hanging on the branch where I had left them. Obviously, nobody else wanted them, and I continued to wear them, my *tukhes*, my *derrière*, literally exposed.

As my rash began to heal, the entire area was covered with crusty scabs and lesions. To add to my misery, lice would crawl into the crevices around the scabs. I would use tiny wooden splinters, the size of toothpicks, to remove at least some of my tormentors who were embedded in the scabs and crust. Yes, we developed lice. We had no changes of clothing. It was getting cold, and we couldn't wash ourselves or our torn clothing very well. The small, pale creatures, with one black spot for a tail, would multiply in the hundreds, even after we did our best to delouse, shaking them off and washing ourselves and our clothing as best we could.

I remember how as soon as we put on our freshly washed clothing, the lice would come out of nowhere within minutes. We developed a real hatred for those annoying creatures; they drove us to a state of insanity, day and night. We were always being bitten and were in constant pain as a result of their bites. I sought vengeance. One night when we were sitting around the fire, I put my hand inside my shirt, which was torn into ribbons, and managed to scoop out a good handful of those nasty creatures. I proceeded to throw them into the fire and listen with glee as they crackled and popped, each one exploding separately, like little firecrackers. I know it may have been a cruel and unusual punishment, but they richly deserved every bit of it. And I do not have any remorse. The lice persisted in staying attached to us even after we left the forest.

Although the lice stayed with us for a long time, we had the good fortune to experience fleas on only one occasion, not in the forest. Fleas apparently don't like the forest; they prefer warm homes. It was night and we somehow ended up in a war zone. There was shooting from all directions. We could see the explosions from a distance and could hear the sound of rifles, machine guns, cannons and artillery. Bullets were flying from all sides. As we ran in a huddle, a kind farmer opened his door and invited us into his house. We were offered some food and, as was the custom of farmers, we all went to bed early, practically at the entrance to the house, ignoring the war outside. We brought our own lice, but as soon as we lay down, we were attacked, not by machine guns, but by fleas. It was as bad as bedbugs but much worse than lice. Fire-coloured fleas bite without mercy and without rest. They are voracious eaters. They tear your flesh like tiny crocodiles and leave marks on your body that can take months to heal. And they don't run — they jump and are not easy to catch. They cause irritation all over your entire body and play with your psyche as they jump on their long hind legs all over you.

It was so bad that, notwithstanding the war outside, the flying bullets and explosions practically at the threshold of the house, I left the relative safety of the indoors and stood outside, looking at the fiery sky and listening to the explosions, pretending to be watching fireworks. I was still afraid of death and dying. But, I decided, if I am to die, I would prefer to be shot rather than torn and eaten alive by the horrible wingless parasites that can jump and leap through the air like circus performers, eating your flesh and sucking your blood. I stood there throughout the night, watching the fury of the battle that lit up the sky like thunder and lightning. Early in the morning, the fighting subsided and I was reunited with my brother and parents, and we continued on our way, back to our shelter in the forest. We never found out who was fighting that time.

My brother and I lived through the most horrific fear during the spring and summer storms. The thunder and lightning that punctuated these storms were nothing but God doing his nasty work to frighten little children so that they would believe in Him. When lightning would appear across the sky, the whole forest would be illuminated. I would shake and shiver, and in a trembling voice, I would recite the blessing over lightning: "Borukh ato adoynoy eloheynu melekh haoylem, oyse maase breyshis"—*Blessed are You, Lord our God, King of the Universe, Author of Creation....* But I never finished the entire blessing. Before I could complete it, thunder would follow, and I would start reciting the blessing on hearing thunder: "Borukh ato adoynoy eloyheynu melekh haoylem, shekoykhoy ugvurosoy moley oylem"—*Blessed are You, Lord our God, King of the Universe, whose power and might fill the world.* The thunder and lightning would continue for hours, without pause, throughout the spring and summer. I would continue to mumble both blessings, mixing them up and never finishing one before starting the other. During this process, I would tremble, even crying and screaming in fear, especially when lightning would strike in the vicinity. Often the lightning would even start a forest fire.

These thunder and lightning storms were also a time when I would question God's wisdom. I understood that we needed rain, even if it got us wet and we might freeze, because rain would make food, like potatoes and radishes, grow. Also, God's rain made the grass grow, and trees — especially wonderful fruit trees, like in the orchard of the Boyko family. But why create the useless thunder and lightning which did nothing but frighten people, particularly children, and even cause fires? It served no purpose that I could see. Neither did vicious bugs. Except to torture people and animals. I was ready to tolerate biting honeybees for obvious reasons, even though I had been bitten by them numerous times. But lice and those vile jumping fleas with their huge hind legs? And, worse than that, why did God create Germans and Ukrainian police, who kill other people — Jews and Roma and even good, decent Ukrainian Christians?

I knew that there was a blessing for everything: on seeing the rainbow, at the sight of the sea, on hearing of evil things or good things, or seeing a Torah scholar or even an exceptional secular scholar. But it was adding insult to injury to force me to say a blessing on thunder and lightning. Surprisingly, there was no blessing, at least that I knew of, on the infestation of lice and fleas, or even mice, which to my mind were equally useless creations. I couldn't understand why God, in His wisdom, created such useless and horrible creatures.

WE ALWAYS CELEBRATED THE SABBATH AND HOLY DAYS

Mother, even without the benefit of a calendar, knew the exact day of the week: when it was Shabbos, Passover, Rosh Hashanah, Yom Kippur, Chanukah and all the other major and minor Jewish holidays. She even knew when it was *rosh khoydesh*, the beginning of the month on the Hebrew calendar, when special prayers are recited.

We continued observing Shabbos, saying the weekday prayers and the holiday prayers, and fasting on Yom Kippur. Fasting was nothing new for our parents; it was a daily practice for all of us. On Chanukah we lit candles made out of the sap of a pine tree, using a wick made from a bunch of threads pulled from our clothing. We said the prayers and sang the appropriate Chanukah songs in Hebrew and Yiddish. The candles were not the best and did not burn properly, but they cheered us up and provided some temporary comfort and hope. Even though we had potatoes, we were unable to make potato latkes, the traditional Chanukah food, because we had neither oil nor a frying pan. Nor did we have a grater or grinder. But we mashed and ate boiled potatoes in the shape of latkes.

As for Passover, when it arrived we had no problem with *khometz*. We had no bread and we had no matzo. All we had to do was *kasher* our single pot, making it kosher for Passover, and replace the piece of rag that plugged the hole. On the eve of Passover, even though we had no leavened foods, Father would go through all the motions of *b'dikas khometz*, the search for leaven, as is the custom. With a large feather in one hand and a container consisting of a large wood chip or slice of a tree bark in his other hand, he pushed the invisible and non-existent leaven into the container with the feather. He would first recite the blessing before the search: "Blessed are You, Lord our God, King of the Universe, who has made us holy through His commandments, and has commanded us about the removal of leaven."

After the search, he would put the feather and the container together and recite, in Aramaic, in a very official almost legalistic fashion, the formula for burning the *khometz*:

> *May all* khometz *or leaven that is in my possession which I have not seen or removed be annulled and deemed like the dust of the earth.*

This would be followed by a repetition of the same mantra with some additional words after burning the *khometz*:

> Kol khamiro vakhamiyo, d'iko birshusi, dakhamitey udlo khamitey, d'viyartey udlo viyartey, livtyl v'lehevey hefker k'afro d'aro.
>
> *May all* khometz *or leaven that is in my possession, whether I have seen it or not, whether I have removed it or not, be annulled and deemed like the dust of the earth.*

Nothing fazed my father. He was not going to stop doing what he had seen his father and grandfathers do and what he had been doing on Passover in his own house since his marriage. One has to serve the Almighty wherever one may be, even in the forest. The Almighty can see and hear even those who are in the forest in distress.

Having burned the make-believe *khometz* and recited the blessings, and after Mother lit the homemade candles made of pine sap, we were ready for Passover and a whole week of rather pitiful celebration under most miserable circumstances.

LOST ON THE WAY TO SAMARY

We never had sufficient food to eat and most of the time we were pretty hungry. But neither were we on a starvation diet. Even though we were skin and bones, our bellies were never swollen. Mother would look at our emaciated faces and cry uncontrollably. I could see the pain in her face. She would argue with Father, the eternal optimist, who was determined to survive and always dealt bravely with every challenge. One of his favourite expressions was "Mir veln tantsn oyf zayn keyver, yimakh shmoy"—*We will dance on his grave, may his name be erased* — meaning, of course, Hitler. Never discouraged or sad, Father always tried to cheer us up with a story or a song, or by surprising us with something special to eat. My father even promised that after the war — as if there were no doubt of our survival — he would bring us all to *Amerike*, to which he felt he had a certain claim because of his father's sojourn there for many years. To me, he promised a special treat when we got to *Amerike*: I could have as much sweet, cold tea as I wanted. As a child, cold, sweet tea was my favourite refreshment, and I have not lost the taste for it. I called it *teyele*, the diminutive for tea in Yiddish, as did everyone else when talking to me about tea. The promise of this tea was reason enough to survive the war and go to *Amerike*.

Mother, on the other hand, was completely distraught. She had lost her will to live and spoke with envy of the dead. She had become a different person from when she had to cope with her survival and the survival of her children alone. After the massacre in Ratno, when we left the farm without Father, Mother was brave, took risks, never failed to protect her children and, in her own way, spoke words of encouragement and hope. At that time, she never thought of dying. Now, she gave up on herself and her family. She wanted all of this to come to a deadly end. No more fear, no more hunger, no more pain — eternal peace and tranquility.

Now her mantra became, "Take us to the Germans and let's bring it to an end." When I would hear this talk of going to the Germans, I would get hysterical, thinking that Father might listen to Mother and go to the Germans. Notwithstanding Mother's comforting words of being reunited with our murdered relatives in heaven, I was against dying and against going to the Germans just to be with Bobeh and Zeyde and my uncles in heaven. But Mother would persist. With tears in her eyes, she would beg Father, "Take us to the Germans. You think you are so smart. You think you will survive the war. You think you are smarter than everybody else. You are having a bad dream. We won't survive. At least our neighbours, friends and relatives were taken out from the comfort of their homes; they were warm and sated and did not suffer, and they died bravely, without going through all this misery, torture, hunger and fear. We, on the other hand, after living like animals, totally dehumanized, are going to die after suffering all the hunger, cold, misery and fear." Then she always ended by assuring us that it is not so bad to die, and with the promise that we would be together in heaven, with all of our murdered relatives, neighbours and friends and the rest of Kortelisy. As for me, in case Father listened to Mother and decided to go to the Germans to be shot, I was making my own plans to run away.

Father must have understood, respected and loved Mother very much to have the patience to listen to her talk like that and not scream at her or even raise his voice, argue. Instead he patiently pleaded with her to give up the idea of going to the Germans. He felt her pain and he tried to comfort her, but no words would console her or calm her down. She would just get more hysterical. Then, as an alternative to going to the Germans, Mother suggested we leave the forest and go back to Samary, which was still untouched and where there were still a few Jews left. She even threatened that if Father did not agree she would take the children and go there without him. For Father, going to Samary was apparently a better choice than going directly to the Germans to be shot. As Father had told Mother on many occasions, he would not even know where to find the Germans; they would have to come looking for him. In fact, Father fought hard to ensure that the Germans didn't find him. But he knew how to find Samary and, of course, it was the better choice.

After weeks of tears and pleading, Father agreed to go to Samary. So, at sunset one day, we started walking. But somehow, even though Father knew the way to Samary like the palm of his own hand, we got lost. We wandered through the forest throughout the night, and we never reached Samary. I think about the way Father later talked about that trip to Samary, and I think it was not by accident that by early morning we ended up back at our shelter, where Adam and his wife were waiting, happy to see us. We were most likely, under Father's careful guidance, walking in circles the whole night.

But later, in conversations with Mother, she ascribed our getting lost to providence. The day after we got lost on the way to Samary, the Germans, as if they had just discovered the village and found the extra time, came to Samary and murdered all the Jews, including the convert and his two beautiful daughters. The Germans could not, however, kill us because we never got back to Samary. And they could not kill Hershl's widow and her triplets. They were already dead and were spared being butchered by the Germans as a part of the "final solution."

DEEP IN THE FOREST

We continued to live in the huge forest with Adam and his spouse as our close friends and neighbours. The forest became our home, our friend and protector. During our stay there, to avoid being detected, we must have changed our location and built new shelters at least four or five times. Every time we moved, we managed to improve on the structure of our shelter. Building it together reminded me of the time we used to spend as a family building a *sukeh* for the holiday of Sukkos.

One time, right after we had settled in a new location, a farmer who was roaming through the forest innocently stumbled on our camp. He ran away in fear and so did we. We moved to another place, even deeper into the forest. My brother and I explored this part of the forest, full of lush green vegetation and different trees, birds, ants and huge anthills, spiders, chipmunks, squirrels, rabbits, snakes, foxes, wolves, mice and fireflies at night. Besides the fireflies, we discovered the most amazing phenomenon: the glittering of fallen petrified trees. They only glittered and shone like gold from a distance because once you came close to the petrified wood and touched it, it became like any other piece of dead wood — dry and drab. We observed different kinds of birds' nests and even once stumbled on a family of vicious wild boars, ready to attack. Lucky for us, our father was nearby and heard our screams. He came running and rescued us by somehow persuading the wild boars to run away from us in the opposite direction.

I once faced a grey wolf on my own. I threw the hatchet I had in my hand in its direction but missed it, and it fled. The sole wolf was not as terrifying as the ones Bobeh Frumeh had described, which were capable of swallowing little children. I guess it must have been a very sated wolf or too proud to deal with a tidbit, a tiny morsel like me. Be that as it may, I lost my deep-seated fear of wolves in that moment. Maybe because now there were other things to fear.

Our diet was always the same. When spring came, we lived off the land by picking mushrooms and berries that grew wild in the forest and which we had picked even before the forest became our home. We traded and bartered with the German soldiers through the local farmers we could trust. We supplied them with dried mushrooms and blueberries, and in return, the farmers would get precious salt from the Germans. The Germans were not aware that the salt was intended for a Jewish family hiding in the forest. We had plenty of water for cooking if we simply dug a couple of feet into the ground.

We also discovered, in the early spring, a small, green, three-leafed clover, which we would boil in water with some salt. It tasted like any other borscht or *schav,* a typical soup made of green leaves that grow wild in the fields. It had a tart taste and would fill up our bellies. It must have been a healthy and nutritious dish, at least for a while. Unfortunately, in the late summer, we realized that eating it could be quite painful, perhaps even fatal. We ate the plant when it was no longer in bloom, and we all became sick with terrible stomach aches. We quickly learned to stay away from that plant after it had lost its bloom.

Besides blueberries, mushrooms and the three-leafed clover in the spring and summer, we ate mainly potatoes. The farmers would bury their potatoes in the surrounding sand dunes for the winter to protect them from freezing in cold weather. My father and Adam, or sometimes my father alone — as our family's needs were greater — would go out at night and dig up the potatoes that had been buried in the sand dunes. It was a long walk to the sand dunes, and it took the whole night to get there and return.

Father would leave at sunset. Before leaving, he always recited the Tefilas Haderech, the prayer for the road:

> *May it be Your will, Lord our God and God of our fathers, to lead us to peace, direct our steps to peace, guide us to peace, and bring us to our desired destination in life, joy and peace.... Rescue us from any enemy or ambush on the way, and from all afflictions that trouble the world. Send blessing to the work of our hands, and let us find grace, kindness and compassion from You and from all who see us. Hear our pleas, for You are a God who hears prayer and pleas.*

It may have been an appropriate prayer to recite under the circumstances. Father asked for the right things; there were ambushes, many enemies and great danger on the road. In view of some of the treatment we had received, I doubted that God was actually listening and helped out. I thought that Father was on his own — only Father. But he didn't think so. Father thought that the Almighty and His angels were always there to protect him. Upon his return, he would immediately recite that special *goymel* blessing, which is recited upon deliverance from peril: "Blessed are You, Lord our God, King of the Universe, who bestows good on the unworthy, who has bestowed on me much good." If there was a God watching Father and considering his safe return, He well deserved this prayer and praise.

Usually, Father would return the following day, at sunrise, carrying a huge sack of potatoes greater than his own weight on his back. It was a life-threatening exercise, but it was the only way. It was our only food at times, and I developed a great deal of respect for the humble potato.

Father suffered from serious asthma and, of course, he no longer had a supply of the special tobacco that he was supposed to smoke to provide him some relief. It happened quite often that his getting sick would coincide with us running out of potatoes. Despite his sickness, he would leave the forest and come back with the usual huge sack of potatoes on his back.

I stumbled on a great idea to create an emergency supply of potatoes that we could use in the event that Father got sick. When Father would return with his heavy sack and nobody was looking, I would take a whole bunch of potatoes — four or five pots worth — and hide them at the back of our shelter, covering them well to protect them from frost in the winter. Whenever we would finish our supply of potatoes and Father was sick but still ready to go looking for more, I would come out with the treasure trove: enough potatoes for another three or four days, giving Father time to recover from his sickness. Eventually, my ruse was discovered, and sometimes I would be forced to deliver the emergency supply even when Father was not sick but just not in the mood to go. Still, my strategic plan was not disrupted. Even when I had to deliver up my hidden supply, I always kept some potatoes in reserve. By some miracle, or most likely thanks to the fresh forest air, my father eventually lost his asthma. It was simply gone.

Father was brave and strong. He never complained and always had a smile and song, in Yiddish, Russian or Ukrainian. For him, life was worth fighting for and he never felt discouraged from doing so. The greater the challenge and threat, the greater became his will and effort to survive. The closer we were to death, the stronger became his will to live. But our fear of Father being caught and killed was real and always on our minds whenever he took off in search of food. Each time our father left the shelter and disappeared into the forest, we would stay up through the night and wait and pray for his safe return in the early morning. Sometimes he would be late, and we would think the worst. We would become anxious and start walking in the direction from which we expected him to return, looking for him, until we saw him through the trees and brush, all bent over, carrying the load of potatoes on his back. Those were moments of great joy and jubilation, and the sight of Father would make us momentarily forget the cold of winter, our fear and hunger. We would express our joy by jumping around our father and holding onto him, eventually pulling him and his heavy load to the ground. Father would hug us back and always had a good word and a story to tell. Sometimes it would be a happy story, but mostly the stories were sad. But he would always cheer us up with a song.

Thinking about it now, many years later, I can recall the sad expression on Adam's face when he saw us children hugging and dancing around our father. Adam's children were not there to greet him and celebrate his return. There was only his wife. And in the morning she was usually inside their shelter, asleep.

Occasionally, Father had a delicious surprise for us. Not halvah, but once he brought some bread. This was a special treat. I had not tasted bread in over a year, and as I took a morsel and brought it to my mouth, I fainted before I could bite into it. On another occasion, the happy mood around Father's return turned bitter when he told us about a bottle of milk a farmer had given him. Even though he had handled the bottle of milk very carefully, like a baby, he had slipped on some ice and broken the bottle, spilling the milk all over the ground. The loss of the milk was painful and sad, but nothing could truly diminish the joy of Father's return from his overnight trips in search of food.

One thing I distinctly remember is that upon Father's return, right after unloading the sack of potatoes, he would crawl into the shelter, where Bobeh Freyde was always resting. Maybe it was just to tell her that he was back. But I always thought that Father had something special to give her. Always thinking about food, I imagined that Father had reserved for her a special treat, maybe halvah.

A year after her husband's death in Ratno, almost to the day, on Tuesday, September 14, 1943, my grandmother Freyde died of typhoid fever. She had stayed with us in the forest from the very beginning but at one point decided to leave us and the forest. She stayed with various friendly Christian families while helping the sick who had been plagued with typhoid fever, which she eventually contracted.

One day, my parents decided to go find her and bring her back to live with us in the forest. On the way, we encountered a farmer, who told us about her death. She had been taken outside, placed leaning against the stable walls, to die a horrible death, all alone, without food or water. The thought of this always brings tears to my eyes because she had always been there to help others, even strangers, Jew or gentile. It is hard to imagine how much she suffered, all alone, before relief came with her death. When Father heard the sad news about his mother's death, in clear defiance of the rule that Kaddish is to be said with a minyan of ten men, he walked over to a tree, pressed his forehead hard against the trunk and tearfully, in a loud voice, recited the Kaddish, screaming in pain, knowing well that there would never be a minyan of Kortelisy Jews to participate and provide a congregational "Amen" to the prayers.

FATHER'S ENCOUNTER WITH WOLVES OF EVERY KIND

Early one morning, Father was returning home through the forest, carrying a load of potatoes on his back, and in the middle of the path cut deep into the snow there was a lone grey wolf sitting on his haunches. The wolf stared at Father and would not budge from the path. Father rightly chose to avoid the wolf by going off the path and walking waist deep into the snow around the wolf. The heavy potatoes he was carrying weighed him down even further into the soft snow. The wolf did not budge; he just sat there, turning his head, watching Father walking around him, deep in snow.

Lucky for us and for Father, the wolf was probably not very hungry or maybe it was just too lazy to go after my father in the deep snow. Or maybe, with the huge sack of potatoes, Father appeared to be too big a target for the wolf to tackle. Anyway, at that time, a wolf could find food without hunting and without a struggle. After all, there were plenty of human carcasses for wolves, foxes and other carnivorous animals to eat without having to attack a massive, moving object.

My father was never afraid. In the forest, he would start up with snakes and kill them by hitting them over the head with a heavy stick while they got ready to attack, rising up on their tails. Fighting snakes, Father probably thought he was performing a mitzvah, remembering the curse God gave to the original snake: "On your belly shall you crawl and dirt shall you eat all the days of your life. I will put enmity between you and the woman, and between your offspring and hers; they shall strike at your head, and you shall strike at their heel." Father, in accordance with the biblical commandment, bruised the snake's head before the snake bruised his heel.

Father's second dangerous encounter involved wolves of the human variety. In search of food in one of the nearby hamlets one evening, Father encountered a couple of young men who were looking for some fun. They grabbed my father and dragged him to the *starosta*'s house. It was late and the community elder was already asleep. The young men shoved my father in front of the sleeping man and, with great pride, announced, "We brought you the Jew — Leiba. You take him to the Germans as your duty demands. If there is a reward, you will share it with us."

My father fell on top of the sleeping man, begging him to spare his life. The *starosta*, now half-awake, quickly found his composure. He pushed my father aside, turned to the two young men and said in Ukrainian: "Ya ne lyuds'kyi rizun"—*I am not a killer*, or literally, *I am not a slitter of throats*. "You take Leiba back to where you found him." He took a further risk by sending them away with a tongue-lashing.

Lucky for the *starosta*, the young men did not report him to the Germans. Had they done so, he and his family would have ended up before a firing squad. But, somehow, the entire hamlet heard about the incident and decided to play a nasty game with the brave and humane *starosta*. A rumour spread among the farmers in the area that *Leiba dorohey*, Leiba is expensive. Apparently, some farmers took advantage of the situation and made the *starosta* pay for their silence. In exchange for a promise not to report him for failing to do his duty, the farmers demanded vodka. Paying off the farmers with pails of samogon was a minor inconvenience compared to the trouble he could have gotten himself into for releasing Father.

AWAKENED FROM DEATH

Early one cold morning, I got up before my parents and little brother and left the shelter in search of some dry wood to start a fire. It was around the middle of April, just before Passover. Spring was in the air, but it was still cold. In some areas of the forest, where the sun did not penetrate because of the thick tree branches, there were still some sheaths of ice and mounds of snow on the ground. Barefoot, jumping over patches of ice and snow, I searched for firewood.

Suddenly, I heard sounds and loud conversations, people yelling, calling to each other in what I thought sounded like German. I panicked. My reaction was swift and instinctive: I began to run away from the source of the noise like I was being chased. After a while, no longer hearing the voices, I calmed down and stopped running. But by then, I didn't know how far I had run from our shelter, and I could not find my way back to it. I started running in circles, trying to find my way, but nothing was familiar to me. I continued running and extending the circles wider and wider, hoping that in this way I would find the shelter, but it was not happening.

I was lost. I panicked again and began screaming and calling out, even though it was dangerous, hoping that my parents would hear my screams. There was no answer. Nobody heard me. I began to realize that it was too risky for me to continue screaming. Someone other than my parents might answer my calls for help. So I stopped. But

I continued walking and running through different sections of the forest that were totally unfamiliar to me. At one point, I reached a hilly area where there were only massive oak trees. The ground was covered with large oak leaves and I found it quite pleasant and comforting. I sat down and decided to just sit there and relax for a while and enjoy the tranquility of the surroundings. But I could not sit still for too long, even though the place was comfortable. Anxiety took over and I began to think that I would never see my parents again, that I would die in the forest from starvation or cold, or that I would be killed and eaten by the wolves or foxes or maybe even vicious wild boars. I jumped up and began to run in circles again, from time to time taking the risk to call out for my parents.

I ran through another area of the forest, where saplings were growing in deep swampy water up to my knees. I managed to extricate myself from the swampy water and reached a dry hilly area filled with pine trees. I rested there for a while and then continued in a straight line and stumbled into a swampy area filled with thin birch trees. Each area of the forest gave me a different feeling — sometimes fear and sometimes safety and even comfort. There were still some patches of ice between the birch trees and the water was very cold. I managed to fall several times, tripping over dead saplings concealed beneath the water. My shorts and shirt were now drenched in cold water. I shivered and trembled because of the cold and because I was afraid of losing my life in the wilderness.

The day had turned to late afternoon and I was getting tired and hungry. I was weak, but I persisted in my search for the shelter and my parents, trying hard to be courageous and not to give up — one more call for my parents and then another, until I finally gave up all hope of finding my way back to the shelter.

Night set in. With the sun down, soaked in icy water, I was shivering even more than before and my teeth were chattering from the cold. I was wet, hungry, exhausted and losing all hope of survival. I began to accept my fate. Realizing that I would never survive the night in my wet and torn clothing without shelter, I stopped calling and began looking for a place where I could keep warm and hide from the wild animals.

Stories of being lost in the forest, told by farmers, came to my mind — people who had died overnight in the forest from the cold. I also remembered the story about a woman who had frozen to death in the winter while inside her horse-drawn sleigh. The woman was dead inside the sleigh when the horse pulled up to her house. Rumours circulated that the woman had been drunk and froze to death. But the brave horse stayed sober and moved in the right direction, delivering his unfortunate dead mistress home. I thought I had at least one thing in my favour: I was sober. The worst thing one could do was get lost in the forest while drunk, especially in the wintertime.

Finally, I found a spot inside a thicket of intertwined shrubs; I would be well concealed and have a fortress against the wild animals. I covered myself with leaves and ferns to protect myself from the cold and hide from the wolves, knowing that if I didn't keep warm I would freeze to death before the wolves could eat me. Still, I resigned myself to not surviving the night, to freezing to death and eventually being eaten by the wolves. I tried to stay awake, thinking that my chances of survival would be much better if I stayed awake. And I held onto a big stick that I had picked up.

It is difficult to say which action or inaction saved me. I was trying desperately not to fall asleep because I knew that falling asleep would be a death sentence. I struggled to stay awake, as I often had at the seder while waiting for Elijah the Prophet. It was hopeless. I fell asleep immediately, in my wet clothes, within seconds of resting my head on the ground. But falling asleep turned out to be a blessing and a lifesaver. In my sleep, I dreamed of my murdered grandmother, Frumeh, who would sometimes visit me in my dreams in the shelter, covering me when I was cold. Although it was only a dream, I would actually feel warm after having been covered by her. This time, instead of covering and comforting me, keeping me warm, she gave me a tongue-lashing and scolded me. I clearly heard her voice: "Wake up you silly, lazy boy. Don't sleep. Wake up. Your parents are looking for you. Wake up." I felt my Bobeh Frumeh's hand on my shoulder, shaking me.

I woke up and I mustered all my strength to call out into the darkness. The answer to my shouts was immediate. It came from my father: "Vu bistu, Pineleh, vu bistu?!"—*Where are you, Pineleh*?! I don't know what happened afterwards and I don't know how my father managed to find me in the dark, hidden in the thick shrubs, all covered in leaves and ferns, because after I heard my father's voice, I did not reply. I must have lost consciousness. When I finally woke up, I was next to the shelter in front of a fire.

My parents pronounced my rescue to be a miracle. I was convinced that my grandmother Frumeh was still protecting me and would always be there with me whenever I was in need. I was saved because she had come to me in a dream and woken me up from certain death.

BECAUSE OF *SHATNEZ*

Sometime after this incident, Adam and his wife decided that it was now safe for them to leave the forest and return home to Hodyn. There were no more Germans in sight in our area and Adam thought the danger of his being targeted had subsided. And so, we were left alone. Actually, I never understood why Adam, who was not Jewish, had not returned to his hamlet after the killings and loss of his children but had, instead, decided to stay in the forest. All the other Ukrainian Christians who had also lost relatives at the hands of the Germans had taken the risk and returned to the village to try to rebuild their lives and homes. We Jews had no such choice. Even though by this time Germans were sparse in our area, there were people about who were ready to kill us or deliver us to the Germans.

Maybe Adam stayed with us in the forest because he liked my father and wanted to help. He certainly did not stay in the forest for my brother and me. We were pesky kids and behaved like kids even during those bad and abnormal days. And sometimes we would behave in a way that Adam disapproved of. Quite often he would look at us and cry. At the time, I did not understand why we made Adam cry. Maybe, looking at me, he was reminded of the time when we had almost drowned in freezing water. Or maybe, looking at us, he cried because he had lost all his own children.

We were not really aware what was happening on the front, who was winning and who was losing. We knew that the war was still going on and that some Germans were still around, especially those moving on the highway, in both directions, getting harassed by the Soviet partisans. Our thinking was that should liberation come, it would come in the distant future, if at all. But sometime in the late spring or early summer of 1943, something new was happening in the evening sky. Planes began to fly in a westerly direction over the forest where we lived. On their flight westward, the planes seemed to be carrying heavy loads and were moving slowly. But on their return east, presumably after completing their bombing mission, the sound of the planes was different; they were light and moved swiftly, each plane zooming by with a single, mighty roar, one after the other in quick succession. We could count the number of planes returning by the sound of each plane as it zoomed by, as if it were escaping. We assumed that these were Soviet planes, flying out in the evening on bombing missions and returning east later the same evening after dropping their bombs. The sound of the planes was encouraging and gave us hope to continue with our struggle to survive. As the planes flew overhead, we would stand up, waving our hands at the sky and cheering; even Mother participated. She began to show some signs of a will to live. We felt like somebody was taking care of us, like we were not abandoned.

But on one occasion, we ended up being the victims of an errant bombing mission that nearly made us fatalities of the Soviet war effort. We later speculated that one of the Soviet planes had been hit by German artillery before the pilot had a chance to drop his bombs and hit his targets. He was forced to return immediately or risk being blown up before disposing of all of his bombs. Fearing a crash landing in enemy territory with all the bombs on board and dying in the process, the pilot probably decided to dispose of his payload in a "safe" place. This place was the middle of the forest where we had the misfortune to reside. Whatever the reasons, we ended up being a target.

It was late at night, and we were sleeping in our shelter when we heard a single plane flying east, but not in the usual sequence of many planes returning east after their mission. This single plane sounded fully loaded; it was moving slowly and made a different kind of sound than the usual sound of the returning planes. Suddenly, all hell broke loose. The ground began to shake and fires appeared all over the place, ignited by lit objects that flew in all directions from the point of the initial explosion. We were afraid to move, even though our first reaction was to run. But we would have been running into fire, which was all around us. We just lay on the ground inside the shelter, paralyzed, while numerous bombs exploded all around us. We didn't know if the bombs were flying from the sky or the ground. But after the explosions subsided, still surrounded by flames, Father thought that maybe what was going on was a German *oblave*, a raid against partisans. We thought we had better run before the German soldiers arrived. We got up and started running through the burning shrubs, grasses and trees, covering our faces, trying to escape.

We managed to escape the area that was on fire and stayed away from the inferno overnight, worrying about pursuing Germans the whole time. At sunrise, we returned to our shelter and looked around. There was destruction all around us. All the trees had their tops chopped off, and in the vicinity of our shelter there were numerous deep pits emitting an awful stench. We had built our shelter up against two different kinds of trees that were fused together, branches and foliage embracing each other. The tops of these trees were lying dead nearby, but somehow their branches still embraced, like warriors that had fallen together. My father stood with folded arms, looking at the destruction, at our burnt shelter, and wondered what had happened. Why were the tops of those two trees against which we had built our shelter cut off? And why were we bombed for no good reason in the middle of the forest, nearly getting killed and having our sleep and rest disturbed? Why was our shelter a target?

Father came up with an answer, one word that he slowly intoned:

shatnez. He pronounced it like it was a chant. The rules of *shatnez* and *klayim*, which prohibit mixing wool and linen, and all kinds of species (including different types of trees) is a biblical prohibition, meaning that this was not an accident. It was God's will. The fusion of two different types of trees, the trees against which we had built our shelter, had offended the Almighty. The Almighty had demonstrated His anger, as He was in the habit of doing whenever He was offended. He sent the Soviet air force to destroy this evil abomination and remind my father of his transgression, almost killing us in the process. It seems that the Almighty was still keeping an eye on my father and insisting that Father, even while hiding in the forest, should obey and observe all the commandments, including the biblical prohibition of *shatnez.* Maybe He was just testing Father, as was His custom and habit going all the way back to biblical days, as He had tested Abraham with His order to sacrifice his only son, Isaac.

After listening to my father's explanation, I wondered whether the bombing would have happened had Adam and his wife, who were not Jewish and not obliged to observe the *shatnez* commandment, still been with us. Unfortunately, we never saw Adam and his wife again. But to this day, I can remember his tears whenever he looked at us, even when scolding us. I think often about Adam and his tiny wife, whose name I never knew.

IN THE FOREST RANGER'S HOME

It must have been the middle of 1943, during the months of May or June when, although we were unaware of what was going on with respect to the war, we started to have the feeling, based on rumours and the constant overhead flights of Soviet planes, that the war was almost over. There were hardly any Germans outside their headquarters in Mokrany, and the survivors of the Ukrainian Christian population in the area were more relaxed and began rebuilding their villages and hamlets and their destroyed lives. We were infected by this spirit of relaxation and decided to move out of the safety of the deep forest south of the highway to the northern part of the forest. This new location put us closer to the sand dunes where the potatoes were buried, as well as to the villages and hamlets, where food was more accessible. It was a risky move, but it made life much easier, especially for Father, who didn't have to walk the long distance in search for food. At times we even stayed overnight in the comfort of some farmers' homes, instead of in the forest.

We developed a particularly close friendship with the local forest ranger, who was married to one of the daughters of the Boyko family, close friends of my parents. We would stay with the forest ranger quite often, even during the day, and spent some nights inside their home. They had three children: the eldest was a boy of about fifteen, and there were two pretty little girls, about eight and nine. There was no school for any of us. The boy would do some chores around the house and take care of things in the huge yard, with my help whenever we were there. The two sweet girls were always cheerful. They wore beautiful peasant dresses with multicoloured ribbons at the bottom and pretty, colourful kerchiefs that tied under their chins. You could see their sparkling blue eyes, mouths and a small part of their faces where they were exposed. In spring and summer, the skin of the exposed part of their faces was tanned, while the part that was usually covered by the kerchief was as white as milk. The little girls never walked; they pranced and moved by making little jumps and hops while singing songs or reciting rhymes. Even while sitting at the table, having breakfast, lunch or supper, they would pass the food by intoning in a singsong, "Here are the cucumbers," or, "Here is the bread. Have some potatoes and tomatoes red," adding another rhyme, "I hope you are well fed."

The home of the ranger was lively whenever we were there: the family told stories and jokes and were always singing. Everyone participated, including my father, who often led the singing. Sometimes he sang solo, particularly the Yiddish songs. One Yiddish song was about a married couple. The husband lives in America and his wife is in the old country, struggling to eke out a living for herself and her children. She feels abandoned and starts the song with these words: "Mayn getrayer man, in d'rerd zolstu mir arayn"—*My dear husband, you should be interred in the ground.* The rest of the song consists of her complaining about her bitter situation, how the children are hungry, and how she even had to pawn his tallis to raise some money to buy food. The song finishes with her getting suspicious that he may have someone else, another woman, in *Amerike*. She declares that if that is so, she has no intention of crying for him. And, if he can't send a letter, then he should just send the divorce papers. This was most likely a song my father had heard from his own mother whose husband had been in America. She had pleaded with him to bring her and the family there. Father also sang a more cheerful song, also in Yiddish, about the *mizinke*, the youngest daughter, who is finally getting married, and how everyone, including the extended family, is happy and excited to celebrate this great event. He also sang some other Yiddish songs like "Itsik hot shoyn khasene gehat" and "Lomir trinken a l'khayim far dem libn khaver Stalin," with the ranger and his family trying to sing along, though they didn't speak a word of Yiddish.

There was also a mischievous Ukrainian song, probably with some sexual connotations, urging a girl to keep on dancing:

> Hyi hrumet hyi hudeh,
> Dryibnyi doschyik hyideh.
> Hulay, hulay dyivchyinonko, ya dodomu zavedeh.
> *There is thunder, There is tumult,*
> *A little light rain drizzles.*
> *Dance, dance, little girl, I will take you home.*

He also sang an old Ukrainian song about a young man meeting a girl in a lush garden:

> Rosprahayte khloptzyi konyi,
> hyi lahayte speechyivat.
> A ya pyidu v'sad zelenyi....
> *Unharness the horses, boys,*
> *and lie down to rest.*
> *And I will go to the green garden....*

There, he meets his young lady while the others are resting. I don't know, the boys may have been Cossacks, including the one who went to the green garden and found love.

My father did not care about the language or contents of a song or whether the ranger and his family wanted him to sing or understood what he was singing. He thought that everyone loved singing in any language, whether it was Yiddish or Ukrainian. Many years after the war, when my father was in his late eighties, I brought him to the veteran's hospital in Montreal. The facility provided entertainment and activities for seniors, and so I left my father there for the afternoon while I went to work. When I returned to pick him up, I saw my dear father on stage, entertaining a mostly French-speaking audience with Russian, Ukrainian, Jewish liturgical and Yiddish secular tunes. I took a seat and enjoyed the concert with the rest of the audience. My father loved to sing. He even sang in his sleep.

One day, when I was in the fields with the forest ranger's son, he did things I found to be strange, even disgusting and repugnant: he defecated and ate his food at the same time. I could not understand how he was able to do it. I had been taught from an early age to strictly separate the acts of eating and pooping. I was also taught to wash my hands before eating and after a bowel movement, even after urinating, and always to say the appropriate blessing after washing my hands, and before and after eating. I learned these blessings by heart even before I knew how to read, even before I knew the *alefbeys*.

On another occasion, I saw the boy, who must have just reached puberty, playing with his penis. I didn't understand what he was doing, even though by then I knew where babies came from; I still did not know the mechanics of baby-making. Through this boy, I learned that not all penises look alike. I did not realize that mine looked different because it was circumcised. I thought I was born that way, even though I had attended many circumcisions and, as a young boy in the village, had the important job of visiting the houses of women who had given birth and were still in bed recovering. We young boys would recite blessings and pray for the health of the newborn and the mother. For this service we would receive candy and cookies. The only other naked boys my age I had seen were Jewish kids in the mikveh or at the lake near Kortelisy. We all looked the same. But this Christian boy's penis had a different shape at the top; it looked to me like the face of a baby carp out of water.

Poor boy. The only sexual pleasure he would ever have was by pleasuring himself. He did not grow old enough to know delightful adolescent puppy love, and he did not live long enough to have a relationship with a woman or know the pleasure of being close to a woman's body or feeling her touch. He was never given the opportunity to experience the agony and ecstasy of being in love or feeling infatuation.

MORE MURDER AND SURVIVAL

Once, after spending a whole day with the forest ranger's family, we were invited by the ranger's wife to stay with them overnight, and we gladly accepted. It was undoubtedly not too safe for Jews to be in the open, but it was so much more pleasant to stay in a warm house rather than in a forest shelter, where we had to sleep on the hard ground. We had a wonderful evening with food, storytelling, *chastushki* (ditties), jokes and, of course, singing. And, as is the habit of farmers, we all went to bed early and got up early.

In the morning, the ranger told us about a horrible dream he had had during the night. He was still frightened by it and was at a loss as to its meaning. He hoped for a positive interpretation. We all listened to his dream respectfully, but we did not make a big deal out of it. The ranger, however, was truly upset by his dream. "Many people have bad dreams," his wife told him. "Just forget about it. Don't let it bother you. You are making a big fuss over nothing." The forest ranger did not appear to be convinced. He was stressed and continued to see doom and gloom.

After a big breakfast, consisting of large quantities of baked potatoes and sour cream, my father and the ranger's brother-in-law, a young man, went outside into the yard to cut some firewood. The rest of us stayed inside the house. They were sawing large logs into firewood on a sawhorse, using a long two-handled saw. My father was facing the dirt road that ran through the forest alongside the ranger's house and yard when he noticed, through the trees, unusual traffic. Wagons were moving in formation along the dirt road. He became suspicious. It looked more like a military convoy than like farmers' wagons. Father told the young man to go back to the house to warn us to leave; he would wait for us at the edge of the forest.

The ranger's house was in the middle of the forest, in the centre of a huge clearing that was in the shape of a perfect square. Immediately after being warned, my mother, my brother and I left the house. As soon as we ran outside, we noticed to our left two men in brown army fatigues, holding guns and walking toward the house. The ranger's big family dog was running at the men, barking and growling, ready to attack. The soldiers approached the dog without fear. The dog continued to bark and growl at them, but now backed up in retreat as the men advanced.

We were close enough to these soldiers to see their faces. In them we saw the end of our lives. But, somehow, we still did not give up hope and surrender. Instinct took over. We turned away from those two Germans and began to run in the opposite direction, toward the forest at the edge of the clearing. As we approached the forest line, however, we saw two other soldiers facing us from inside the forest, lying on the ground with machine guns at the ready. They were dressed in the same brown fatigues as the other soldiers and were camouflaged. As if in a well-rehearsed movement designed to trick them, we pretended not to see the camouflaged soldiers and continued running toward them rather than away, hoping that they would not shoot. When we neared the edge of the clearing, metres away from where the German soldiers lay in wait with their machine guns pointing at us, Mother suddenly stopped and quickly removed the slippers she was wearing to make it easier to run. She grabbed us by our hands and pulled us into the forest to our immediate right. Once we were inside the forest, Mother let us go, and we ran as fast as we could. We continued running, ignoring the soldiers' screams of "Halt!"

We managed to get well into the forest before all hell broke loose and we found ourselves under a hail of gunfire. Bullets started whizzing past us, some of them hitting the birch trees in front of us. The two human beasts were shooting to kill a mother and her two young children. Suddenly, I felt as if a hot compress had hit the bottom part of my left leg. At first I thought that I had touched some poison ivy. But it was not the familiar sensation and burn of poison ivy. As we ran deeper into the forest, the shooting finally ceased. We stopped, and I could see blood dripping from my leg, through my pants, which I had recently acquired and which now suffered a modest circular tear at the point of entry and exit of the bullet. Luckily, neither my mother nor my brother had been touched, and I had only a modest flesh wound, so we were able to continue running. Either those German killers were poor shots and could only kill immobile people, or we were protected by the trees, which had received the brunt of the bullets. But even now, when I think about our narrow escape and how close we were to being killed, I get the shivers. My father, who was watching from a distance, thought that we were saved by the intervention of angels. I thought that we were saved by the trees.

The young man, the ranger's brother-in-law, had taken my father's advice and left the house at the same time that we did, managing to avoid the Germans and survive. But the ranger, seeing no reason to run, stayed with his family inside the house. There was no limit to German inhumanity. The ranger, his wife and children — they were all murdered inside their home. The boy and the two beautiful, innocent little girls were murdered before they reached their prime, inside their home, where they had always felt safe and happy, always singing and prancing about, and where we had had so much fun and pleasure being together. Their parents were unaware of what the Germans were capable of, even though neighbouring Kortelisy had been destroyed. The message had not been received because no one with a human heart and brain could imagine such viciousness, such cruelty, such inhumanity.

My only hope was that, before they were slaughtered by those vile and brutal men, the ranger and his beautiful family did not think that the reason for their death was because they were harbouring a Jewish family. This was certainly not the case because those Germans had taken time away from the front, where they were losing, to come to the middle of nowhere with the sole purpose of killing the villagers, Ukrainian Christians, in the area around destroyed Kortelisy, based on the suspicion that they were supporting *Banditen*, partisans. Neither the ranger nor any member of his family supported the partisans.

There were no more Jews to kill in the area. We were the only Jewish family from Kortelisy still alive. When those two German soldiers were shooting at us, they most definitely did not think we were Jewish. That same morning, other soldiers had already done some killing in other places in the area. As we were running away from the bullets, we encountered a woman running from the opposite direction. She had survived the killings in a nearby village, and her kerchief had been shot through by Germans trying to prevent her escape. We told her not to run any further, because she would run into more Germans. She told us the same thing, not to continue running because there were Germans further down, at the other edge of the forest and in the nearby hamlets and villages. None of us moved, and we stayed together at the place of our encounter, waiting for the slaughter to end.

As we were sitting in the forest, trying to conceal ourselves as much as possible, expecting the worst, we could smell smoke coming from the direction of the ranger's house. After killing the family, the German soldiers burned the house down with the murdered family inside. Throughout the night, we could hear the ranger's dog crying and wailing, not unlike a human being. The dog did not cease his plaintive howling until the morning. When we met up with the ranger's brother-in-law the next morning, the dog was still sitting on top of the ashes of the ranger's home, refusing to leave. We had to forcibly remove him from the burned remains of the house and the murdered family. As we pulled the dog away, he turned his head several times toward the burned-out house, showing human-like feelings about his loss, in stark contrast to the two-legged killers, the barbarians who had perpetrated the murders.

The Germans continued their killing spree throughout the morning and the rest of the day, moving from village to village and from hamlet to hamlet in separate detachments, murdering men, women and children, the old, the sick, and those with physical and mental disabilities. Later, we visited some of the homes of those who had survived, and I particularly recall two victims who had been seriously wounded. One was an older man, the head of a clan, whose entire family had been killed — brothers, sisters, children, grandchildren and in-laws — as they sat at their long table for an early breakfast. This lone survivor had been sitting at the head of the table and was shot through the neck as the Germans gunned down the rest of his family. He survived, but his vocal cords were shattered, and he was now unable to speak. He was also unable to eat solid food. Somehow, without the benefit of a doctor, the local villagers had managed to fashion a tube that enabled him to consume some liquids. I watched him drink tea from a big earthen pot through that tube. I can still see the painful vision of this man.

Another victim who had been terribly wounded was a little boy. He lay in bed, probably dying. I walked over to him and stood there looking at him sadly, almost in tears. He had been shot through and through, like a sieve, and was lying in a pool of coagulated blood. There were no doctors to help. All the years since then, I have felt grief for that little boy and wondered whether he survived.

Seeing the seriously wounded older man and the young boy, both seemingly on the verge of death, I began to realize how lucky my mother, brother and I were to have dodged the bullets. Even though I was wounded in my leg, it was nothing compared to the injuries received by the older man and the young boy. I was also lucky that I didn't develop an infection. There was no penicillin, not even iodine, and no doctor to tend to my wound. I had never heard of Pasteur or microbes, but I knew I had to keep my wound clean, change the bandages often and keep the creepy lice away from it. I fashioned bandages from big leaves, which I washed in clean water and then wrapped around my wound, tying them with strips of wood.

In spite of my efforts, as the wound began to heal, a crust about a foot long developed on my leg, and the lice crawled into the cracks and crevices around the wound, making it their home. This was very irritating and annoying, driving me to insanity. Employing the technique I had used when I'd had the *krets*, I used a splinter of wood the size of a toothpick to remove the lice.

PEOPLE WITH GUNS, LOOKING FOR CAUSES

Now living in the forest not far from the ranger's destroyed house, we were still in the vicinity of other hamlets and villages, and instead of Father walking alone in search of food, we would go together. We were once again close to Kortelisy, and the urge to see our village was very strong. It was hard for us to accept the fact that all of Kortelisy and its inhabitants, Jews, Christians, Roma, were now dead and there was nothing to see except for piles of ashes and exposed chimneys, the sole monuments to a vanquished village.

One day, we started walking in the direction of Kortelisy, as though we were walking home as free people. But we were in a dream; it was just make-believe. As we drew nearer to our former home, sanity prevailed and we began to realize that there was nothing left in Kortelisy. It was not safe to go there and it was no longer home; no family was waiting for us. We turned back. We would have to wait for another day and another time to see our destroyed village again.

We were still concerned about the Germans. They were apparently running thinner and thinner in the area, and around the end of 1943 were no longer permanently stationed in the region. This generated a vacuum for other hostile groups, some fighting each other. Thus, in addition to the spectre of the Germans, we remained worried about the disgruntled Ukrainian police, who were still around, though they had been disarmed and disbanded by the Germans. The police were now fighting both the Germans and the Soviets, as they had become Bulbovtsi or Banderivtsi — and they now lived in the same forest as us.

We were also concerned about the newly formed partisan groups that were in the forest or inside fortified camps they had built in some of the hamlets. The partisans were becoming more and more active. They would attack German convoys that were moving to and from the front. They would ambush, plant mines and blow up German military vehicles on the highway that ran through the forest. After an attack, the partisans would run, and the Germans, in pursuit of the partisans, would come pretty close to our shelter.

So this period presented a triple threat: the Germans did not disappear completely, and we lived in constant fear of the disbanded but still dangerous former Ukrainian police — and even of the newly formed Soviet partisan groups, who were indistinguishable from the Bulbovtsi and the Banderivtsi in dress and appearance. All the groups were ready to shoot, not only Germans, but anyone suspicious who crossed their path. It would seem that people with rifles, no matter what side they were fighting on, were anxious to use them, just for the sake of it. It was also great for a group's morale to find a scapegoat and hold an execution, to shoot someone as a spy or collaborator, even though the victim may have been completely innocent.

Every time we accidentally encountered those Soviet partisans, they would accuse us of being spies for the Germans. Once you were accused of being a German spy, no proof was necessary. The accusation alone was sufficient to seal your doom. No argument, no discussion, no proof of innocence, nothing could save you. Father would point to me and my brother and argue with them that we were not spies. He would explain that we were Jews and in hiding, running away from the Germans, that we were all born and raised in the neighbouring, now destroyed, village of Kortelisy. This explanation made them even more suspicious of us. They asked "clever" questions and made up their own answers: "How did you and your family survive? If you survived the destruction of an entire village, you must be collaborators. Otherwise you could not have survived." Ironically, they now failed to recognize us as Jews; the so-called Jewish accent did not help.

After a thorough and cruel interrogation during which we were threatened with death if we were lying — and with the truth being decided on a whim — they concluded that we were not spies after all. They let us go with a warning to Father: "Leave your family. Go out, kill a German, get his rifle and join us. If you don't do as you are told, next time we see you, we will kill you all." Their attitude toward us would suddenly change: instead of wanting to kill us as spies, they would kill us if Father refused to join them. We tried to avoid them but it wasn't always possible.

The first fearful stage of each of these encounters was determining if the group was former Ukrainian policemen or Soviet partisans. It was always a relief to find out that they were partisans, because with Ukrainian police, we would have been dead without the benefit of interrogation or trial. With the partisans, there was the chance of survival.

On one occasion, a whole group of Soviet partisans were marching through the forest, carrying a slaughtered hog. They stopped at our shelter to prepare it and have their lunch. This encounter turned out to be the happiest and most wonderful occasion. With these partisans around, we felt free and safe. Some of the partisans even spoke Yiddish. They played with us children, let us touch their guns and even offered us some of the grilled pork. Of course, even though we were hungry, we could not accept it because it was not kosher.

ON ACCOUNT OF A SACK OF BUCKWHEAT

It was now April 1944. Spring had arrived, and in addition to the potato, we could now rely on fresh mushrooms and all sorts of berries, as well as the three-leaf clover, to fill our bellies. In the spring and summer, we always had enough to eat from what grew in the forest, maybe enough not to die of hunger. It was just before Passover, and we were ready with a little sack of buckwheat flour that Father had pronounced kosher to use for our Passover matzo. The weather was sunny and beautiful when suddenly, completely out of season, a most ferocious winter blizzard hit our area.

Along with the huge amount of snow came a great deal of heavy gunfire: machine-gun bullets and artillery shells flew overhead from all directions, but especially from the direction of nearby Mokrany. At night the sky would light up from projectiles flying in all directions. We assumed the Germans were combing through the forest in search of partisans, who had become more and more active. Skirmishes were a regular occurrence between partisans and German forces, and from time to time the Germans would launch an *oblave* against the partisans living in and operating from the forest.

We were lying low, trying to stay concealed. Because of the bad weather, there were no mushrooms, berries or potatoes. The only thing we had in the way of food was the little sack of buckwheat, which we were saving for Passover. We decided that between the snow and the fighting it was too risky to leave the forest, so we would stay put and rely on the sack of buckwheat for our survival. This pure delicacy of buckwheat boiled in melted snow was enough to satiate our hunger, and it lasted for at least a week.

Now, without any food remaining, we were confronted with two choices: leaving the forest or starvation. We started walking, sometimes crawling, through deep snow, holding on to the trees, until we reached a path. The path had been cleared of snow and was well-trodden, indicating that many people wearing boots had walked it before us. Father immediately decided that this was no ordinary path dug by farmers. He declared that it was a military path, dug by soldiers, and concluded that Germans must still be in the vicinity. But we had to risk it. We continued walking along the path very carefully, looking out for Germans. The path led us out of the forest, and we saw some farmhouses in the distance. Everything looked peaceful. Smoke was coming out of the chimneys, and farmers were walking or running about their farmyards and in and out of their stables and homes. There were no Germans or any other people with rifles. A farmer noticed us as we approached his house and waved at us. As we came closer, he began talking and he sounded unhappy. First, he naturally complained about the unseasonable weather. He was worried that his entire crop would be ruined, and his family and animal stock would die of starvation. Second, he blamed this on the ungodly Soviets, who had brought this horrible and unnatural weather. They upset the seasons given to us by God Himself, so that we may live. Now we were going to die because of the ungodly Soviets.

My father looked at the farmer without understanding what he meant by the ungodly Soviets creating ungodly weather. Everybody knew that the Soviets do lots of ungodly things and make people suffer, especially farmers. But the weather? God still controls it, not the Soviets; He didn't hand control of the weather to the Soviets. Father thought for a moment and inquired, "What do the ungodly Soviets have to do with the weather?" The farmer explained that the unseasonable snowfall had come to this region at the same time the Soviets had arrived in the area. They came here and made the nice spring weather vanish and brought on the huge snowstorm. The farmer continued cursing the Soviets for bringing the snowstorm, for changing spring to winter. After a lengthy back and forth discussion, we finally realized what the farmer was saying: the big snowfall had come with the arrival of the Soviet army, and they had been in the area for about a week, moving as far west as Mokrany before having to retreat from the Germans. It had been the Soviet soldiers, not the Germans, who had dug the path in the snow and who had been doing all the shooting. Imagine our disappointment. Had we left our hiding place and come out of the forest a little earlier, we would have been liberated by now. But because we had misread events and because of the intervention of a little sack of buckwheat, we remained under German occupation. There was no relief for our disappointment and anger at the little sack of buckwheat. After gathering some food, we sadly returned to the forest, where we were condemned to a life of fear for at least another two months. If not for the buckwheat, we would have been forced to leave the forest, in spite of the weather and the shootings, and our liberation would have already come.

FINALLY, LIBERATION

By the end of July, the Soviet army had returned, this time without bringing a snowstorm. Brest-Litovsk, which was a bit west of Kortelisy, was liberated on July 28, 1944, a little over a week after my bar mitzvah, while we were still hiding in the forest. I never did have a real bar mitzvah, but I had learned what it meant to be a Jew in other ways, and paid a heavy price for it.

Before reaching Brest-Litovsk, the entire Soviet army just ploughed through our home in the forest. Soldiers and equipment moved in all directions. As we watched, trenches were dug and an army kitchen was set up with huge cauldrons to feed the soldiers. While some of the soldiers continued fighting and shooting in the direction of Mokrany, others would show up in the middle of the forest, exhausted. They would put aside their rifles and line up with canisters in hand to pick up their food rations. And when they finished eating, they would return to their rifles and continue shooting, still in the direction of Mokrany. Then another batch of soldiers would line up, pick up their food and follow the same pattern. Some would barely start their meal and fall asleep with their canisters in their hands, still full.

I noticed soldiers using their spoons or army knives to scoop out chunks of food from big cans that had non-Russian writing and a picture of a big eagle with spread wings on them. The food was delicious-looking — reddish chunks of pork they called *svinaya tushionka*, apparently shipped from America for the Soviet army.

Artillery shells and bullets continued flying overhead in all directions, and all the soldiers would duck when hearing them whistling and thundering overhead. But we were not afraid or even bothered by the sounds of war; we didn't even duck. The soldiers urged us, "Idite v tyl"— *Go back* — get away from the war zone; save yourselves; leave this area before you are shot. But we were too happy to be concerned with flying bullets and explosions. At last, at last, we were free and nothing could hurt us. We felt indestructible and wanted to continue staying with our liberators. We walked erect and mingled with the soldiers. They were friendly and hugged and embraced us, especially my brother and me, even grabbing and lifting us up and throwing us into the air. We were hungry, but food was not on our minds. We were too busy enjoying the moment, excited by all the war activity and the attention we were getting, especially from the soldiers who spoke Yiddish.

For the first time, we had the luxury of not dealing with our survival. We could turn to mourning and think about our relatives and friends from Kortelisy who had not made it. Of course, we felt regret and sorrow for those who had perished. My parents broke down and began to cry hysterically, remembering our village and its murdered inhabitants at the same time that they began to realize that they had survived. As soon as they stood up from this hysterical outburst, as if from sitting shiva and observing the seven days of mourning, the first thing we did as free people was return to our destroyed village, like some invisible power was pulling us there. It was instinctive though dangerous, this life-threatening homecoming to where there were no more homes. On the way, we stopped at the green grazing fields outside the village, where Zeyde Berchik and Bobeh Frumeh, together with a number of other Jewish victims, were buried. The huge common field was flat. Hundreds of white daisies and yellow dandelions grew all over it, as if their bright appearance could conceal the ugliness that permeated the field. It was impossible to locate the actual burial spot. We poked around for a while, looking for possible signs of a grave, but it was to no avail. The ground was flat. All signs of disturbance of the earth were healed beyond recognition and we gave up looking. The field was one big cemetery without a single tombstone.

We continued to Kortelisy, which, unlike the green fields from which we had just come, was totally devastated, burned to the ground. There was not even a wilted weed sprouting from the scorched earth, not even a blade of grass. Not a single building or shack remained standing.

We stood in front of the site where Zeyde Berchik's house used to stand. It was a pile of rubble. The only thing that remained standing, like a monument, was the brick chimney, with spent bullet shells all around it. There had obviously been some fighting over the rubble of Zeyde Berchik's house, with the brick chimney used as a cover. There was nothing left of Zeyde Meyer's house either; it too was burned to the ground, including the huge stork's nest. Even the little lilac tree was gone, and the nearby church with its blue-green roof was also turned to ashes. There was no sign of our house or that of our neighbours, the Sheftels. Nothing remained standing. The old cemetery across from our house was still intact, as were the brown sand dunes and the new cemetery on the other side of them.

I thought of our neighbours and the children with whom my brother and I used to play and how much more time we would have liked to spend with them. I ran over to the remains of the Sheftel house, as if looking for my dead playmates. Of course, I didn't find them, but I remembered the spot of my encounter with the German soldier in the doorway of the Sheftel house, and I looked toward the sand dunes and remembered our dog running down the dunes with red blood gushing from his little body, shot for no reason by a Ukrainian policeman in front of my eyes.

Father stopped for a moment to look at the sand dunes. He was probably thinking about the times he had returned there to dig up and steal potatoes to feed his family. There were no storks; there was no sound of birds or even of the lowly cricket. There was no animal life, in flight or on the ground — not a butterfly, grasshopper or even a horsefly, not even a dragonfly, which had always been in great abundance in Kortelisy. I remember catching them, holding them between my thumb and index finger around their waist and legs and feeling their muscular strength as they tried to free themselves while looking at me with their big eyes, as if saying, "Don't be nasty, kid. Let me go." Finally, I would let them go and see them fly high, spreading their powerful double wings.

Kortelisy was a wasteland of scorched earth, empty of life. Even the single street had disappeared. There was nothing but emptiness. In the trenches and ravines, which had always been full of greenery and a multitude of bugs, there was not a blade of grass. This was the place where my grandfathers had walked proudly, as if they and their families lived in biblical Canaan. There we were now, alone.

While my parents were standing around, tearfully observing the destruction and most certainly thinking of family and those who had perished, I decided to visit my favourite place — the lake. I ran as quickly as I could through the empty and barren fields, and within minutes I reached the lake and surrounding marshes, which brought different memories, like an electric shock, of events we had lived through in the marshes — of hiding and of hearing the agonized screams of "Shema Yisroel!" and the cries of wandering toddlers who had just lost their parents, only to be silenced by the sounds of a gun.

Seeing the lake also brought back pleasant summer memories, when every Friday the entire Jewish population would go to the lake to bathe — not to swim, only to bathe and splash in the shallow waters.

On the shore of the lake, I found an old abandoned rowboat, waiting to be taken into the water. I obliged and started rowing. I hadn't rowed too far when I noticed that the boat was leaking and accumulating water. Quickly, I started rowing back to the shore, but before I was able to get there, the boat became completely submerged with me in it. Luckily, I was able to walk back to the shore with my head above the water. Like all Kortelisy Jews, I had never learned how to swim, and had I rowed just a bit further into deeper water, I could have drowned in my very favourite place immediately after being liberated.

When I think about our Kortelisy visit now, I realize that the visit itself was more dangerous than that boat ride. Maybe my parents recognized the danger but decided to risk it anyway. Of course, there were no more Germans to fear. But, there were still the former Ukrainian police, who would have loved to kill some Jews. We were smack in the middle of the area where they would gather and were pretty lucky not to have encountered them during that visit.

Everything appeared to be a matter of luck, including my survival of the boat ride and avoiding an encounter with the former Ukrainian police — just a lucky break. Life itself, surviving the war, the whole unhappy and tragic ordeal of my family was one big accident. Did we merit surviving because of some intrinsic goodness? There were members of the Kortelisy community with far greater merit who deserved survival and who had perished. Father would say that it was simply the will of God and there is no sense in looking for an explanation or rationale. God has His own way of doing things and one should not seek explanations for the actions of the Almighty.

Or maybe we would have avoided the entire ordeal had my grandfather Meyer decided to stay in America and bring his family over instead of returning home to Kortelisy. On the other hand, had my grandfather brought his family to America, my father would never have met and married my mother, and I would not have been born. You can't create your own destiny. One's destiny is created by factors that come into existence even before one's birth. Or are there invisible, powerful and unimaginable forces controlling and guiding our lives, deciding and determining our destinies?

After the incident on the lake, I rejoined my parents, who were still wandering around the destroyed village. I was soaking wet and tried to explain my condition, which they found bizarre and hard to understand. I wasn't going to tell them that I had almost drowned. I had to stay on their good side as I still wanted to see one more place which they had no interest in seeing: the *mayak* outside the village, which I had been prevented from seeing by the local boys when it was being built. Even though my parents wanted to see the marshes and visit the burial site of the victims of the Germans disguised as Ukrainian women, they somehow agreed to go to the tower, just to please me.

We reached the structure and I quickly ran up the hill and touched the bottom of the tower. I looked up. It was tall and erect — obviously neglected and partly in ruin, but still the most impressive and magnificent, and the tallest, structure I had ever seen, with its antennas and wires still intact, protruding from the top. I thought of the kids who had come running with me to see the tower when it was being built and who were no longer alive; they would never be able to see it. I cried for them, but at the same time, I was happy to be alive and totally relieved of the burden of the fear of dying. Finally, I felt free, free enough to stand before the tower without fear. I stood there for a while admiring that beautiful, wonderful structure.

My parents were calling me. I tried to stand on my hands and walk down the hill on them like the Soviet soldier had years before. I still wasn't able to do it. Instead, I lay down and rolled down to the bottom of the hill, where my parents and my brother were waiting.

PART III

FULL CIRCLE

We left Kortelisy and walked toward the highway, crossing empty fields and dirt roads. We encountered Soviet soldiers in mechanized vehicles and wagons drawn by horses. Some of the soldiers stopped to talk to us. Some even spoke to us in Yiddish and were delighted to see us, hugging us and giving us their food rations. We told them our story in brief, and we cried together. One of the soldiers, seeing my father in his long johns and me in my torn pants, was able to find us fresh military outfits. We continued walking and finally reached the highway. The *shosey* was packed with traffic moving in both directions, the air filled with the emissions from exhaust pipes of Soviet army vehicles, tanks and trucks that were filled with soldiers moving toward the front, and open trucks carrying the wounded that were heading in the opposite direction. I stood there watching this life drama, smelling the emissions of the exhaust pipes of the various army vehicles congesting the *shosey*. I still enjoy the smell of gasoline.

We hitchhiked. A truck carrying wounded soldiers stopped and gave us a lift in the direction of Ratno. Some of the wounded soldiers were unconscious, others were screaming in pain and still others were lying in dead silence; all were covered in bloody bandages. We reached the Pripet River. The bridge over the Pripet had been destroyed by the retreating Germans, and parts of it protruded from the water below. We crossed the river on two parallel steel planks, the truck swaying all the way. As soon as we had crossed the river, we disembarked from the military truck. We had come full circle back to Ratno. Instead of arriving on foot in the middle of the night, this time we arrived in broad daylight.

We settled in Ratno, where there were a few survivors who were nice enough to accommodate us and find us an "abandoned" house to live in, the owners having been murdered. Besides my immediate family, there were no other Kortelisy survivors, except for our black-and-white cow. She showed up one day, mooing from the shed that was attached to the house. I heard the mooing and went to the shed, asking myself what a cow would be doing there, when lo and behold, I recognized our big white cow with the black patches — our precious, heroic milking cow who had provided all the milk we could drink. It was like finding a lost relative, a member of my own family: this was a Jewish cow who had survived the Holocaust and the Kortelisy massacres. We all hugged the cow and tearfully held onto her neck for a long time.

Now the cow belonged to a farmer who lived on the outskirts of Ratno and who had somehow ended up with her after we abandoned her in our stables. He was not about to return the cow to us. My father consulted the local judge, who was his drinking buddy, and who without hesitation rendered judgment off the bench and told my father, "Let the cow go. What will you do with a cow in Ratno? You should be happy to have survived the war, to be alive." We let the cow go, but it was like parting with a family member. Later, when we left Ratno in an open truck, I anxiously eyed the grazing fields on the border of the road, hoping to see the cow again, to have a final glance at our beautiful cow before departing from Ukraine forever. But even though there were many cows grazing in the field, I didn't see our cow.

For a while we also had to give up our father, who was "invited" to join the Soviet army. The head of the local NKVD was looking for collaborators to send to the front without even a minimum of training. According to this NKVD *nachalnik*, or Commissar, anyone and everyone who had survived the war in western Ukraine was a collaborator, and such a person should now serve — and be prepared to die for — the Motherland. This Commissar was also my father's friend and drinking buddy, yet this connection was not a consideration. He decided to send my father, who had just survived the war, to the front to serve as fodder. My father was picked up immediately and sent to Kowel for induction.

Father had been separated from us a few times during the war, but Mother was not prepared to lose him again. She followed him to Kowel with the intention of having him disqualified. She thought about Father's asthma, but he'd had no trace of it since we lived in the forest. She remembered that one of the things that would trigger his asthma, besides dust, was eating or even smelling onions. And so, the night before his very cursory and superficial medical exam, Mother stayed up with Father the whole night, feeding him onions. By the time he appeared before the army doctors, Father had the worst asthma attack he'd ever had. He couldn't stand on his feet or even hold himself up; marching or holding a rifle appeared out of the question. He was gasping for air. In addition, after a sleepless night, he looked pale, hardly holding on to life. He was disqualified by the examiner on sight — even as fodder for the German front.

I started Soviet school again. I don't know what grade I was in, but the curriculum was the same; everything we learned was in praise of Stalin and the destruction of the enemies of Soviet power, especially Nazi Germany, under the guidance and wise leadership of Comrade Stalin. But there were also still the local enemies, the dastardly kulaks.

Ratno was safer than Kortelisy and we did not fear for our lives. Yet the Jewish remnants made no signs of planting their roots again in Ratno to rebuild a Jewish community. It seemed to me that the attitude of the local Ukrainians toward Jews hadn't changed. A generous Ukrainian family invited us to stay with them while we were looking for a permanent home in Ratno, and when I claimed that Ukraine was my home, their teenage daughter told me angrily, "Ukraine is neither your home, nor your land. Neither is Ukrainian your language." I felt as if I had been told that I didn't deserve to live and had no right to breathe the air, as I had felt when I had been subjected to the "Jew test" before the war. This was shocking and painful for me to hear, and especially because the young lady was so very beautiful and I wanted to be her friend.

I don't know how my brother and I ever survived Ratno because, during our free time, we would explore and play in the trenches, where mines and bullets and other explosives were scattered. It was by sheer accident that we did not stumble on or play with any of the explosives left by the German and Soviet forces. A great number of people were killed or wounded by abandoned ordnance. I remember attending the military funeral of two Soviet sappers who had been killed in the process of dismantling a mine. I also remember seeing lines and lines of wagons holding the wounded and dying, who were covered in coagulated blood, waiting patiently in front of Ratno's only clinic to be seen by the one doctor on duty.

We had to have some money to buy food, even though our accommodation was free. Somehow my parents knew or had recently acquired the art of making moonshine, in this case samogon, which I would sell to the Soviet soldiers in their trucks on the highway passing through Ratno. I am not sure it was legal. Probably not, but it was a living. Some people became very rich doing it. My father didn't. He eventually found a decent job and did not continue in the liquor business.

Unfortunately, while still in Ratno, Mother got very sick with typhus fever. Although the sickness is highly contagious and deadly, the rest of my family and the other people who lived with us did not contract it. Miraculously, Mother recovered from this horrible malady after several months of high fever, without medicines and without the help of a doctor. We prayed and did everything we could to make her comfortable, mostly feeding her hot tea and warm soups. We had nothing else to offer except our love and devotion.

MOVED BY AN INVISIBLE HAND

We remained in Ratno until, one day, my mother appeared in my school. She pulled me out from the classroom, and suddenly we were on our way to Kowel, a city some fifty or sixty kilometres southeast of Ratno. I believe that the move from Ratno to Kowel was part of the beginning of a master plan to leave the Soviet Union and our ancestral habitation. My grandparents had thought that in Kortelisy we lived in the best possible world. My grandfathers would not exchange it, not even for *Amerike, di goldene medine*, America, the golden land, where the streets are paved with gold. But we were leaving.

When we arrived in Kowel, there were already other Jews there whom we had previously met in Ratno. The words I heard again and again were "waiting for instructions." We were moved by an invisible hand and secret codes. I believe my parents didn't exactly know what was happening. The only thing they knew was that we were waiting for instructions together with the other Jews in Kowel. We were leaving Mother Russia for an unknown destination with false identities in our hands and hope in our hearts.

In one of our explorations around Kowel, my brother and I walked into a big and impressive building, a synagogue that had been partially destroyed. Inside the synagogue, the white walls were covered as high as the hand could reach with writings in Yiddish and other languages, with many messages containing the word *nekome*, revenge. The Jewish victims who had been gathered into the synagogue before being taken out and murdered had left those desperate messages pleading for a revenge they never got to see.

One day the order came: pack your belongings, limited to bare necessities, and show up at the train station. The invisible hand had finally moved. My brother was already an experienced train rider from his early childhood trips to doctors in Brest-Litovsk. I, on the other hand, was a novice when it came to trains, and I had to listen to my brother's instructions on how to behave on a train. The last time I had been at a train station, I was with my father at the Mokrany station before the war, and I had run when I heard the train coming, not realizing that trains move on tracks. Now, my brother told me that when the train was moving I should always sit, and I should always hold on to something in case the train makes a sudden stop. And I should never, but never, run in the aisles, but always walk slowly and hold on to the seats.

When we walked into the wagon, it was packed. All the seats were taken. People were standing pushed up against each other, speaking Polish, Ukrainian, Russian and Yiddish. Some travelled in groups, some in families and others alone. Some were running away from home; others were returning home. Most had something to hide and showed fear when they were disturbed by officials and Soviet soldiers. My brother did not have a solution for how to ride the train without a seat. From now on, during most of our travels, we would be in packed trains, and I eventually found a way to avoid standing — I was able to crawl into a baggage net that was attached to the wagon wall and even sleep there.

As the train was moving from Kowel deep into western Poland, sudden panic and fear developed among the Jewish passengers as rumours started to circulate about incidents where Jews had been removed from trains by armed Polish resistance groups and killed. Actually, those rumours were based on facts. According to some historians, hundreds, if not thousands of Jewish survivors were killed in Poland after the war. And far-right resistance groups like the Narodowe Siły Zbrojne (the National Armed Forces, or NSZ), though originally formed to fight the Germans, were now fighting the Soviets; they accused Jewish survivors who had escaped to the Soviet Union but who were now returning home to Poland of bringing communism with them.

Even on a moving train, facing fear and possibly death, life goes on. Mordkhe and Magultse, who were originally from around the Ratno area, had survived the war, as my family had, by hiding in the forest. They had fallen in love and wanted to be married. So when at one point the train stopped, most of the Jewish passengers got off the train to form a congregation, and my father solemnized their marriage and recited the *shevebrokhes*, the seven blessings traditionally recited at weddings. The travellers pretended to hold glasses filled with wine and drank to the health of the new couple, bestowing all the blessings on the bride and groom. The couple eventually settled in Canada.

The train continued to Gliwice or, as it was called in German, Gleiwitz, where we disembarked and my family was installed, of all places, with a German family. There was a woman whose husband was either dead or a Soviet prisoner of war and a nineteen-year-old son who had probably just left Hitlerjugend, the youth movement of the Nazi Party. A friend my age who travelled with us from Kowel was staying in a nearby house, and he always tried to get the German teenager into a dark alley so that he could beat him up. We once succeeded, and were poised to strangle him, when we changed our minds and let him go. In revenge, he somehow managed to get hold of a picture of one of my murdered relatives. He tore it up in front of my eyes while I tried to grab it from him and save it. I felt as if he had just murdered my relative again, and I reacted immediately. I ran outside, angry as hell, found a stone and shattered one of the glass windows of his mother's house. Unfortunately, the window was in the room where my family lived.

We stayed in Gliwice for several months, awaiting further instructions. During that time I visited some bombed-out ruins in the area. I remember walking into a ruined mikveh with white tiles and marble floors. (The Kortelisy mikveh had been a poor imitation.) I also walked into the ruins of a synagogue, with prayer books, Bibles and scrolls scattered all over the place. I wanted to take it all with me. I picked up a prayer book with an inscription in German that indicated it was a gift from one family member to another and took it with me. I was unable to save any of the other sacred books and scrolls.

In Gliwice I also discovered the marketplace. I would watch Soviet soldiers stealing, grabbing merchandise off the tables and running, and merchants screaming after them. I once observed two Soviet soldiers approaching a table laden with watches and jewellery. One of the soldiers picked a number of items off the table. As he walked away with the items, he turned to the anxious merchant and pointed to the other soldier and said, "He will pay." The merchant was relieved, but not for long. When the soldier who was left behind also started walking away, the merchant asked for payment. The soldier informed the merchant that he didn't even know the soldier who had picked up the merchandise.

It was in this marketplace that I started selling household items for the German woman with whom we lived. She was very happy when I brought her the profits, and she would reward me with a commission. The last item she gave me to sell was a crystal piece in the shape of a basket with a handle. But, before I could sell it, a Soviet soldier grabbed it from me and ran. I chased him, screaming in Russian, and with the help of another Soviet soldier, I got it back. And then, before I could sell it, my mother somehow found me in the market. She was excited and agitated, and she grabbed me and took me to the train station; we were moving again. Unfortunately, there was no time to return the piece of crystal to the German lady. It still bothers me after all these years. The piece is still here, reminding me of my involuntary transgression.

We were now on a train to Prague, crossing the Czech-Polish

border, which was controlled by the Soviets. We were travelling with forged Greek identity cards. My first name was Panagiotis, and I was supposed to be a Greek citizen returning from incarceration in Auschwitz. We were told that unless we spoke Greek, we should pretend to be deaf; some comedians suggested that we pretend to speak Greek by reciting the Aramaic prayer of Yikum Purkan. We were especially warned not to speak Russian. There were a good number of families on the train who were returning from the Soviet Union, where they had survived the war, and who, upon finding their homes in Poland destroyed, decided to leave Poland. Their children spoke Russian. Mothers were covering the mouths of their children with their hands for fear that they might say something in Russian and be detected as being the unthankful deserters and traitors to the Motherland that the Soviets deemed them to be.

We succeeded in crossing the border and arrived in Prague late at night. Years later, I heard from people who had crossed the same border on forged Greek identity cards that the Soviets had known exactly who we were and had been bribed to let us through. In fact, I do not recall any of us being questioned or our papers being checked. When our train reached the border, we stayed inside the train for a while. One person, the leader of our group, took our papers and showed them to one of the Soviet soldiers carrying a machine gun on his shoulder, and then we were on our way.

Once we arrived in Prague, we began to walk. I could at last see the entire group of refugees, carrying their meagre belongings inside suitcases, sacks or pillowcases, struggling to stay awake, dragging their feet. Some were carrying their sleepy children. We moved in the dark in this strange, medieval city like a massive formless and faceless body. None of us knew where we were going; we just followed each other. We kept walking aimlessly. Exhausted, we were finally led into a hotel and into a huge room where the floor was covered with mattresses. We were told that we could now go to sleep and were sent to bed without supper. I was hungry, but I fell asleep as soon as I hit the mattress.

The wonderful thing about the hotel was not the accommodation. It was the movie house inside the bowels of the building, which I was able to sneak into for free any time of the day or night to see as many Soviet war movies as I wanted. The movies showed the heroic deeds of the Soviet army and the great leadership of Comrade Stalin. It was the first time I saw cowardly German soldiers and it warmed the cockles of my heart. I had never before or since seen that many movies in one week, which was the length of our stay in Prague.

I wandered the streets and saw the Jewish cemetery, as well as other Jewish landmarks, and was mesmerized by the clock with the Hebrew alphabet standing in for numerals. I was enthralled by the Jewish sites, though at the time, I didn't know the Jewish history of Prague. I was just stunned by what I saw and felt a certain warmth and closeness to the city and its people.

One day while I was walking down the street, I stopped in front of a bakery window displaying the most colourful and deliciously appealing pastry. I stood there in my torn shirt and pants, unkempt and unwashed, salivating at the sight of all that enticing pastry. A woman inside the store motioned with her hand for me to come in. I was frightened, but nothing could stop me from getting close to that pastry. She gestured for me to pick one piece of pastry. It wasn't easy, but I managed to do it very quickly, before she changed her mind. I chose the biggest one. She paid for the pastry using her ration cards. I still remember the woman's face, even the clothes she wore. I ran out of the store quickly, like a wild animal, holding on to the pastry with both hands. It was a most delicious morsel of food, and the taste of it has never left me.

Our next stop was Bratislava and then Budapest. There, my brother and I ended up in the Jewish hospital, probably because of exhaustion and malnutrition, and there we received the most miserable treatment from bedbugs. It was worse than the lice in the forest. You could kill lice and, in some measure, relieve your frustrations. But with

Budapest bedbugs, you were always faced with a serious dilemma: you could kill them but, when you did, they emitted a most horrible smell, which was even worse than their bite.

Bugs aside, the hospital stay was a new and strange experience for us. For the first time, we met people who claimed to be Jewish but didn't look like the Jews I had known in Ratno and Kortelisy. They looked like *goyim* and spoke a strange language. They were not allowed to boil water on the Sabbath, even to help the sick, but it was alright to smoke a cigarette on the Sabbath. On one Sabbath, Mother asked the nurse in attendance where she could get some warm water, and the nurse, with a cigarette in her hand, bluntly told her, "You can't. It's the Sabbath." The nurse probably never heard that "pkiakh nefesh doykhe Shabbos"—*the saving of a soul defers the Sabbath.*

Despite these differences between us as survivors and refugees, we were treated like royalty. My brother and I were pampered by doctors and hugged and kissed by nurses, although we could not communicate with them. After we were discharged from the hospital, one person even continued visiting us at the transit camp. He showed me around the city and even took me to a movie. It was *The Count of Monte Cristo* in English with Hungarian subtitles. I understood neither of the languages, but I thoroughly enjoyed the movie.

In Budapest I was introduced to paprika. I purchased a paprika pepper, probably for several hundred *pengős*, the local currency, not knowing whether it was a fruit or vegetable. It was a shock to me to discover that so beautiful a vegetable had so bitter a taste. I have since acquired a taste for paprika in its variety of colours and flavours.

My brother and I recovered before our departure from Budapest. We then ended up inside the American Zone in Vienna, where we slept overnight on the floor of one of the Rothschild palaces before departing for Linz, the regional capital of Upper Austria. The area around Linz supported several centres for refugees, survivors of concentration camps, returnees from the Soviet Union and other Jewish survivors from Poland, western Ukraine, Hungary and Romania.

My family stayed in a relatively luxurious displaced persons (DP) camp in a suburb of Linz, called Bindermichl, where we were housed in the *Hitlerbauten*, Hitler buildings. We had a whole house to ourselves, except for one little bedroom, where the authorities placed a succession of young women. Whenever the ladies had male visitors, my mother insisted that the door to the room remain open and that there be no overnight stays. This was an unbending rule. One morning my mother came across the American soldier who was courting the young lady leaving her room. Mother chased him out of the house and into the street, warning him not to show his face there again, while other residents of the camp ran after my mother in fear, warning her that she was dealing with an American soldier who had guns. But Mother kept screaming about protecting her children. I didn't understand how we were being protected by Mother screaming and chasing the American soldier.

The camp inhabitants managed to organize a rich and lively cultural life. There were political parties, religious and secular organizations, a theatre and a school, even an orchestra. There was also a soccer team with some champion players. (When Austria played soccer internationally, they always picked two or three players from our team in Bindermichl.) In the centre of the camp, there were wooden barracks where all the social and cultural activities took place, including theatrical performances by local and visiting entertainers. I will never forget seeing a performance of Peretz's *Bontshe shvayg* (Bontshe the Silent) with Aba Igelfeld. I was completely absorbed by the story and by Igelfeld's great performance and expressive face. The audiences always displayed good taste. On one occasion, the audience did not like the performance of a magician. He was first booed as a warning of things to come, then physically attacked and chased out of the camp.

The camp also published a Yiddish newspaper, called *Oyfgang*, using the Latin alphabet. There was a Jewish school for children and a technical ORT (Organization for Rehabilitation through Training) school for vocational training located near the Wegscheid DP camp. I first attended and then graduated from the Jewish elementary school, where I learned mostly Jewish history, Hebrew and Yiddish languages, and a subject called "Palestinography and *zmirah* (singing)." Then I studied electricity at the ORT school nearby and received a graduation certificate in electro-engineering, but with a level of only "good" marked on the graduation certificate. When I was admitted to the Jewish school, I was placed in a class based on my age rather than my knowledge, which was poor. I found myself studying equations and trigonometry before I even knew the multiplication tables. For some unknown reason, my knowledge of math improved at the ORT school.

At the Jewish school, I regained my childhood at age thirteen or fourteen. I had friends, older and younger, to play with. Some of them spoke Yiddish or Russian. Others spoke Polish or Romanian. But we understood each other. The children who came from the Soviet Union were the most assertive and had greater confidence than the children who had survived in the forests and bunkers; the latter were timid and frightened. The children who came from the Soviet Union were also the best soccer players, boxers and tap dancers. I tried everything, including playing Ping-Pong, roller skating and boxing. I also played soccer and other games I had never heard of before. And I finally learned how to ride a bicycle. I managed to get hold of a bicycle, found a path with an incline, and started out late one night, practising the art of bike riding. I fell off the bike many times and suffered some cuts and bruises. But I was pretty determined. Again and again, throughout the night, I practised. By early morning I had become an expert bike rider. The sight of a bike still reminds me of my uncle Shmilke, who had promised to teach me how to ride a bike but was murdered before he could.

We lived in the Bindermichl DP camp till June or July 1948, when we received an invitation from the Canadian consular office for an interview. The interview went well. The interviewer was impressed by my grandmother Freyde's maiden name, Rothchild, as was the Canadian government, apparently. Canada was ready to receive us. As it happened, the two orphaned boys my bobeh Frumeh used to tell me about in her stories about Cossacks, Phillip and Jack Ruttenberg, my mother's second cousins, arranged the papers and documents for my family to come to Canada. Their sister had ended up in the United States.

Within weeks of the interview we were on our way to Canada via Italy. First we travelled by train to a place called Grugliasco, a community not far from Turin, which had been partly converted into a transit camp. We waited there for our boat, the *Sobieski*, to arrive at the port city of Genoa. In Grugliasco we were practically under house arrest. We were not allowed to leave the camp, which was surrounded by walls and wires. I got to know a fellow my age, Yekhezkiel Berezniak, who had survived Auschwitz and was also in transit and lived in Italy after the war. He spoke Italian and asked the *carabinieri*, the police guarding the gate, to let us out. They always refused. But they had no objection to our leaving the transit camp by climbing over the wall and barbed wire, in their presence, right next to the gate they guarded. I was always afraid that one day they would use us for target practice and shoot at us.

After a month or so in Grugliasco, we were taken to the *Sobieski* and were served our first meal of overloaded plates of spaghetti on the open deck. I had never had spaghetti before and didn't quite know how to handle it. After the meal, we were placed with other passengers of equal rank in the hull of the ship with all of our *galakhutches*, our belongings. On the Mediterranean, it was calm, smooth and pleasant. I had a wonderful time exploring the ship, and I even found a place with a shower and helped myself to a salty douche. Unfortunately, the trouble began as soon as we crossed Gibraltar into the Atlantic. I became seasick and developed a serious urge to stop the misery by jumping into the huge waves. I guess I loved life too much and persisted in my struggle to survive this new, horrible ordeal of seasickness. It stopped suddenly, the same way it had started, as soon as we approached Halifax.

BREAKING OLD HABITS

We arrived in Montreal on September 18 or 19, 1948, and slept in various homes until we moved into one of the rooms of a home occupied by two bachelor brothers on St. Urbain Street. There, we slept on sofas and on the floor and in the kitchen. It was better than the shelter in the forest or the train, or even the boat. Mother found a job in a cookie factory, and Father found a job through the benevolence of the owner of a furniture factory, a person he'd met in the Anshai Ukraina synagogue on St. Urbain Street. The synagogue — which later became Zichron Kedoshim — had been built by Jews who came from Ukraine. My father's job was to polish and varnish the furniture. Unfortunately, my father was not used to that kind of work, and he was never instructed by factory management how to do it and, in his inexperience, he managed to burn his hands with the liquid solution of the furniture polish. I am convinced that the management was more interested in having the furniture polished than in the safety of my father's hands. Eventually his injuries were so severe that he could no longer work in the factory and they sent him home.

Father was without a job for quite a while, so he had all the time to attend synagogue, where he mixed with *landslayt*, his countrymen of Ukrainian origin. Indirectly, he found a job at the abattoir on Iberville Street, working for the Vaad Ha'ir, the Jewish Community Council, as a *mazhgiekh*, inspecting kosher meat, and for the Canadian

Pacific Railway, owners of the abattoir. Even though my father didn't go to the synagogue to look for a job, attending and mixing with synagogue-goers helped him find one. Considering our circumstances, it was a good and honest job, even though Father had to pay a "commission" to the man who introduced him to the job and, after the man passed away, to his widow, for a good number of years.

Now, we were able to rent a place on Durocher Street, in one of the row houses at the corner of Lajoie Avenue. With the help of a subtenant, a family of four who lived in one room and had kitchen privileges, we were able to pay the rent. It's amazing how we lived together in peace and harmony. However, I always argued with the man about communism and, as he called him in Yiddish, *Khaver* Stalin. It was terribly funny. The man had been born in Poland and ended up in the Soviet Union during the war. His wife had been born in the Soviet Union and she always took my side. It would appear that the wife and I, both of whom had received a Stalinist education, had lost our love for Comrade Stalin. But the man worshipped him. He spoke of Stalin as the embodiment of all wisdom and enlightenment, as saviour of the world and, most of all, a bulwark against the evils of capitalism and colonialism.

Then it happened: capitalism was good to our subtenant. He found a decent job and was then able to rent a place for his family. Eventually they immigrated to the capitalist United States of America to join his sister and open a liquor store.

~

With only two-and-a-half grades of Soviet schooling and some time in the school in Bindermichl behind me, now in Montreal at the age of sixteen or seventeen, I was too old for elementary school and possibly too old, as well as unprepared, even for secondary school, and I spoke neither English nor French. My mother, who firmly believed in a good education, desperately wanted me to go back to school, any school, after the lengthy interruption of my education by the war.

Mother always said she didn't want me to end up working in a factory. So she tried to have me admitted to one of the Jewish schools.

We visited with Shloime Wiseman, principal of the Jewish People's School, who received us while lying on his office couch, complaining of chronic backaches. He informed us that I was too old for the primary school, which he was running, and unprepared for high school. He suggested, maybe a bit ironically, that if I could not be a student, then maybe I could become a teacher, and for that I could see Yoyneh Braverman, principal of the Jewish Teachers Seminary.

With a cigarette drooping out of his mouth and smoke covering most of his face, Braverman informed us that I would have to be at least eighteen to attend his seminary and, in any event, without a high school diploma, I couldn't attend the seminary, no matter what my age. Noting our disappointment, Braverman did not dismiss us immediately. He continued asking questions and testing my Hebraic and Jewish general knowledge. Maybe he kept us there and continued talking to us out of interest in Holocaust survivors, but I got the feeling very early upon our arrival to Canada that no one was very interested in Holocaust survivors and their stories. As I discovered when I became a student at the seminary, where I was finally admitted, my Canadian-born classmates and instructors, even though they were educated people with curious and inquiring minds, never asked me questions about how I survived the war. My friend and classmate Yekhezkiel Berezniak, who had survived Auschwitz, was never asked about the number tattooed on his arm.

Braverman decided to admit me on a trial basis, maybe because I was a Holocaust survivor, or maybe because I was able to recite by heart numerous passages from the *sider* and from King Solomon's Shir Hashirim (Song of Songs) and parts of Akdomus. I had been chanting the poem since I was in cheder and heard it recited in the synagogue every Shavuos, without necessarily understanding its meaning. But it seemed that Braverman was impressed.

At my first lecture at the seminary, I was duly shamed and

embarrassed when I was asked a question by one of our most wonderful teachers, Yankev Zipper. I stood up in Soviet style to answer and evoked a great deal of laughter from my classmates when Zipper told me, "Megst zikh avekzetzn, Pinchas," that I may sit down and give my reply to the question while seated. I learned my lesson quickly. The next time I answered a question or posed one, I sat firmly in my seat, although not very comfortably. I had to fight my compulsion to stand and had a hard time breaking an old habit acquired in childhood.

It was quite difficult for me to understand or accept the behaviour of my Canadian-born classmates. My basic beliefs, convictions and childish perceptions that I had picked up in my village were being challenged now. Respect for your elders had always been central. Respect for your elders was categorical, no questions asked. It was hammered and dinned into me so strongly and with such great force that it continued to be a constant guide even into my adulthood. It even followed me when I attended law school. On one occasion one of my French-Canadian classmates at McGill's Faculty of Law made a derogatory remark about one of our professors, F.R. Scott, whom I greatly admired and respected. I, in turn, terribly annoyed by his remark, chastised my classmate and told him to have more respect for this wonderful professor. "Why?" my classmate inquired. "Because he's older?" It was strange for me to hear him say that. It was as if he was reading my mind (of course, it was because he was older). Perhaps he had been taught to have the same respect for elders and authority that I had been taught, but for the church instead of cheder and the Soviets. Benefiting from a cosmopolitan environment in Montreal and a broader education than my own, he had probably abandoned this rule of conduct long ago, while I retained it. I began to realize at this late stage of my life that something might be wrong with the principled notion of obedience and respect for your elders and total submission to authority, as I had been taught in the Soviet school system, the cheder and in my village as a whole. Not all elders should be respected.

One of the instructors in the seminary — I will call him Gefen — started out as a communist in a Polish shtetl, and later in life, when in Canada, turned to religion and became extremely Orthodox, even questioning Darwin's theory of evolution. The poet Irving Layton taught English to the newcomers who attended the seminary and, at one point, he discussed Darwin's theory with us, which was an idea that was new to me. Some of my classmates reported this to our Orthodox teacher, Mr. Gefen, whose rebuttal in Yiddish was swift and brief, if not very scholarly: "Der mentsh kumt aroys fun a monkey, er [Darwin] iz aleyn a monkey"—*Man is descendant of a monkey, he* [Darwin] *is himself a monkey*. That was his most powerful argument against Darwin's theory — that Darwin himself was a monkey. Even I understood that there was something wrong with his argument, though I had never heard of Darwin and his theory before.

But what irked and shocked me even more was that a former communist who had been born in the shtetl and had written books about it, who came to Canada as an adult, could make a very sweeping and dismissive statement about the feelings, faith and behaviour of religious Jews living under Hitler, showing total ignorance about shtetl Jews and their strong faith in the Almighty during those difficult days and years. During a lecture on the *sider* and on prayer in general, Mr. Gefen mentioned how fasting was an essential part of the Jewish religion and how the gates of heaven open during the Yom Kippur fast. I thought that I would contribute to the discussion by telling the class and Mr. Gefen how strongly Jews had prayed under Hitler. I mentioned the fact that both of my grandfathers fasted every Monday and Thursday during the war years, hoping that the Almighty would listen to them and save them, their families and the rest of the Jews from annihilation. Gefen's response to my intervention, completely in contradiction to his previous remarks on fasting, came quick and sharp: "Your grandfathers' fasting was nothing but *gavtones* and *yehires*." He was all angry and flustered as he proclaimed that my grandparents' fasting was pretentious, arrogant and without merit, that their fasting was nothing but a delusion of grandeur, assuming undeserved dignity and importance.

I was speechless. His remarks, carrying the full meaning of the Yiddishized Hebrew words of *gavtanut* and *yehirot*, were terribly hurtful. He failed to see that there wasn't an ounce of pretension in my grandparents' bodies and souls. And like my grandparents, the Jews in my village prayed and fasted every Monday and Thursday sincerely and without pretension or arrogance, simply believing that the Almighty was listening. Their faith was strong, and they turned to God honestly; unfortunately, it would appear, after all is said and done, that He was not listening. And my very religious teacher, with all his knowledge about the shtetl, was ignorant and did not understand the heart and soul of the shtetl Jew and the Jews of my village under Hitler. I was hurt by Gefen's words, but I did not have the strength to stand up to him and defend the murdered villagers.

~

The fear of celebrating birthdays that had been planted in me since childhood ended abruptly when I was a counsellor in Camp Kindervelt in the Laurentians, the mountains north of Montreal, in 1949. One day, during lunchtime, the entire hall full of campers, counsellors and staff erupted in singing "Happy Birthday." I was not familiar with the song, and I did not understand what the commotion was all about. At first, I didn't even realize that it was all about me and my birthday, or even that it was my birthday — not even when my name was shouted out in the song. A couple of counsellors grabbed me, tore off my shirt, carried me up to the little dining room stage and started bumping me, to the delight of the other diners. I did not understand the ritual of the bumps, of which I counted eighteen, but combined with the song and my name being shouted, it suddenly dawned on me that it was part of the birthday celebration and that everyone in the dining hall was celebrating my birthday. It was a double surprise — the party itself and the fact that it was the date of my birth, a day that had, up to this time, always been ignored, a day that would pass like any other ordinary day.

It was truly delightful to at last have a birthday party, to be the centre of attention and a minor celebrity, at least for a while, to experience a special pause, a most delicious interruption in the passage of time. It was my special day, and everyone celebrated and greeted me with a smile throughout the day.

My parents didn't have their birthdays celebrated until my brother and I started doing it for them. Their reaction to those celebrations was not very enthusiastic. Offers to celebrate any of their anniversaries were always politely declined with a wry smile, and whenever we insisted, they would simply say, "We are not coming!" It seems to me that they were, at their age, unable to abandon the taboo of counting.

IN SCHOOL AND ON THE STAGE

By 1954, with the help of two mortgages and a loan from the Hebrew Free Loan Society for a down payment, my parents were able to buy a newly built duplex on Plamondon Avenue. A Canadian-born family rented the upper apartment and supported the purchase and the payment of the mortgages. Father turned out to be a good businessman and financial juggler. After several years, my parents also purchased a two-door white Ford vehicle from Sternthal Motors in my name, even though I had no earnings and didn't yet know how to drive a car. Neither did my parents. One day, after a number of driving lessons, my friend Donald Hamilton was teaching me how to parallel park in front of our house, while my mother, the eternal optimist, stood in the entrance, offering her encouraging words: "You will never learn how to drive." By then I knew how to drive and had even taught my father how to drive. Donald was just showing me the trick of parallel parking. Instead of driving himself, my father preferred that I give him lifts and pick him up from work, which I cheerfully did. I even helped him out with his work in the abattoir in the early mornings. Even in later years, before and after my classes at McGill's Faculty of Law, I would help him with his deliveries. Because of this job at the abattoir, the McGill administration provided me with a precious parking permit on the campus grounds, making me the envy of my classmates. To those who inquired how I was so lucky to get a parking permit, I told them it was because I had a wooden leg.

It was through my father that, at nineteen, I got a little job with the Vaad Ha'ir, where I met the rabbis of the city, including Rabbi Herschorn and Rabbi Pinchas Hirschprung, as well as the executive director, Mordechai Peters, who had changed his name from Pietrushka. He was an excellent boss with a wonderful sense of humour. I still remember how difficult it was to supervise the production of kosher food and establishments that served kosher food. Once, it came to our attention that a non-kosher salami was being sold with a forged Vaad Ha'ir certification. I was delegated to purchase a sample and then give it to an actual detective who, with salami in hand, was hired to find the culprit who was manufacturing and distributing the *treyf* salami as kosher with our certification.

Mordechai Peters was a religious man. However, he was also worldly. One of the *shoykhtim*, a ritual slaughterer named Shloyme, was a Jew with long *payes* (sidelocks) and a massive beard. He was able to test the *khalef*, a special knife used for slaughtering, for sharpness and for nicks and chips invisible to the eye by using his tongue. But also, the crotch of his pants was always unbuttoned, completely exposing his privates. I remember Peters pleading with him: "Reb Shloyme, farbahalt di kharpe"—*Reb Shloyme, hide the shame*. I once asked Peters why Shloyme didn't button up; didn't he realize that he was exposing himself? Peters explained it this way: "You see Pinchas, Shloyme is a follower of a saintly, miracle-working rebbe. His rebbe, who is always preoccupied with *dvorim elyoynim*, godly matters, forgets to button up. Shloyme saw his rebbe unbuttoned, and he thought it was part of the religion, so following his rebbe, he deliberately leaves it open."

One day, Peters gave me a special assignment. He tore a Montreal telephone book into two equal parts. He gave me the first half of the telephone book and told me to pick out the Jewish names, telephone them, and ask them where they bought their kosher meat, and if they did not buy kosher meat, I was to ask them why not. I had a little argument with Peters about the name Cowan. Peters thought that behind every Cowan, there was a Jew. I thought otherwise but, following his instructions, I also telephoned all the Cowans. And I got funny answers from the Cowans, mostly "none of your business." I received similar answers from some Jews, even some Jewish Cowans. I didn't argue with the non-Jewish Cowans. I apologized. But I argued with those with Jewish family names, telling them what a fine institution we were and how we needed their support. By buying kosher meat, they would be supporting Jewish life in Montreal. I did manage to convince some to start buying kosher meat, including some secularists.

One conversation brought tears to my eyes — a conversation with Mrs. Rosenberg. After assuring me that she was indeed buying kosher meat, she cried about how her children had turned against God, *arup funem glaykhn veg*, had chosen the wrong path. A few years later I met one of her sons, Harold Ross. He was running a prep school, and it was with his help and guidance that I was prepared for Sir George Williams College. He was secular, but he considered himself Jewish. He was also a chain-smoker, and I saw him smoking on the Sabbath, but I also saw one of his daughters eating matzo on Passover. As for Mrs. Rosenberg's other son, Fred Rose, he was a member of the Canadian Communist Party and was charged and convicted with espionage and sentenced to jail. After he was released, he moved to Poland, where I believe he stayed for the rest of his life.

Peters gave the second half of the telephone book to a woman who thought it was a waste of time to call. She wrote her reports on little cards containing the name, address and telephone number of each person, and the answer to our question. But she didn't bother to call; she made up answers of her own choosing.

The Vaad Ha'ir did not give up easily. We wrote letters to those who said that they were not buying kosher meat, and we urged them to start, providing them with the name of a kosher butcher in their neighbourhood. The whole thing blew up when a number of people from the second half of the telephone book, whom the fine lady had identified as non-buyers of kosher meat, received our letter urging them to switch to kosher. They were indignant, and they called or wrote back that they did have a kosher home and did buy kosher meat. I ended up calling those people with our apologies and started working on the second part of the telephone book. I learned an important lesson from this incident: to be honest and not to cheat because you will eventually be caught. So, I was honest in all my dealings, even when I became a lawyer. Not so much because I was actually honest, but because I was a coward, afraid of being caught.

I graduated from the Jewish Teachers Seminary after I had learned from some wonderful teachers like Yankev Zipper, Shimshon Dunsky and Yisroel Rabinovitch, who made *dikduk* (Hebrew grammar) interesting and exciting, and, of course, Irving Layton, who taught us greenhorns English. I taught Grades 2 and 4 at the Solomon Schechter School, where Pinchas Lifshitz was principal, for four years. At the same time, I decided to go back to school, and I was accepted as a mature student at Sir George Williams, where I earned my bachelor's degree in literature, philosophy and political science. Considering entering the legal profession, I also took a course in beginners' Latin, thinking it would be useful if I were to become a lawyer. Sir George Williams was a lifesaver in terms of advancing my education, accepting me without having a high school graduation certificate.

I had very little income, but thanks to my parents, who provided me with a home and with encouragement, after receiving my degree, I stopped working and applied to the McGill Faculty of Law. I had first decided I would be a rabbi and I applied for entrance to the Jewish Theological Seminary of America in New York to study for the rabbinate. On account of some strange reasoning on my part, I changed my given name from Pinchas to Percy at this point. I travelled to New York and did my entrance exams, consisting of oral and written tests. I particularly remember the exam I had on Talmud with the world-famous scholar Hillel Bavli. I chose the tractate of Brokhes, which begins with the matter: *M'eymosay* — from when does one recite the evening Shema. There are at least half a dozen schools of thought and opinions about that. But even though Bavli thought I had picked the easiest tractate in the whole Talmud (he was right) and I was openly accused of that, I was accepted. After a torturous and agonizing inner struggle, I decided that I was too weak in my faith to preach religion to others. I did not have the strength and conviction to be a religious preacher.

I decided on law and applied to McGill in 1954. I was accepted. In the first year, out of eighty-two students, only thirty-two passed. There were some very bright and exceptional students in my class. Some of them became judges, politicians and public figures. One of the students in the first year was Leonard Cohen, but he never showed up to the second year. Instead of becoming a lawyer, he decided to become a world-famous poet and balladeer. Still thinking of myself as a simpleton (in light of my mother's comments relating to my birth in the month of Tammuz), I was terribly worried about my ability to graduate from law school, particularly considering the fact that the graduates of the class of '58 were so very bright. But I passed the first year, and I did very well in some of the courses, especially in constitutional law with F.R. Scott. I graduated with a BCL in 1958, and it was the proudest moment in my life.

I was in the middle of studying for my bar exams when, at the invitation of a friend, Bernard Herman, I took a break and ended up watching a rehearsal of a Yiddish play by Sholem Aleichem, *Dos groyse gevins* (The Lottery), directed by Dora Wasserman. She was the great persuader and, when needed, a shameless flatterer. She asked me to read the part of the matchmaker Soloveitchik, which she kept on assuring me was a part I was made for, saying how happy she was that she had kept it open. I couldn't do both — the bar and the play. But I chose my first love, going all the way back to Soviet school, where I had participated in plays and tasted the stage. I didn't require much persuasion or flattery from Dora. I deferred the bar exams for six months and chose to be in *The Lottery*.

It may have been irresponsible of me to defer the exams but I believe, in hindsight, that the decision may have been therapeutic, may have prevented a nervous breakdown and saved my life. As soon as I decided to be in the play and defer the exams, I felt a heavy weight drop off my shoulders. I wasn't tense, and I was able to breathe again and even enjoy the weather. As soon as I finished with the play, I went back to my books, studying for the bar. But now I was relaxed, confident and felt I had all the time in the world to study and prepare. The six months of the deferral expired. I travelled to Quebec City by train the day before the exam, stayed overnight in a hotel next to the courthouse, wrote the exams in the morning and afternoon, and then travelled back home in the evening. I passed the exams. It was a long time ago. I do not remember the questions or the answers or a great deal of the law that was dealt with in the exams. But I still remember the colourful spittoons at the courthouse, placed in strategic spots all over the floor. When I visited the Quebec courthouse as a lawyer years later, I noticed that the spittoons had been removed, and I wondered what happened to the spitters afterwards.

At my graduation from law school on the McGill campus, which my mother attended, I told her that it was her doing and that she deserved all the credit, reminding her that my education had started with her dragging me before Wiseman and Braverman. I know, had I refused to walk to those institutions of learning she was prepared to lift me up and carry me, just as she had across the muddy puddles when I was a spoiled child.

~

After working many jobs, including helping my father at the abattoir, as a shipper for Eaton's, in a few restaurants and bakeries, at the Vaad Ha'ir, at the Jewish public library under David Rome and as a teacher at Solomon Schechter, I lived, breathed and worked as an amateur

Yiddish actor and professional attorney for five decades. Quite often, I would be in a dress rehearsal till 4:00 a.m. and would then have to plead a case later in the morning, followed by an evening performance on opening night. I was never paid to be an actor and I earned my living as a lawyer. I had enough to get married, raise a family and live in relative comfort — take vacations, travel, go to concerts and the theatre.

I enjoyed being a lawyer. I enjoyed working with people, being of help, solving problems and doing research in preparation for trials. I had wonderful partners and sometimes we would turn the office into a social club and have discussions and lunches together. (Regretfully, one of my partners, Bernard Gardner, died of a massive heart attack during one of those lunches.) Thanks to one of my American clients who had real estate investments all over Quebec, for a time I was involved in proceedings throughout the province, and I had trials in almost every judicial jurisdiction, which provided me with the opportunity to travel throughout most of the province.

As for my acting, it was sheer pleasure, without the strain that working as a lawyer entailed. In court, you sometimes, maybe deservedly, lose. But you never lose on stage; you always win. Being on stage, unfettered by your dignity, losing your shyness, assuming in mind and body a different life and persona than your own, portraying the different characters in Jewish literature, which I studied and loved, provided a satisfaction equal to winning a case, maybe even greater. We actors were loved and applauded by the audience. In court, arguing a winning case with some humour, I was applauded only once, which was stopped by the judge after his own brief chuckle. I was even awarded the J.I. Segal Award for my artistic efforts and achievements on the Yiddish stage. In my legal practice I travelled all over Quebec, once to Russia and once to New York City. With the Yiddish theatre, I travelled to many cities in Canada, and to other countries: Israel, Switzerland, France, Russia, Austria, Ukraine and the United States.

Visiting Ukraine was an emotional roller coaster, between the good and the bad, the happy and the sad. This was the country where I had been born and had experienced, as a child, the cruellest taste of inhumanity under a vicious German occupation; and it was the place where life had been wonderful and fulfilling. From the distance of Kyiv, which I had never visited before, I thought of Kortelisy and remembered the good times, whether it was under the Polish or Soviet regimes. The tiny tucked-away corner in western Ukraine had been my happy home, the place of a real, though short, childhood, filled with family that loved and cared for me. In Kyiv I didn't see any traffic signs with the Kortelisy name on it. But, I saw a sign with the name of Kowel on it, which brought tears to my eyes.

Even though I had never seen Kyiv or Odessa before, when visiting those two cities, everything, besides the Soviet symbols and monuments, was so familiar — the buildings, the streets and the people. I remembered it all from my readings of Mendele Mocher Sforim, Sholem Aleichem and other Yiddish authors. After all, this had been the heart and cradle of Yiddish life and literature and Jewish revival. This was the part of the world where Hovevei Zion (Lovers of Zion) had started and the voices of Ahad Ha'am, Trumpeldor, Jabotinsky and Pinsker were heard. And, considering the warm receptions we received in both cities and wonderful meetings we had with some of the Jewish literati and leadership, the thought that there might be a Jewish and Yiddish revival in Ukraine crossed my mind.

In Kyiv we played in a community centre called the Officers' Club, which had a theatre and a stage, and where I noticed busts of Stalin and Lenin tucked away, out of sight. In the audience there were men and women, most likely Jewish, in army uniforms, their chests completely covered in medals. Similarly, in Odessa, Jewish audiences freely came to see Yiddish theatre. There were receptions after the performances and inspiring speeches, not about Stalin or Lenin, but about the revival of Yiddish and Jewish culture. Seeing all this, I thought that somehow there would again be Jewish life in Ukraine and the Soviet Union. I guess I must have picked up the biblical vision of the revival of the dead from my cheder years, from the prophet Ezekiel, chapter 37, where he speaks of a great revival. After all the severe punishments and curses of the Jews, God speaks to the dry bones and gives them flesh. I thought that this might also be a prophecy foretelling the revival of the Jews in Ukraine and the Soviet Union. I was naive. I saw in a Kyiv square a huge statue of Bohdan Khmelnytsky, who had directed the ruthless massacre of Jews in the years 1648 and 1649, and I was overtaken by a terrible fear and an urge to run. I left the park as quickly as I could.

SECOND SON

As the years passed, Father continued to retell the miracles of his escape from the massacre in Ratno with increasing conviction. But he still could not explain — maybe he did not need an explanation — why God would allow the killings of the Jews, saving some and murdering others.

"Tayerer Tateh"—*Dear Father*, I would say. "You are defying, contradicting and denying your own logic."

"How's that, my son?"

"Just listen to yourself," I would continue with some cockiness. "You believe in a great, invisible, righteous God, who judges fairly his righteous and humble believers, and others, equally, with the same measure. He surely judges with greater fairness than our earthly courts, where I earn my living and see firsthand the wheels of justice turning, not always in the right direction" — adding the words "especially when I lose" for a touch of humour. "Unlike human courts, the Almighty knows and sees everything. He doesn't depend on witnesses, who may sometimes, even without malice, be wrong and even deliberately lie. He doesn't miss a thing and has all the evidence and facts, even those facts that have not yet happened. And I know you believe that those who perished in Ratno and Kortelisy were as righteous as you were and equally deserving to survive. Why did they perish, if God's judgment is fair and equal for all and more righteous than human courts and judges? The only conclusion I can arrive at, in view of the horrible events and based on your logic, is that there was no God and, if there was a God, He is a cruel God and He had nothing to do with your escape. It was you and you alone — your determination to live. Or, you were just lucky. You made the right moves at the right time."

And I would continue: "If there is a good and merciful God and everything moves in accordance with His will, why is there so much evil and injustice in the world? Why do babies die, and why is there sickness altogether? The righteous man does not always flourish like a date palm and grow tall like a cedar in Lebanon, as it is written in Psalm 92."

At this point, Father understood me well, and he didn't like what I was saying about God. He would become terribly angry. In my father's eyes, I had become not only the third son in the Haggadah, as I had been dubbed by my dear mother, but now also the second son — the *roshe*, the wicked one. With my words, I withdrew from the community and became a *kofar b'iker,* denying the essential and basic principles of my faith. In reaction, Father would jump up, and in a pleading voice, almost in tears, make his usual, oldest, most powerful and standard Orthodox religious argument — the same response reserved for any difficult question that truly has no answer, including questions relating to the existence or non-existence of a Creator. He would jump up and say, "Why? Why? Why? How do I know why? You think you know all the answers and the ways of the Almighty. You won't find an answer in *dayne narishe goyishe bikhlekh un filosofyies*, your silly secular books and philosophies. When, God be willing, the Messiah will come, all the difficult and unanswered questions will be answered and all problems will be resolved. Everything will be explained to you *apikorsim*, you heretics."

~

My parents, who had always been close to each other and their children, but who never publicly demonstrated affection or made a fuss over us, in their old age finally learned to hug their grandchildren. Or maybe, more correctly, they learned to respond with hugs to the hugs of the grandchildren. As a child, my daughter, Happy, would talk to her Pepe, her grandfather, and would try very hard to teach him to say, "I love you." She would repeat again and again, "Pepe, say it. Say I love you." The words just would not come out of his mouth. Why say the obvious, just sentimental mush? Of course he loved her. Years later, when he was in the hospital, Happy would visit him and help him with his meals. "Pepe, do you like the food?" she would ask him. He could not bring himself to say that he liked the food. His standard reply would be, "I like you better." Later on, he developed a taste for what he called banalities. Breaking with tradition and superstition, Father enjoyed the celebration of his ninetieth birthday while in the hospital, very much like I did my eighteenth in Camp Kindervelt. But, still fettered by superstition, he participated and celebrated with a great deal of restraint and reservation, not showing too much exuberance.

SURVIVOR

I consider myself very lucky and am moderately proud of my modest achievements in life. I had the strength to survive the war as a child — though really through the efforts of my parents — and, in adulthood, I first survived my divorce and then cancer. As a young man, I was too comfortable in my parents' home to think about marriage. But when I did marry, the marriage was good, and three beautiful children arrived in quick succession: Jonathan, Robert and Happy. Then one day, on a Sunday morning, while I was watching cartoons with the children, I learned that my marriage was over. It was a shock; I thought I would never survive. I thought of the terrible stigma attached to divorce, and I walked the streets and public places with the mark of Cain on my forehead. In my practice I handled many divorces, and they were never pleasant. I was hoping for reconciliation, and we went for sessions with social workers and psychologists, but in the end we were divorced.

My children survived the divorce and grew up well and succeeded in their endeavours. They managed to maintain a balanced and good relationship with me and their mother, notwithstanding the divorce. They are happy, as am I, with their spouses and my grandchildren. I am also happy with my partner in life for the last twenty-six years, Gisele Rucker.

The other shock, the diagnosis of colon cancer at age seventy-four, was the second-worst piece of news I had to deal with. I wasn't ready to die. I could not run or hide from the scourge of cancer as I had from the murderous German soldiers, and I could not turn to my childhood fantasy that Jews don't die. Again I was lucky and survived. After surgery, my wonderful surgeon, Dr. Nancy Morin, came into my room, sat on my bed, and calmly told me that the cancerous part of my colon had been removed and I would not require chemotherapy or any other therapy. I was completely cured of cancer. And now, left with a "semicolon," I have been free of cancer for fifteen years.

I willingly retired from the legal practice and was also retired from the stage, which was difficult to accept. It was like being thrown out of my own house. I miss both law and acting, and it took me a while to get used to retirement. For a number of years, throughout the day, I would walk around with a feeling of abandonment and failure. There was always gnawing at my brain the feeling that I was missing something, without knowing what. I have since recovered and try to enjoy my time. I used to have similar feelings, of something missing in my day, when I started skipping the daily practice of putting on *tefillin*, phylacteries. Eventually I got used to it.

~

The older I get the more I think about my childhood and how we lived in constant fear under the Germans. My heart still sinks and I am overtaken by fear when I hear the sound of a motorcycle, which always announced the arrival of German soldiers. I also still remember receiving my first boots, my parents doting over me, helping me to put them on and teaching me how to make a knot. It was those boots I left at home for fear of spoiling the leather when we hid in the wet marshes.

My mother died in 1984, on the first day of Chanukah. The night before, *erev* Chanukah, I visited her in the hospital. She wanted to hear Father recite the blessing over the candles. I telephoned home and over the receiver she listened to Father recite the blessings and sing Ma'oz Tzur. The next day, she passed away at age seventy-six.

Father died in 1999 on the twenty-third day of the month of Adar at age ninety-five. I left work in the early afternoon to visit him at the hospital. He died in front of me that same afternoon, bravely, the way he had lived. He never lost the expression of confidence and strength in his face, always facing death without fear. When he died, I stood for a while, frozen over his dead body. Then I pulled the bedsheet over his face, exposing his legs. I looked at his legs, still carrying the colour of life, and I thought of the miles and miles those legs had walked through forests and villages, in all weather, carrying heavy sacks of potatoes to feed his family.

I observe the yahrzeits, the yearly anniversaries of the deaths of my wonderful and devoted parents, by lighting a memorial candle, as is the custom. I have accepted their deaths and am not tortured. I am, however, still tortured by the murders of my grandparents and uncles, even though they happened many years before the deaths of my parents. I have horrible visions of my grandfather Meyer, my uncles Shmilke and Ben-Tsion and the other Jews of Ratno and Kortelisy standing before their graves about to be shot. I can still visualize the murder, after Havdalah, of my zeyde Berchik and bobeh Frumeh. I cannot recover from the horrible sight of the killings in the marshes and the sounds of the screams of Shema Yisroel. I will for the rest of my life be a witness to depravity, to man's inhumanity to man, even though I only experienced a small sample of pure evil, of the vast scope of industrialized murder. I cannot forget. I am doomed to remember and suffer with these memories.

I will not even attempt to answer why and how it happened. There is no answer. It is beyond any rational explanation. I am not qualified to present an analysis of antisemitism, which culminated in genocide, the worst cruelty toward the Jewish people or any other people. Even though throughout our history, there have been numerous brutal and despicable acts perpetrated against Jews who live in the Muslim and

Christian worlds, it is not within the scope of my story to touch on those. My story is only a small sample of what the Holocaust was — the story of the terrible destruction of a small village whose inhabitants were murdered, some only because they were Jews. Although, after the war, my family found a good home in Canada, I still feel uprooted and I will always think of Kortelisy as my home, where my basic beliefs and mindsets were formed. I feel possessed, maybe unreasonably, by a strong nostalgia for my village, which I should have put behind me a long time ago. The older I get, the more controlling and forceful it becomes; I am focused on a little boy in a tiny village and on a community that is forever in the past.

GLOSSARY

Ahad Ha'am (1856–1927; Hebrew, "one of the people") The pen name of Asher Ginsberg, an influential Zionist leader and writer from Ukraine. He believed that Zionism should focus on the revival of Hebrew and on the Land of Israel as the centre of a cultural and spiritual renaissance.

Aleichem, Sholem (Shalom Rabinovitz; 1859–1916) A prolific and beloved writer of modern Yiddish literature who raised the cultural status of Yiddish writing through his writing, publishing and literary criticism. From Ukraine, Sholem Aleichem wrote in Hebrew, Yiddish and Russian. His plays, novels and humorous stories about shtetl life touch on themes of antisemitism, immigration, Zionism and modernity and have been translated into dozens of languages. The 1964 hit musical *Fiddler on the Roof* was based on his collection of stories *Tevye der milkhiker* (Tevye the Dairyman).

American Jewish Joint Distribution Committee (JDC) Colloquially known as the Joint, the JDC was a charitable organization founded in 1914 to provide humanitarian assistance and relief to Jews all over the world in times of crisis. It provided material support for persecuted Jews in Germany and other Nazi-occupied territories and facilitated their immigration to neutral countries such as Portugal and Turkey. Between 1939 and 1944, Joint officials helped close to 81,000 European Jews find asylum in various parts of the world. Between 1944 and 1947, the JDC assisted more than 100,000 refugees living in DP camps by offering retraining programs, cultural activities and financial assistance for emigration.

American Zone One of four zones in Germany administered by the Allied powers between 1945 and 1949. The other three zones were administered by Britain, France and the Soviet Union.

Asch, Sholem (1880–1957) A prominent and sometimes controversial Yiddish novelist and playwright from Poland. Asch settled in New York in 1914 and became a writer for the Yiddish newspaper *Forverts* (The Forward). His short stories and novels depict the lives of Jews in Eastern Europe and explore themes of faith, love and spirituality, as well as the conflicts experienced by Jewish immigrants in America. Asch was one of the founders of the American Jewish Joint Distribution Committee (JDC). *See also* American Jewish Joint Distribution Committee.

Babi Yar A ravine on the northwest outskirts of Kyiv, Ukraine, that was the site of mass killings during the Holocaust. On September 29–30, 1941, Babi Yar was the site of one of the Nazis' largest mass murders, with over 33,000 Jews murdered by Einsatzgruppen (mobile killing units) and other German and Ukrainian forces. It is estimated that 100,000 Jews, Roma, Soviet officials and prisoners of war were murdered in Babi Yar during the German occupation of Kyiv.

Ded Moroz (Russian; Grandfather Frost) The Slavic version of Santa Claus, a mythical figure who was associated with winter and giving presents to children. Ded Moroz was banned by the Bolsheviks as a religious figure but was reinstated by Stalin and has become an important element of Soviet winter festivities, specifically on New Year's Eve.

feldsher (from German; field surgeon) A healer or folk doctor. *Feldshers* originally served as field medics in the German army in the seventeenth century and then began to practise in rural settings across Eastern Europe, where trained physicians were scarce. Most rural communities had at least one *feldsher*, some of whom had partial medical training and were licensed. *Feldshers* practised cupping, blood-letting and other medical interventions of the time, as well as folk remedies and magical cures for physical, emotional and spiritual ailments. The term is still used in some Eastern European countries to refer to paramedical workers.

Feter Yishmoel (Yiddish; Uncle Ishmael) A reference to the Arab population of Palestine. In Jewish and Muslim traditions, the biblical patriarch Abraham's two sons, Ishmael and Isaac, are the progenitors of Arabs and Jews respectively, making Arabs the descendants of "Uncle Ishmael."

Great Famine A famine caused by Stalin and the Communist Party in Soviet Ukraine in 1932–1933, also known as the Holodomor ("death inflicted by starvation" in Ukrainian). After Stalin's decision to collectivize farms, peasants in Ukraine rebelled, and the Communist Party, worried about an uprising, banned many areas in Ukraine from receiving food, resulting in mass starvation. An estimated 3.9 million Ukrainians died of starvation during this time, and Soviet policies and restrictions of food supply and population movements were significant factors in the deaths. The famine was accompanied by a program of persecution and repression of Ukrainian language and culture. The Soviet authorities suppressed information about the famine, and most details only came to light after the collapse of the Soviet Union. The Holodomor was recognized as a genocide by Ukraine in 2006 and other countries have followed suit since then.

Hovevei Zion (Hebrew; Lovers of Zion) Followers of Hibbat Zion (Love of Zion), an association of organizations established in Eastern Europe in the 1880s to advance a national identity for the Jewish people and to promote Jewish agricultural settlement in the Land of Israel. The movement was the forerunner of political Zionism.

Jabotinsky, Vladimir Ze'ev (1880–1940) A Zionist activist, writer and leader who split from the official Zionist movement in Europe to found the Revisionist Zionist party in 1925. He also founded a new branch of nationalist Zionism, the New Zionist Organization (NZO), or National Military Organization, in 1935. Jabotinsky advocated for the mass immigration of European Jews to British Mandate Palestine, promoting the ideals of Jewish self-defence and self-determination, and for Jewish sovereignty over the entire territory of the British Mandate. In 1937, he became the commander of the Irgun Zva'i Leumi (Irgun), which carried out armed struggles against the British and the Arabs in Palestine between 1937 and 1948.

Khmelnytsky, Bohdan (c. 1595–1657) A Cossack officer who led a series of uprisings to free Ukraine from Polish domination. The Khmelnytsky Uprisings (1648–1657) were accompanied by brutal attacks on Jews, who were seen to be associated with the Polish nobility and were frequently the target of violence during times of unrest. It is estimated that tens of thousands of Jews were violently murdered, thousands fled and many Jews were sold into slavery. The violence against Jews occurred mostly during the first years of the uprising, which became known in Jewish communities as Gzeyres Takh-Vetat (Yiddish for the "[evil] decrees of 1648–1649"). The destruction of numerous thriving Jewish communities in Ukraine had a devastating impact on Eastern European Jewry and is seen by many as one of the great calamities in Jewish history.

Kishinev pogrom An anti-Jewish attack that took place in April 1903 in Kishinev, a city in the southwest of the Russian Empire. The pogrom was instigated by a blood libel — the false accusation that Jews kill Christian children to use their blood for ritual purposes. Over two days, local residents murdered 49 Jews, raped and injured hundreds more, and ransacked Jewish homes and businesses. The first pogrom of the twentieth century, and the first to be photographed and well-documented, the Kishinev pogrom came to the attention of the international community and became synonymous with Jewish persecution.

Komsomol (Russian; abbreviation of Vsesoyuzny Leninsky Kommunisticheskiy Soyuz Molodyozhi; All-Union Leninist Communist League of Youth) The youth movement of the Soviet Communist Party established in 1918 and geared toward youths between fourteen and twenty-eight. The Komsomol mainly functioned as a means of transmitting Party values to future members. Members were frequently favoured over non-members for scholarships and employment; becoming a young officer in the Komsomol was often seen as a good way to rise in the Party ranks.

kulak (Russian) A term used in the Soviet Union to refer to a class of people who owned a certain amount of land and were considered prosperous. During Joseph Stalin's campaign of forced collectivization, the kulaks were persecuted, with their property confiscated and many deported to camps in Siberia.

mezuzah (Hebrew; doorpost) The small piece of parchment containing the text of the central Jewish prayer, the Shema, which has been handwritten in ink by a scribe. Many Jews place this parchment on the doorposts of their homes, often in decorative cases.

Narodowe Siły Zbrojne (NSZ; National Armed Forces) An underground Polish right-wing resistance organization established in 1942 to fight the German occupation, Soviet partisans and communists. The NSZ continued to carry out attacks on communist institutions after the war and on Jews who were returning to their homes in Poland after the Holocaust.

New Soviet Man (also New Soviet Person) The ideal human being as conceived of by the Bolsheviks in the early twentieth century who was thought would emerge from and embody the moral superiority of Communist society. The New Soviet Man would be educated, strong, selfless, hard-working and able to master his own nature and the environment.

NKVD (Russian; acronym for Narodnyi Komissariat Vnutrennikh Del; People's Commissariat for Internal Affairs) The Soviet Union's security agency, secret police and intelligence agency from 1934 to 1946. The organization's dual purpose was to defend the USSR from external dangers from foreign powers and to protect the Communist Party from perceived dangers within.

Paderewski, Ignacy Jan (1860–1941) Polish musician, composer, philanthropist and politician who championed Polish independence and served as prime minister of Poland in 1919.

phylacteries (in Hebrew, *tefillin*) A pair of black leather boxes containing scrolls of parchment inscribed with Bible verses and traditionally worn by Jewish men on the arm and forehead at prescribed times of prayer as a symbol of the covenantal relationship with God.

Piłsudski, Józef (1867–1935) Polish socialist leader and revolutionary who was the first head of state of the newly independent Poland, from 1918–1922, after more than a century of Poland's partition between Russia, Austria and Prussia. Piłsudski organized a coup d'etat in 1926, after which he served as minister of defence and remained politically powerful and popular among Polish citizens, including many Jews because of his opposition to antisemitism. Piłsudski attempted to form alliances with western powers and other European countries and signed non-aggression pacts with the Soviet Union and Germany in 1932 and 1934 respectively.

Pinsker, Leon (Lev) (1821–1891) A Polish-Russian Jewish physician and leader of the Hibbat Zion movement. Pinsker promoted the integration of Jews into Russian society until the anti-Jewish riots and pogroms in Russia in the 1870s and 1880s changed his views. In 1882, he published a pamphlet, *Autoemancipation*, in which he argued that antisemitism was deeply embedded in European society and that the only solution for Jews was to establish their own homeland. *See also* Hovevei Zion.

Purim (Hebrew; lots) The Jewish holiday that celebrates the Jews' escape from annihilation in Persia. The Purim story recounts how Haman, advisor to the King of Persia, planned to rid Persia of Jews, and how Queen Esther and her cousin Mordecai foiled Haman's plot by convincing the king to save the Jews. During the Purim festivities, people dress up in costumes, feast, read the story of Purim and send gifts of food and money to those in need.

Red Sea (splitting of) The miraculous event recounted in the book of Exodus where God parted the Red Sea so that the Children of Israel, who were fleeing slavery in Egypt, could pass through and escape the pursuing Egyptian army.

Roma (singular male, Rom; singular female, Romni) A traditionally itinerant ethnic group originally from northern India and primarily located in Central and Eastern Europe. The Roma, who have been referred to as Gypsies (now considered a pejorative term), have often lived on the fringes of society and been subject to persecution. During the Holocaust, which the Roma refer to as the Porajmos — the destruction or devouring — Roma were stripped of their citizenship under the Nuremberg Laws and were targeted for death under Hitler's race policies. It is estimated that between 220,000 and 500,000 Roma were murdered in the Holocaust. Roma Holocaust Memorial Day is commemorated on August 2.

Rydz-Śmigły, Edward (1886–1941) Marshal of Poland and Commander-in-Chief of Poland's armed forces until Poland fell to the Germans in 1939.

seder (Hebrew; order) A ritual meal celebrated at the beginning of the festival of Passover. A traditional seder involves reading the Haggadah, which tells the story of the Israelite slaves' exodus from Egypt; drinking four cups of wine; eating matzah and other symbolic foods that are arranged on a special seder plate; partaking in a festive meal; and singing traditional songs.

Shavuos (also Shavuot; Hebrew; weeks) A Jewish festival celebrating the giving of the Ten Commandments at Mount Sinai. Shavuos occurs seven weeks after the first Passover seder.

Simchas Torah (also Simchat Torah; Hebrew; rejoicing in the Torah) The holiday that marks the end of the annual cycle of readings from the Torah and the beginning of a new one. The holiday is celebrated in synagogue by singing and dancing with the Torah scrolls.

Stalin Constitution (Also known as the 1936 Constitution of the Soviet Union) The second constitution of the Soviet Union, adopted into law on December 5, 1936, to replace the constitution of 1924. The constitution provided a new framework for the Soviet government that was in place until 1977. It purportedly reflected the successful spread of socialism and civil rights to all citizens of the Soviet Union and guaranteed universal suffrage. In reality, it centralized the power of the Communist Party and its adoption was followed immediately by a campaign of political repression.

sukeh *See* Sukkos

Sukkos (also Sukkot; Hebrew; Feast of Tabernacles) An autumn harvest festival that recalls the forty years during which the ancient Israelites wandered in the desert after their exodus from slavery in Egypt. The holiday lasts for seven days, during which Jews traditionally eat meals in a sukkah (or *sukeh*, in Yiddish), a temporary structure covered with a roof made from leaves or branches.

Torquemada, Tomás de (1420–1498) A Spanish cleric and advisor to Queen Isabella I, and the first grand inquisitor of Spain during the Spanish Inquisition, which tortured and burned those who did not believe in Christianity. Known for his cruelty, Torquemada was responsible for the deaths of thousands of Jews who had been forced to convert to Christianity but practised Judaism in secret (Crypto-Jews or Conversos), as well as other nonbelievers. Torquemada supported the expulsion of Jews from Spain in 1492.

Trumpeldor, Joseph (1880–1920) An early Zionist activist from Russia who died defending Tel Hai, a settlement in British Mandate Palestine, and is regarded as a Zionist national hero. While still in Russia in 1918, he founded HeHalutz, a youth organization to settle young people in the Land of Israel.

Zerubavel, Ya'akov (1886–1967) A Labor Zionist leader and journalist from Ukraine. Zerubavel immigrated to Palestine in 1910, where he was a leader in the Labor Zionist movement Poalei Zion and edited the movement's Hebrew newspaper. He fled the country after he was imprisoned for his criticism of the Turkish authorities and returned to Russia and Poland, where he became the editor of a Yiddish newspaper. He immigrated to British Mandate Palestine in 1935 and continued to publish Yiddish-language publications.

PHOTOGRAPHS

1

2

3

4

1 Pinchas's great-grandfather Eliyahu Rothchild. Ratno, circa 1800.

2 Pinchas's paternal grandfather, Meyer Blitt. Kowel, 1905.

3 Pinchas's maternal grandmother, Frumeh Ruttenberg, with Pinchas's mother, Adele (standing), and Adele's cousin. Kowel, circa 1911.

4 Pinchas's mother with his uncle Yerakhmiel. Kortelisy, circa 1926.

1

2

3

1 Pinchas's uncle Shmilke Blitt. An inscription on the back of the photo reads in Yiddish, "In remembrance, for my friends in America I send my picture as a sign of friendship." (Translated by Pinchas Blitt.) Kortelisy, 1938.

2 Pinchas's uncle Ben-Tsion Ruttenberg. Ben-Tsion gave this picture to a relative who was leaving Kortelisy for South America. On the back, Ben-Tsion wrote a Hebrew rhyme: "Go in peace on your road and arrive quickly on your morrow, may your road be lucky and escape all sorrow." (Translated by Pinchas Blitt.) Kortelisy, February 15, 1938.

3 A group of friends and relatives from Kortelisy and Ratno, including Pinchas's uncle Moyshe-Dovid Blitt and his wife (third and fourth from the left), his uncle Yerakhmiel (centre, back), and his uncle Shmilke (far right). Kortelisy, 1935.

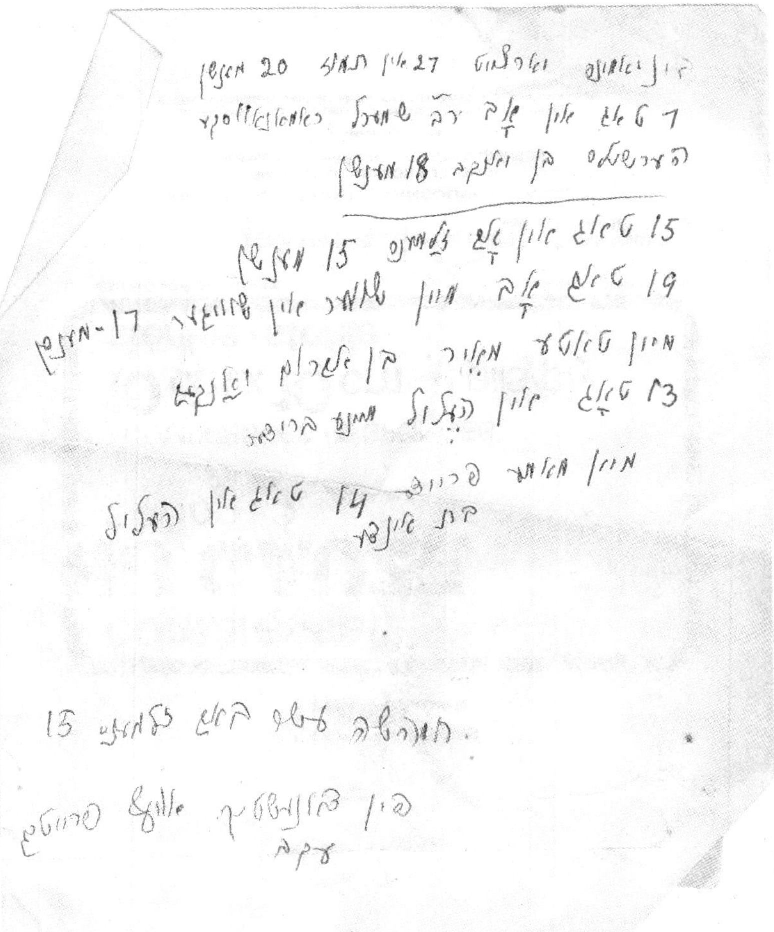

One of Pinchas's father's notes, in Yiddish, marking the dates and names of relatives and neighbours who were killed. He recorded the Hebrew dates, how many people were killed and names of some of the dead, listed by first name, ben or bat (son or daughter of) and a parent's first name. The dates listed range from July 29 to August 1, 1942. The note reads:

Binyamin's yahrzeit 27 Tammuz 20 people / 7th of Av Reb Shmerl Romanowski Hershele ben Yakov

---

15th Av Zalmen 15 people / 19th day Av my father-in-law and mother-in-law 17 people / My father Meyer ben Avram Yakov / 13th of Elul my brother / My mother Freyde bat Hinda 14th day of Elul / 15th Av Zalmen 15 / from Thursday to Friday / Eikev [the weekly Torah portion of the week these murders took place]

1

2

3

1 Pinchas standing proudly with his bike after learning how to ride in the Bindermichl DP camp. Linz, Austria, 1946.

2 Pinchas carrying a flag to a demonstration at the Bindermichl DP camp. Linz, 1946.

3 Pinchas (standing second from right) with other students in the Bindermichl DP camp and the emissary from Palestine (sitting third from right) who taught the history of Zionism. Linz, 1946.

1

2

1 Pinchas's family and one of the women who lived with them in the Bindermichl DP camp, Magda. From left to right: Pinchas's father, Mordechai-Leib (Leiba); his mother, Adele; his brother, Laizer; Pinchas; and Magda. Pinchas's family kept in touch with Magda after they, and later Magda, moved to Canada. Linz, 1946.

2 Pinchas (second from the right) with some of his friends at the ORT school near the Bindermichl DP camp. Linz, 1947.

1

2

1 Pinchas studying electro-engineering at the ORT school near the Bindermichl DP camp. 1947.

2 Pinchas receiving his diploma in electro-engineering from Mr. Zitzer, the director of the ORT school near the Bindermichl DP camp. 1947.

1

2

1 A demonstration against the British in the Bindermichl DP camp, during which Pinchas read a poem he had written. Pinchas can be seen in conversation with Simon Wiesenthal in the middleground of this picture. Linz, 1947.

2 A group of students from the Jewish Teachers Seminary standing in front of the Peretz Shule on Duluth Street with their teachers Yankev Zipper (far right) and his brother Yekhiel Shtern (far left). Pinchas is standing at the back, second from the left. Montreal, circa 1949.

1

2

1 Pinchas (centre, back) and his mother (in front of him to the left) and father (far right) with relatives from New York. Montreal, 1948.

2 Pinchas and his mother in front of the duplex they bought in Montreal, 1954.

1

2

3

1 & 2 Pinchas at his graduation from the McGill Faculty of Law. His mother looks on with pride as he shows his diploma to well-wishers. Montreal, 1958.

3 Pinchas's mother and father. Israel, 1973.

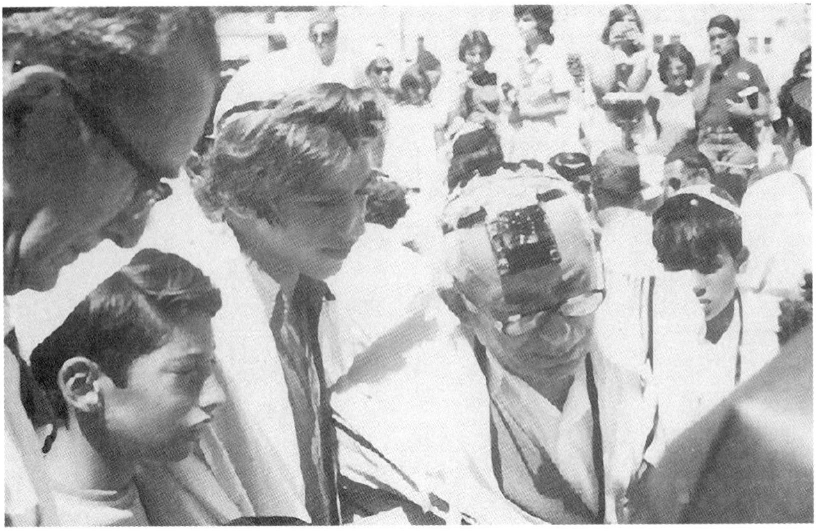

1

2

3

1 The bar mitzvah of Pinchas's nephew Dubi Blitt at the Kotel, the Western Wall. Left to right: Dubi's maternal grandfather, Lou Malus; Pinchas's nephew Yaneev; Dubi; and Pinchas's father. Jerusalem, 1973.

2 Pinchas's father and mother with Laizer's sons, Yaneev and Dubi. Israel, 1973.

3 Pinchas and his son Jonathan, leaving a *kvitl* (a note with a prayer) at the Kotel, the Western Wall. Jerusalem, 1977.

1

2

1 A replica of the shelter Pinchas and his family made while hiding from the Nazis. Pinchas reconstructed the shelter with his children while on vacation in Vermont in the 1970s.

2 Pinchas's father lighting Chanukah candles with Pinchas's children. Left to right: Jonathan, Robert and Happy. Montreal, 1980.

1

2

3

1 Pinchas playing the role of Reb Yosef Loksh in *The Sages of Chelm*, by Abraham Shulman. Montreal, 1978. Photo courtesy of Ron Diamond.

2 Pinchas playing the titular role in the play *Uncle Moses*, by Sholem Asch. Montreal, 1980. Photo courtesy of Ron Diamond.

3 Pinchas and his life partner, Gisele, in a performance of Isaac Bashevis Singer's *The Ball* at the Saidye Bronfman Centre (now the Segal Centre for Performing Arts). Montreal, 1988. Photo courtesy of Ron Diamond.

1

2

3

4

1 Pinchas in the airport, heading out on tour with the Dora Wasserman Yiddish Theatre group. Montreal, 1990.

2 Pinchas at the Babi Yar memorial near Kyiv while on tour with his Yiddish theatre group. Soviet Ukraine, 1990.

3 Pinchas and his brother, Laizer, cooking together. Montreal, 1997.

4 Pinchas and Gisele. Montreal, 2000.

1

2

1 Pinchas's father's 92nd birthday at the Jewish General Hospital, with Pinchas's daughter, Happy, doing all the preparations. Montreal, 1996.

2 Pinchas's children Happy (left) and Jonathan (right) with his father at a Passover seder. Montreal, 1998.

1

2

3

1 Pinchas with his sons, Jonathan (left) and Robert (centre), at Robert's wedding. Cleveland, Ohio, 2006.

2 Pinchas and his son Jonathan. Montreal, 2011.

3 Pinchas and his daughter, Happy, at her wedding. New York, 2012.

1

2

3

1 Pinchas with his family at a birthday celebration. Seated (left to right): Pinchas's grandson Idan, Pinchas, Pinchas's grandsons Noah and Abe, and his daughter-in-law, Stephanie. Standing (left to right): Pinchas's partner, Gisele; his daughter, Happy, and son-in-law, David, holding their daughters, Rebecca and Juliette. Hilton Head, South Carolina, 2016.

2 Pinchas's son Robert with his wife, Stephanie, and children (left to right) Idan, Abe and Noah. Knoxville, Tennessee, 2018.

3 Pinchas's daughter, Happy, with her husband, David, and their daughters, Rebecca and Juliette. New Jersey, 2018.

Pinchas and Gisele celebrating Passover during a pandemic. Montreal, 2021.

INDEX

The Azrieli Foundation was established in 1989 to realize and extend the philanthropic vision of David J. Azrieli, C.M., C.Q., M.Arch. The Foundation's mission is to support a wide spectrum of initiatives in education and research. The Azrieli Foundation is an active supporter of programs in the fields of education, the education of architects, scientific and medical research, and the arts. The Azrieli Foundation's many initiatives include: the Holocaust Survivor Memoirs Program, which collects, preserves, publishes and distributes the written memoirs of survivors in Canada; the Azrieli Institute for Educational Empowerment, an innovative program successfully working to keep at-risk youth in school; the Azrieli Fellows Program, which promotes academic excellence and leadership on the graduate level at Israeli universities; the Azrieli Music Project, which celebrates and fosters the creation of high-quality new Jewish orchestral music; and the Azrieli Neurodevelopmental Research Program, which supports advanced research on neurodevelopmental disorders, particularly Fragile X and Autism Spectrum Disorders.